THE INNOCENT CADET

BECOMING A WORLD WAR II BOMBARDIER

BY

CHARLES N. STEVENS

To Sean,
Best wishes
Charles N. Stevens

authorHOUSE®

AuthorHouse™
1663 Liberty Drive, Suite 200
Bloomington, IN 47403
www.authorhouse.com
Phone: 1-800-839-8640

First published by AuthorHouse 6/25/2008

ISBN: 978-1-4343-8828-5 (sc)

Library of Congress Control Number: 2008904823

*Printed in the United States of America
Bloomington, Indiana*

This book is printed on acid-free paper.

TABLE OF CONTENTS

INTRODUCTION

I have written an account of a particularly eventful and meaningful period of my life, that between child and man, when I was 18 and 19 years old. It covers the time period from the day I entered the service until I left for overseas to England as a flyer in World War II. During that time, away from home and usually homesick, I assiduously maintained my ties to my family by writing letters nearly every day. They, in turn, wrote me as frequently. My mother saved all my letters, tying them together in neat bundles with kitchen string and stacking them in several department store gift boxes. When my parents passed away, I found the boxes of letters among other containers of keepsakes and old photographs. The letters, written over a period of 13 months in 1943-1944, contained a detailed record of my life in the Army Air Corps. Upon reading and rereading the letters, the details came rushing back, each one saturated with all the emotion originally connected to them. Those memories, in turn, stimulated others that had never found their way into my letters.

What I finally wrote were pieces written in chronological order around what I considered important or meaningful themes. It is not a day-by-day record. Most of the information comes from my letters, passages of which are sometimes quoted in italics. Where details are skimpy or missing, I've supplied them from my best recollections. In some places I've used personal photographs, bombardier's manuals and cadet yearbooks to help supply details. Periodically, when relevant, I have inserted memories from my life before the service. Some of the names have been changed when the material has been sensitive or very personal.

I have written the account in first person present tense to make the writing more immediate. I want the reader to travel through this personal adventure with me.

I was raised by a loving, church-going family. They were conservative yet tolerant. I was not familiar with the dark side of life although I heard something about it in the locker room banter when I was on the high school track team. Compared to other men my age, I was an innocent young man. My innocence became even more apparent when I joined the service and began to compare the lives of those men with mine.

Even though I see much of my present self in the accounts of the young man of over 60 years ago, I've changed emotionally, intellectually and spiritually. Sixty-plus years of living, education, experience, maturation and pure accident have altered my life since that time. Now at 83, some of the ideas that I held so fervently as a young man have been altered or dissolved by time as new ones have reshaped them or taken their place.

Every period of my life has been an adventure. My life right now is an adventure. My childhood and my adult life after the service are just as important as what I have written about, but no part of my life has been so well documented and pivotal as the time in the service reflected in my letters.

* * *

For reasons I don't fully understand, it's important to me that my great grandchildren, my great- great grandchildren and all who follow them know who I was. I simply want them to appreciate me as an individual who once walked the earth, loved his life and wrote about it. I want to be more than an obscure name that someone in the future might stumble upon when exploring the dusty web of family connections. I have nothing to leave---no morals, lessons or messages. I present myself only as I am, or was then, leaving future judgments about my strengths and weaknesses to others. I have set a small part of my life down in a cryptic stream of words, hoping they will convey to my future family all the juices of a living, breathing human being with his bag of experiences, thoughts, dreams, emotions and sensations. In this way I hope to live again in their minds.

I have seen enough leaning slate headstones in old graveyards, the rock weathered, encrusted with lichens, flaking away so that the name of the buried is lost forever. Vanished too is the life of a once living, breathing, sensing man or woman who many years before had laughed and wept and loved, had known the fragrance of flowers and the sound of wind in the trees.

I don't want to be one of those old photographs without a name written on it, some future family member not having the slightest idea who I am. Will I be thrown out with the trash, stuck in a dark drawer, thrown into a box of unknowns?

Even permanent, well-maintained brass markers with embossed names lie cold and sterile in cemetery grass. The expression of a single thought on an old post card by the deceased is more significant than a gravestone. In the faded ink of the script lies the warmth of life. An old yellowed letter may mean even more---a tender expression of love, the enjoyment of a picnic down by the river, the sorrow over a death in the family.

I know little about my grandfathers and grandmothers. My childhood memories of them still float in my mind along with stories about them told to me by my parents. I have a few of their old letters and several photographs pasted in a tattered album, but that's all. I know even less about my great-grandfathers and great-grandmothers, only the remnants of their lives remaining in faded photographs, a few brittle newspaper clippings and isolated story fragments. Any kin existing before my great-grandparents I know nothing about, not even their names. It is as though they had disappeared without a trace---whole lives lived, then forgotten forever.

I neither believe in an afterlife nor cling to the universal dream of immortality. To me, my father's "immortality" consists of my memories of him and to some extent several photographs, letters and memorabilia, but when I die, the vivid memories I have of his kindness, bravery, tenderness and inventiveness will die with me. So too will pass memories of my mother's sweetness, unswerving love and delicateness. Only words can preserve those virtues.

What I write will be my immortality, my contact with my future family---as long as natural disasters, wars or fires do not destroy my words. Or a family in the distant future, cleaning out an attic and deciding what to keep and what not to keep, does not toss it out as too old or remote to have any meaning.

*   *   *

I wrote this account not because I thought I was anyone special or did anything outstanding. I was simply a young man like thousands of other young men caught up in the collective passion of the times---an individual player in a cast of millions swept into a grim drama, the great aberration of wartime. Every young man could have written similar accounts about his particular experiences, but what I have penned is the way it was for me. Neither proud nor ashamed, I did what nearly all of the boys on my block, my classmates and my fellow choir members did--- joined the service.

I would particularly like to thank my wife, Dolores Seidman, a former English teacher and counselor, who read all my first drafts and gave me valuable feedback then edited the final draft. A huge thanks also to Bill Robbins, an excellent writer and superb editor, who gave me numerous suggestions and kept my grammar in check in the early chapters. Finally I would like to thank my writing group, Davin Malasarn who organized the Wordknot group--- Marie Shield, Frances O'Brien, Maggie Malooly, Alice Hayward and Sue Coppa. They carefully read and listened to my chapters and provided me with grammar pointers and helped remedy points that were unclear.

THE TROLLEY RIDE

The draft board officials give each of us tickets for the Red Cars, the big Pacific Electric trolleys that fan out over four counties in southern California. At the Sixth and Main station, a tall building with trolleys moving in and out at both ends, a group of us board a car bound for San Pedro.

We roll eastward out of the busy station over a sloping ramp that gradually lowers to the city streets below. Some of the young men who ride in our group are from Inglewood, my hometown. I know a few of them, especially Henry Berman, a classmate of mine from high school who now sits in the seat next to me for the trip to Fort MacArthur. He had been a member of the football team and popular on campus whereas I, except for brief moments of glory on the track team, had simply blended in with the shrubs, the old buildings and the rest of the average faces. Although pudgy, he's well built, his curly blond hair crowning an almost handsome face. Because of a sinus problem, his mouth sags open when he's not talking, his lower lip dropping into a soft curve. His condition gives him a wonderful resonating voice that when combined with a cultured vibrato allows him to sing like a band crooner. I feel uneasy being with him because he'd been one of the elite at school and I, by parental example, had been indirectly taught to be humble in the presence of "superiors."

After an infinite number of stops on the city streets punctuated with hissing air and the squealing of brake shoes, we sail on to the separated stretch of straight track leading to the harbor. The two-car train accelerates into a hollow-toned swaying as we hurtle down the tracks. A few open windows scoop up air, tumbling it through the aisles, rustling hair and fluttering newspapers.

Henry and I talk about our days at high school and about what had happened to people we knew, particularly what branch of the service they joined and where they were sent. Every young man our age not classified 4-F is in or about to be in the service. Henry and I had both passed our physicals and our written examinations for entrance into the Army Air Corps, only waiting until we were drafted to begin our cadet training.

"I really don't want to leave right now," he says. "I've just met a girl that I like. She works in the ticket booth at a show in Redondo Beach. I asked her out, and we ended up making love. It was really difficult because she was a virgin, but we managed to do it."

He chuckles under his breath as he talks, clearly bragging about his conquest. He relates the incident with all the smoothness and self-assurance of a guy who believes he has passed the supreme test, has earned his passage into manhood. I listen to him attentively out of curiosity and politeness. I smile with him, but I'm uncomfortable with the story; I don't know what to do with it, how to field his words.

"I went back to see her a few days later," he goes on. "She told me she'd really enjoyed it, but that she was sure sore afterwards."

He slumps slightly in his seat, turning his head toward me, laughing softly and checking my reaction. Outside, the shacky houses of Willowbrook and Compton flicker by.

Having never had an experience like Henry's, I have no comparable story to tell him, no lurid tales to swap about women or my conquests of them. As usual, I listen, struggling to react without offending him even though I disapprove of what he had done. I also struggle with myself. I wrestle with a perplexing blend of curiosity about and interest in his account and my own sense of right and wrong. Perhaps because I have a sister close to my age, I immediately feel sorry for the girl. I think about her soreness, about what she now thinks of herself and what she really feels about him. I wonder if she regarded the act as casually as he did. I picture her in my mind, dispensing tickets in a curvy Art Deco booth, her dark hair tumbling down to her glassy, golden jacket, bearing all of that dull pain inflicted on her by my curly-headed schoolmate who now sits next to me. I think about how she would feel if she could hear him talking about her, revealing to his friends the secrets of their most intimate act.

At Dominguez Junction our trolleys leave the main line that goes on to Long Beach. We skirt around the harbor and the docks to San Pedro, stopping near the ferry terminal at a small station. A Point Fermin bus whisks us off to a stop directly in front of Fort MacArthur. A cold, ominous wind nearly blows us off the hill as we walk down the grassy slope toward the main gate.

After assignment to our company, roster and barracks at the checking station, we amble over to the mess hall where the men on duty lead us to the kitchen and a large refrigerator. The cook picks out thick, succulent steaks that he grills for us. We devour them. If life in the service is like this, it will be a wonderful experience.

That first night in the quiet darkness of the strange barracks, I think about the girl again and am sad.

DON OLSON AND THE DISCONSOLATE RECRUIT

Gathered around a bunk in the dim barracks, the men talk seriously, their voices low. While the others stand, one man, his brow furrowed, his chin tucked into his hand, sits on the bottom bunk, a closed copy of *Esquire* magazine beside him. He looks down at the wooden floor, only occasionally rolling his sad eyes upward at one or another of the men. One of them is Don Olson, my friend, whom I had come to see.

I had come upon this tableau after walking over from my own barracks, the same type as this one--two-storied, plain, simple and spartan. The feeble afternoon light glows through the paned windows revealing tombstone-like rows of bunks and a dull array of shadowed olives and browns. A musty smell pervades the room, the scent of wool blankets and mattresses, the dust in the rafters and the essence of the thousands of bodies that have passed through.

"Knowing what's happened to me," says the dark-haired recruit sitting on the bed. "I think it's cruel of you to show me the cover on the magazine. You guys just don't know how rotten I feel about it."

"Oh, come on," says one of them. "We didn't mean anything by it. We were just kidding. We just thought it was a funny coincidence when we saw the magazine in the PX."

"Well, I don't think it's so damn funny," he replies.

I stand at the edge of the small group, not knowing why the guy is so disturbed.

He shifts his black-rimmed glasses, runs a nervous hand through his disheveled hair.

"Look at the magazine cover, Stevens," says Don as he sweeps it off the bunk and hands it to me. "He's just taking it too hard." It shows in caricature an astonished buck private sitting on a park bench while a master sergeant with his chevrons and machismo leads away the private's frizzy-haired blond girlfriend who had just been sitting beside him. The sergeant smirks triumphantly as the woman, her arm linked around his swollen bicep, proudly walks off with him. I have no idea why this should affect him so, but the other men seem to know.

"Why does this bother you so much?" I ask.

"Because it's exactly what happened to me," he moans. "I was sitting on a bench with my girlfriend. This cocky sergeant walks by, leering at her as he passes. Suddenly she just gets up and joins him, leaving me sitting there. She walks right out of my life. She was my life. She was everything to me."

"Are you sure it wasn't a joke?" I ask. "Maybe she'll come back to you."

"I know damn well it wasn't supposed to be a prank."

"Gee, I'm really sorry. You must feel like hell."

"I'm devastated. Thanks anyway for your concern. That's more than I get from these guys."

Suddenly Don laughs at me, then taunts me.

"Come on, Stevens. It's not your problem. You don't have to listen to him. You're just too damn nice."

It was not the first time Don had chastised me. As seniors in high school only one year before, Don and another friend, Bob, had asked me to join them for a round of golf at the local course. Being a novice at the game, I hesitated but then agreed to go with them. We walked to Manchester Boulevard which led straight east to the low hills. Traffic sped by on the boulevard, the pungent smell of car and truck exhaust hanging in the air. I headed directly for the bus stop, thinking we would take one of the old yellow buses that plodded up Manchester, but Don and Bob stepped out to the edge of the busy street and hoisted their thumbs for a ride. I was appalled to see them there, their arms up, moving back and forth, attempting to catch the attention of the drivers. Surprised that I still stood by the bus stop, Don yelled at me.

"Come on, Stevens. We'll get a ride in a minute."

"No," I protested. "I'm going to take the bus. I don't want to hitchhike."

My mother, having warned me ever since I was able to understand about kidnappers and strangers and what heinous acts they were capable of, left me wary of people I didn't know. Hitchhiking was out of the question. Don teased me and begged me to get out in the street with them. I remained steadfast.

"You go ahead. I'm taking the bus."

Reluctantly they sauntered back towards me.

"Okay. We'll go with you," laments Don with an expression of resignation. "The trouble with you, Stevens, is that you're too damn honest."

Despite his condemnations of my "righteousness," we had been good friends, and I was happy to see him at Fort MacArthur among the crowds of uniformed strangers. We were pals through junior high and had run on the track team together in high school. Always taller than I, his friendly, easygoing qualities drew me to him. His smile revealed a chipped front tooth, and his eyes always seemed small and squinty from the constant expression of glee on his face. In our senior algebra class we chatted so much together that our teacher, Mr. Benson, moved our seats far across the room from each other.

"My God," Don had said when we first spotted each other at Fort MacArthur, "Every guy down here has done it. They've all had women. That's all they talk about."

I imagine that the young men, just released from the ties and taboos of their families, friends, communities and jobs, had suddenly assumed an easy freedom and a loosening of their tongues, valuable in setting up their status. Don and I, with our lack of experience and not prone to tell lies to prove our prowess, keenly feel our differences from the others.

Among the rattle of metal trays, the clanking of silverware and the murmur of the men in the mess hall, I think again about the disconsolate recruit. I had genuinely sympathized with him and was interested in his story. The poor guy had been about to ship out to a distant part of the country and wanted the woman to love him and wait for him. The brazen woman revealed her shallowness by walking away with the sergeant. I can feel his sorrow and share some of his sadness.

By the time I place my food-stained dinner tray on the kitchen conveyor in the early evening, it occurs to me that the coincidence between the scene depicted on the magazine and his own woeful tale seems almost too striking to be true. Perhaps traumatized by his being drawn into the service and seeing the cover at a newsstand, he had fantasized that the incident happened to him. Somehow it's more comforting to me to think of him as being disturbed rather than hurt. As we all shall soon scatter to unfamiliar cities and wastelands all over the country, I'll probably never know.

THE SHOWER

Angry and pouting as I wander about the grounds with the other slackers, gold bricks and rule-breakers, I can hardly swallow the injustice of it all. We each carry a bucket handed to us by a grim sergeant who orders us to police the area near the recreation hall. We spread out, combing the asphalt, dirt, grass and bushes for cigarette butts, candy wrappers, crumpled cigarette packages and bottle caps. The crisp air smells of the sea and the pungent creosote of the nearby pier pilings. A ship slips slowly through the still, green water of the harbor, probably laden with supplies for the Pacific War Zone.

My parents, at least, had always listened to my side of a conflict, but the corporals and sergeants in charge of us at Fort MacArthur are ruthless, insisting that only what they think matters. There is no recourse; there is only one side, theirs. Having to pick up trash wouldn't ordinarily bother me, but what irritates me is that I had been blatantly misjudged and now must bear the humiliation of being disciplined for an infraction I didn't commit. I bend down for the stained cigarette butts, dropping them in my bucket, but I see only injustice in the bottom.

An orderly assigned another man and me to clean the showers in the barracks. The corporal in charge thrust buckets, scrapers and stiff-bristled brushes at us and explained what he wanted us to do. After an unending parade of naked bodies had scattered water and soap, a scummy film had accumulated on the galvanized iron walls of the showers. It was our task to scuff and brush it away until the metal underneath gleamed again.

The other man was from Compton and was black. We spoke very little to each other as we scraped and peeled the thin gray skin of soap from the walls. The tools grated, and our furious brushing echoed in the metal enclosures. We dashed water on the dislodged flakes of congealed soap.

I had never associated with a black man before. I ran against several of them while competing on the high school track team and had them for classmates in junior college, but I had never known any very well. Although rather quiet, this man's face was friendly, and he possessed a relaxed manner about him that appealed to me. I didn't know what to say to him, and he seemed not to know what to say to me. Our few brief sentences to each other concerned only the work we performed.

The incessant scraping and especially the brushing finally wore me down. My arm ached from the constant motion, and weariness spread through my legs. My partner, more relaxed and smoother with his work, labored on unabated. Eventually I had to stop to catch my breath and relieve my tightening muscles. At the precise moment that my rear touched the wooden shower bench, the corporal suddenly arrived to check our progress. His instant impression was of me sitting on the bench resting while my partner continued to sweep his brush over the metal wall.

"Oh! So that's how it is!" he shouted indignantly. "You sit on your butt and let him do all the damn work! We'll see about that!"

The slender noncom, his cap tilted on his sandy hair, fumed. His face flushed crimson, and his eyes sparked with vengeance. He not only accused me of slacking, but also implied that because my partner was black that I had taken advantage of him and expected him to do the work while I just sat and watched. I explained to him that I had been working constantly, and that I had just that moment sat down, but he preferred to storm away with his instant assessment. My partner chose to stay out of it, saying nothing, apparently wanting to avoid trouble. Early that evening the corporal ordered me to report to the other side of the fort for two hours of extra work, my punishment.

Evening shadows creep across Fort MacArthur as we stoop for our last bits of rubbish, our sentences having been served. Lights flicker on along the docks and warehouses as the coming night's chill slowly settles. We dump our buckets in a trash bin and walk toward our respective barracks. My pride still smarts from being misjudged, but I learn that fairness is not a virtue the Army respects.

WORK DETAILS

My arms are still sore from a merciless barrage of shots inflicted at the dispensary several days before. I gingerly hoist myself over the tailgate into the rear of an olive-drab truck with the other men. All of us wear gray-green fatigues as we are on our way to another work detail. In my scrambling to get in I smash my swollen, festering upper arm, the result of a smallpox inoculation, against the truck's steel body. I wince but bear my pain, taking a place on the crowded rows of bench seats.

We stood in long, unhappy lines, finally entering the room where we faced a gauntlet of hypodermic needles. The medics, lined up on both sides, gave us all our shots at once. A few stung like bees, and several of us sat on the floor with our backs against the wall to let our dizzy heads clear.

By the following morning I was immobilized.

Instead of clear vibrating bugle notes wavering through the morning air to gently awaken us, the way it had always been in the movies, a crude orderly yelled through a squawking loudspeaker, "Okay! Roll out! Hit the deck! Drop your cocks and grab your socks! Come on! Get moving! Line up outside!" As I stirred under the heavy blanket, I found that my arms throbbed and a dull aching penetrated all my joints. A fever flushed my skin. As I would have done at home, I stayed in bed. The rest of the men hustled into their clothes and washed up.

"Hey guy! You better get out of that bunk," said the recruit next to me.

11

"I'm sick. I can't make it," I answered.

"You're gonna get in trouble. You better move it anyway."

A few moments later the orderly charged up the steps to check the barracks and saw me still in my bunk.

"Why the hell are you still here?" he yelled. "Get your ass out of that bunk and report outside!"

"I'm sick. I have a fever, and I can hardly move. I'm sore all over," I pleaded.

"Okay. I'll let it go this time," he said. "But you get your butt out of the sack and report right now to the dispensary for morning sick call!"

"Yes, Sir."

* * *

We bounce along in the truck over the streets of San Pedro, none of us knowing where we're going or what we'll be doing when we arrive. Only obedience and carrying out our duties are important in the army. My arm still smarts. I can only hope the work ahead won't be too strenuous.

Several days before, they dumped us at an old warehouse, formerly a chemical plant built during the last war. We loaded boxes on trucks and boxcars, then moved other cartons around on the dusty concrete floor. We didn't know what was in the boxes, why they were stored there or why they had to be positioned in such a specific way. While we waited for our truck to return, we heaved rocks at the few remaining glass panes of an even older and abandoned warehouse next door. As the ancient windows were several stories up, it took us a long time to hit one. Fragments tinkled down the side of the concrete wall as we yelled in triumph. We were still boys.

The truck hurtles around Point Fermin before it winds up into the San Pedro Hills, its gears whining and grinding. We stop on a knoll low on the flank of a hill. Spring grasses green the slopes that sweep down to the cliffs and the breaking waves below. The jagged outline of Catalina Island emerges out of a light haze. Except for several gun emplacements, the scene is idyllic.

The corporal in charge tells us that we have to dig down nearly five feet with picks and shovels to an old buried cable that must be removed. Other work details before us had dug a long trench, revealing the twisted, rusted wire beneath, but apparently it's long enough that unearthing it completely would take the combined labor of new soldiers for years to come. None of us, of course, know why the cable is there or why it is so important that it be ripped out. It appears to me that it would be perfectly all right to leave it in the ground. Despite my sensitive arm, I swing the pick and shovel dirt nearly all day, a pungent, earthy smell seeping out of the damp soil. Inch by inch we expose more of the corroded cable.

During our breaks I chat with my working partner, a handsome, rather slender man some years older than I. Like a fly that circles a wedge of chocolate cream pie, and finally in ever-tighter spirals lands on the sweet fluff, his coiling conversation eventually leads to sex. Somehow he thinks I will be interested in his sexual exploits. Perhaps he wants me to swap stories with him. He leans casually against the side of the ditch.

"I even went out with a married woman once. I picked her up at her own house. I went inside, and her husband was sitting there in an easy chair reading a newspaper. She said good-bye to him, and he just waved to her from his chair as we left." Then, grinning and obviously pleased with himself, he adds, "She was the best piece I ever had, too."

My eyebrows arch and my lower lip drops. My head buzzes at the enormity of what he has said. I had never heard anything like it before. I imagine the episode as my pick bites into the damp earth.

"I see the wife's husband, comfortable and blasé, reclining in his favorite chair, the newspaper rustling slightly between his outstretched arms. I see him let go of the paper with his right hand, the pages slumping as he waves to his departing wife. His face is somewhat fleshy but handsome, his black, abundant hair curly but dry. He neither smiles nor scowls, his expression remaining neutral with a trace of sadness around the eyes. His wife smiles, but it is a distant one without the full, genuine curve of her lips. She looks toward the door, her wavy brunet hair cut short, her eyebrows plucked, her lips crimson with fresh lipstick. As they edge toward the front door, she links arms with my work partner, the same arm that I now see dangling only a few feet from me. He, looking uncomfortable and anxious to leave, urges her toward the closed door."

Exhausted from digging, we jiggle on our benches as the truck rumbles back toward the barracks. We had uncovered only a few feet of the corroded wire, so there is plenty left for work details that follow. My partner's astounding story still sails silently along the cables of my brain. I run the scene over and over again, my head full of questions.

"Had their love shriveled like an old banana, its disgusting blackness driving them in separate directions? Had they married, agreeing that "free love" was still permissible? Had they agreed not to divorce, but to live in the same house even though their marriage had ended? Did he enjoy the same privileges as she?"

In the bunk at night my muscles ache even more from hefting the heavy pick all day, and my upper arm still throbs from the inoculation. I think about what useless labor I'll be asked to perform the next day. In the darkness the men breathe heavily, a few snore or shift under their covers. My partner's story still hovers in my thoughts like a sinister drama I don't understand.

THE CORPORAL'S FLOOR

As our brushes and sandpaper sweep across the wooden floor of the corporal's room, we vow that we'll always look around first before we ever make any more rash statements. The floor presses painfully against my knees as I push my weary arms in broad arcs over the boards, the scrubbing and scraping sounds filling the room, the smell of wood and dust scenting the air. We work like novice housemaids beneath his desk and around the legs of the corporal's bed, its blanket properly taut and smooth. If only he hadn't said it. I, who had never uttered a word, the victim of another's chance remark, am now forced to scour the corporal's quarters.

Most of the men on our roster had been assigned K.P., but for some miraculous reason four of us were left off the list. After the unfortunate men marched off to the kitchen, we, feeling smug about our luck, lazed about the barracks, eventually moving toward the porch steps where we chatted in the morning sun.

One of the new recruits, a self-proclaimed authority on Army life, declared in his wisdom, "One thing you have to learn about the Army is that you never volunteer. If you ever do, they'll have you pushing a wheelbarrow or worse."

Directly behind us the corporal in charge of the barracks stood listening. "Oh, you should never volunteer, huh!" he blurted.

We whipped around. There he was, standing tall, a satisfied grin playing along his firm lips, the grin of a cat that has just cornered a mouse and knows it can't get away.

"Well, I have a volunteer job for all of you," he snapped. "You'll find brushes and sandpaper and blocks of wood in the supply room. I want you guys to transform my floor for me."

We sheepishly comply, suddenly trading our short-lived comfort for the drudgery of this unpleasant task.

As I scrub, I try to take the incident good naturedly, but the injustice of it annoys me. Why had the corporal not simply punished the man who uttered the ill-fated remark rather than making us all suffer? In a camp of raw recruits any man wearing stripes on his sleeve is akin to a god, one who clearly understands his power and enjoys exercising it on a whim. "RHIP," they say, "rank has its privileges." Any man who outranks another, regardless of his lack of education, character or competency, can demand that those beneath him obey.

My friend Don Olson, who mistakenly wandered with several other men into a ping-pong room reserved for non-commissioned officers, scrubbed floors for an entire afternoon as punishment. We continually worry that we'll break an unknown rule, make mistakes or offend a person of rank. A private first class challenged me to play ping-pong with him. I trounced him in seven straight games then feared that he would put me on K.P. in retaliation. I felt lucky that he didn't.

The quick shift, from lounging in the sun to scrubbing, upsets my sense of order. I like the future to be as definite as possible; I feel secure when I know what's going to happen next, more in control of my life. Not knowing what the hour or moment ahead will bring disturbs me.

It was always happening. One afternoon, while idling in the barracks, a jarring voice blared over the loudspeaker, "All of you men in the barracks! Fall out between Barracks One and Two!" We hustled out the doors, milled around for a moment then assembled in orderly lines. The corporal in charge shouted, "You guys have five minutes to change into your fatigues and report back out here." Inside the barracks we quickly slipped out of our uniforms, taking some care to hang them up, then stepped into our pale gray-green fatigue suits, none of us knowing what job they had in mind. We rarely ever knew because it was not our place to know; ours was to obey and do. Three other men and I swept the test rooms and the officers' quarters then the classifying room and even the telephone booths. Our relaxation and camaraderie in the barracks had been shattered with the suddenness of a work detail. The sweeping was not unpleasant, but the abrupt, unexpected change was.

We near the end of our task as we rub the floor around the wastebasket and near the door, the corporal standing just outside with arms folded. I think about sudden change and how I never know from what source it will arise.

Several of us attended the movies one night, returning to our barracks in the dark, long after "lights out." We groped as quietly as possible through the inkiness of the barracks, searching for our bunks. One man tripped over something, staggering and causing a loud thump. I felt an object brush up against my knees, discovering that someone had placed broomsticks between the beds at about knee level. If I hadn't stopped at first contact, I would've plunged into the blackness with a racket that would've pleased the tricksters. One returning man slipped into his bunk only to find that someone had folded his sheets halfway down so that he couldn't stretch out. A boyish nature still lingered in some of the men, taking them back to their summer camp days. The night before, the pranksters sabotaged a man's upper bunk bed by removing the hooks that secured it. He crashed down, bedding and all, much to the mirth of the onlookers. Seeing no humor in the situation, he set the barracks aflame with his expletives.

Finished now with the floor, we slowly carry our tools back to the supply room. The corporal, looking very pleased, says with a cruel smile, "Remember now, that work was strictly voluntary."

THE UNHAPPY RECRUIT

Standing on a gravely patch of ground outside the mess hall, the lonely-looking recruit appears lost. While the others wait for the mess hall door to open, he hovers around the group's edge, talking to no one. Older than I, his fleshy abdomen bulges around his belt, spoiling the look of his new uniform. His mouth turns down at the corners, his forehead furrowed. After last night's brief showers, the mid-day sun streams brilliantly through a glass-clear sky, bringing out the deep green of the San Pedro Channel behind us.

Perhaps because I'm not talking to anyone, he catches my eye and sidles slowly toward me.

"I hate being in the service," he says in a dull monotone. "I want to get out as soon as possible. I'm too used to having my freedom and being able to do exactly what I want. I feel all caged up and miserable here."

"I really don't feel that way", I respond.

A look of disbelief passes over his face. "How can anyone like being in the damn Army?" he asks. I don't answer.

I feel honored to be in the Army, despite having to give up some of my freedom. I think the disheveled soldier should show some pride in serving his country. He seems shallow for not sacrificing at least some of his self-interest for a cause as important as winning the war.

Even though the useless work details and the callousness of some of the enlisted officers annoy me, I consider them necessary irritations. I mesh rather easily into the routine of military life. At times I resent the unpredictability of the moment and the sporadic injustices, but they fall within the flexible limits of my tolerance.

On occasions I liked losing my identity. Blending with the others somehow smoothed over the differences between me and the other men, many of whom were older, and, I believed, much more experienced with life. Dressing alike, sleeping in identical barracks in identical bunks under identical blankets, arising at the same time and eating the same food was strangely comforting.

Marching had taught me to be an intricate part of a "soldier machine." As each man had to become just like the next, there was no room for individuality. Each recruit stepped to the same beat, exactly at arm's length from the next man, all in a perfect line. We marched flat-footed, bringing heels down first without rising on toes, lest heads bounced and spoiled the unwavering evenness of the line. Every man executed the same commands with precision.

Groups competed on the parade grounds, the steady boom of bass drums and the stirring brass of Sousa's marches dictating their rhythm. My body blended into the beat, heels timed to the drum's thunder, steps to the mirror image of those beside me, heavy shoes pounding on the bare earth, churning up clouds of dust.

I relished the excitement of my new life and being at the edge of adventures that lie ahead. I welcomed the prospect of new places, states and countries and especially fresh experiences. I was ravenous for mess hall food; even the powdered eggs that the army cooks mixed with water and spread out like thin yellow lava over their massive grills.

I liked being up in the freshness of the early morning. After spring showers during the night, the grounds still damp, I walked to the mess hall in the dark, the first gray tones of dawn showing over the dark silhouettes of the harbor warehouses. I inhaled the cold clean air scented with the fragrance of wet earth. Lights still twinkled on the docks and the barracks and on the great white hospital ship with its huge red cross moored on the other side of the channel. I was hungry and healthy and at peace.

When I have a chance, I edge away from the dour recruit, joining some friends who had just arrived. I have little sympathy for the unhappy man. I think only about his pathetic whimpering. Why can't he bear to lose at least a part of his ego to a cause larger than himself? Of course I don't know what his life was like on the outside, but if everyone were like him, I think to myself, how would we ever win the war?

AN ACT OF FIRMNESS

"Charles N. Stevens!" the officer shouts over the loudspeaker as he reads the names of the men who will ship out that evening. At last the time has come when I can leave Fort MacArthur to begin training as an Army Air Corps cadet. My spirits soar. Finally, after the ordeal of all of those Air Corps tests and the thoughts about what it will be like to fly are about to come together.

But my excitement gradually fades when I notice that many of the men being called with me don't look or act like potential cadets. Some appear rather dull or vacant, slouch about with empty or resigned looks on their faces. At first I think that I'm misjudging them, but it seems strange that none of the men that I know to be waiting for cadet training is called. Since no one is told where he's to be sent, I suddenly fear that the officers have made a colossal error, that I'm about to be isolated from any cadet training base. On the one hand I trust the officers in charge of my fate, but on the other I'm suspicious that they've snared me in some dreadful mistake.

I worry half the morning, speaking to no one. I walk through the day carrying my burden of heavy thoughts. A haze dims the sun, dulling the rows of barracks and suffocating the gentle hills behind us. People appear to mope around in slow motion. Questions take their turn in my mind--- popping up like numbers in a cash register. Should I trust my superiors and leave obediently with the group, hoping that the men really are leaving for cadet training? If I were to be sent somewhere else, would it be possible to transfer to a cadet base later? Shall

22

I tell someone about my apprehensions and remind them that I'm officially a cadet? Finally I can bear the tension no longer.

With resolve alien to my usual disposition, I stride confidently into the office where all orders are cut, and I explain my fears to the sergeant.

"Yeah. What's your name?" the sergeant asks gruffly.

"Charles N. Stevens, 39569857," I reply.

He fumbles through a stack of orders clamped to a clipboard, searching for my name. He stops turning the pages, running one finger down a column of names.

"We gotcha on the orders for the Transportation Corp in New Orleans. Something the matter with that?"

As he suddenly looks up, our eyes lock.

"Yes, there is something wrong with that," I tell him. "I've passed all my tests for Aviation Cadet training. All the papers were to be sent here to Fort MacArthur."

Annoyed, a scowl creasing his forehead, he says, "Well, we don't have any papers on you like that."

"If you call the Army Air Corps office in Los Angeles," I insist, "they'll confirm what I just told you. I also have copies of my papers at home and can have them brought here by early this evening."

Backing off, he agrees to cross my name off the list but demands that I bring him the papers. "I'll get them," I reply as I walk buoyantly out of the office, letting the screen door slam behind me.

I had always been apprehensive about whether I would be placed in Aviation Cadet training because of the method of enlistment. I had been accepted as a cadet, but no one was allowed into training without first having been drafted. Once that happened, we were to be guided into the Air Corps through the classification system. In downtown Los Angeles the army clerks had stamped "Special Assignment--Aviation Cadet" on my papers. Always unsure, I had asked a clerk in the classifying room at Fort MacArthur about it as I swept the floors on a work detail. He assured me that "Aviation Cadet" was written on my papers and that there was nothing to worry about.

Although relieved by his assurances, my doubts arose again when the days passed without my name being called. At least one group had shipped out to San Antonio for cadet training, but I was not on the list. Now this. My trust in the military begins to slip away.

In the early evening I receive a message that my parents are waiting for me just outside the main gate. I walk briskly across the grounds between the geometric rows of barracks. The afternoon sea breeze whipping around the soft San Pedro Hills and up the harbor channel has whisked away the earlier haze. I easily spot the old tan Ford V-8. My mother and father, smiles lighting up their faces, watch me intently as I cross the street, my boyish face grinning beneath my cap. I'm proud of my uniform and pleased to have them see me in it for the first time.

I slide into the back seat of the car. We talk for nearly an hour as they ask questions and listen to the stories of my adventures. Even though I've been away less than two weeks, I feel comforted by being with them again. Their love soothes me. They listen to me and treat me with respect. To them, I'm a special person. For a while I settle deliciously into the warmth of their gentleness and kindness.

I walk back across the grounds clutching the Photostats of my papers. Their short visit lets me know how much I miss the tenderness of my family, yet I look forward to new adventures ahead. I still bask in the glow of my firmness with the sergeant, my not giving in to him, and my not being passive about where I was to be shipped. I feel that I may have changed the course of my life, and I had brought it about myself. I realize that for once, I had not been self-conscious, that the focus of my energy had been entirely on the problem.

I hand the papers to the sergeant in the office. He looks straight at me and says, "That's really the way to get things done."

DESERTS AND FIREFLIES

As the sun edges up over the distant mountains, the troop train of old Pullman cars rolls slowly into Yuma, Arizona, the brush and saguaro cactus casting long shadows over the sand. The angled sun bathes the desert in a golden light, an ethereal glow that is at once strange and exciting. As the wheels of our car click slowly over the rail joints, the men stir from their beds, some with sleep-ruffled hair and half-opened eyes. Others glance outside or walk the narrow aisle to the bathroom. My berth partner, Carlo, looks out the window with me from our disheveled bed as the train passes from blue-shadowed embankments into splashes of sunlight. The muted babble of men's voices blends with the deep steady roll of our Pullman.

As I gaze at the desert in the first light of day, I feel that I've been transported mentally as well as physically. The peculiar light, the sage and creosote bushes, the sharp mountains and the pungent dry fragrance are mysterious and unearthly to me. I bask in the wonder of it all.

I had never been out of California before except for a train trip to Indiana to see my grandfather. I was so young then that all I wanted to do was run up and down the aisles screaming with my little sister. Otherwise our family, out of financial necessity, traveled by car within California. I now look at Arizona with a freshness that only first-time travelers know.

Nearer the center of Yuma, billboards advertise quick marriages and list the addresses of local ministers and Justices of the Peace. Later we pass several small church-like parlors with small steeples and stained glass windows. The phenomenon is as new to me as this part of the desert, and I make a mental note to write home about how unusual it all is.

*   *   *

Our dusty troop train had left Fort MacArthur in the early afternoon, bypassing the harbor and docks then heading up the long, straight Southern Pacific tracks to Los Angeles and the Union Station. While switch engines busily shunted cars from one track to another, making up new trains with different destinations, Carlo and I waited in the station with our duffle bags. Uniformed men from all branches of the service clustered in groups both inside and outside, talking and smoking or daydreaming in quiet boredom. Several of us stood outside near the great Spanish-Moorish entrance arch and the slender towering palms. To our right a covered walkway led to the busy Fred Harvey Restaurant. From private cars and taxi cabs crowds passed briskly through the entrance, the women's heels clicking and echoing over the polished red-tile floors. Tired of standing in one place, we walked inside past the dark wooden ticket booths that seemed dwarfed in the cathedral-like room and gilded by the subdued amber light filtering through the high windows. We wandered into the cavernous waiting room with its beamed ceilings where we found deep, comfortable leather chairs. I was startled when a woman sitting across from me suddenly uncrossed her shapely legs then reached under her skirt to remove her silk stockings. It was really brazen of her, I thought, but somehow I enjoyed it, felt it deep inside.

By 8:30 in the evening our train charged out of the station, the Southern Pacific locomotive gradually gaining momentum as it thundered by Mission Tower close to the dark Los Angeles River. Some of my friends who were also to be Air Cadets were in the same car with me, so I knew I was going to the right place. We flashed through the lights of the Alhambra station. Before we turned in for the night, our train streaking out across the California desert, Carlo and I had given each other a short sketch of our lives.

*   *   *

By the time the train reaches Phoenix, it's nearly noon, and the heat is unbearable. At the station the sizzling temperature brings out swarms of flies. They stream through our open windows, dart through the aisles, buzz around the seats and land on our arms and faces. We wave them away, but they quickly return.

"These damn flies! Why don't we shut the windows for a while? At least 'til we get going again," yells an irritated future cadet.

"Hell no," shouts another. "What do you want us to do, smother in here?"

"Well, these flies are driving me nuts."

We all hope the train will leave soon so that the air will again blow in, ridding us of the pests and cooling us off.

When we finally arrive at Tucson, I'm impressed with the city's cleanliness and modern buildings. Near sunset the train stops again at Douglas, Arizona, a small town close to the New Mexico border where the officers allow us to get off and stretch our legs near the tracks. Volunteers from the town had established a canteen for soldiers in the station, so many of us push our way into the depot for punch and cookies served by pleasant, smiling men and women near the ages of my own parents, and whom I suspect had sons or daughters in the service themselves. In an odd way, they make me feel homesick.

We see little of New Mexico as we pass through it entirely at night. Early in the evening our train hits an unfortunate skunk, its sharp odor flowing in through some of the still open windows.

"My God! What's that?" complains one of the men clamping his fingers to his nose.

Another winces, his eyes nearly screwed shut. "Close the fuckin' windows!"

"Nah. That stink will go away," shouts a man down at the far end. "We need the air to flush it out."

The evil smell becomes the only image we have of New Mexico except for its vast darkness. Sometime after midnight, the train stops. I raise my head from the pillow and see the still-lighted windows of fifteen-story buildings in El Paso, Texas, all appearing eerie and dream-like.

The next day we speed across the flat, barren emptiness of West Texas. The land varies only with the amount of open space between its scrawny bushes. It's a day of unchanging desolation when most of the men nap, read, chat or play cards. Through my open window flow the hot scents and the dust of the wasteland. Even though my eyes are weary and bloodshot from constant exposure to the dry wind, I look out at the passing brush thinking that something new may appear, possibly a hill, a river or even a curve in the track. Like a child I become tired of the unending sameness and the insufferable straightness of the tracks that knife through the sage land like a surveyor's line. I feel the beginnings of a sty in the corner of one eye. My mouth is dry and my tongue sticks to my palate, but still my stubborn curiosity keeps me at the window. I think about how I wouldn't give anyone a nickel for the whole of West Texas.

In my growing restlessness I wash out a handkerchief in the swaying restroom. I wring out the water into the metal basin then hold it out of the window, the hot, arid flow of air drying it completely in two minutes. Now and then we rumble through small sun-warped towns that appear as barren and parched as the land around them. We stop briefly at

Valentine, Sanderson and Marfa so that the locomotive can take on water, giving us just enough time to exercise our stiff legs on solid ground.

Finally, after a full day of gazing at the same parched scene, the tracks begin to follow the contours of the Rio Grande River at the Mexican border. The green cottonwoods and willows along the bank, and the light blue clarity of the river sooth my abused eyes. The train stops at Del Rio, a pleasant town near the river where Henry Berman, my friend from Inglewood, and I have enough time to walk to a small store close by where we buy a pint of ice cream to cool and caress our dry throats.

Not until one o'clock in the morning does the train reach San Antonio, our final destination, where the night air is still too warm for comfort. Tired, hot and sleepy, we wait in the station with our duffle bags for nearly an hour before two Army trucks rumble up to take us to the base. We bounce around town, stopping once before the trucks whine out over the road north toward the Aviation Cadet Center. The lights of San Antonio twinkle in the dry air, the street lamps occasionally casting ghostly light on houses or commercial buildings. The strange sights I see from the truck all seem unreal to me.

Once out of town, the trucks bound along the road. The cooler night air of the country flows beneath the protective tarpaulin. At last we become more comfortable despite the metal-hard seats. As the wind stirred by our trucks rustles the shrubs and bushes at the sides of the road, the night becomes alive with the sparks of fireflies, hundreds of them blinking brightly, their tiny luminescent lights darting in all directions. I'm mesmerized by the spectacle. Like the golden light and long shadows of the Arizona dawn and the glitter of the El Paso buildings at night, the fireflies are new and strangely wonderful to me.

By three o'clock we arrive at the base. It's a scattering of lights, shadows and cream-colored barracks visible only in the cones of dim illumination from overhead lamps. We sign papers, a doctor briefly examines us and a sleepy-eyed orderly issues our bedding. By the time we make our beds and slither into them, it's four o'clock in the morning.

MORE ABOUT CARLO ZUNIGA

Struggling with our cumbersome barracks bags, a group of us search the narrow aisles of the Pullman car for our berth numbers. Stepping awkwardly around several men, I discover my place on the right hand side. The broad, green upholstered seats of the berth face each other on either side of a large window. Outside, in the feeble light of the station, other passengers walk briskly to their trains. Coaches wait on the track next to us, a wisp of steam escaping near their couplers.

A few moments later my traveling companion arrives, checking the seat number again to be sure he's in the right place. He slides his bag under the seat opposite mine then faces me, introducing himself with a firm handshake and an open, friendly face.

"Carlo Zuniga," he says with a broad smile, his prominent but even teeth gleaming in the dull light. "I'm from the Imperial Valley. I've lived everywhere from Calexico to El Centro at one time or another."

We shortly learn the vital statistics about each other. Because he merely presents himself the way he is without any aggressive blather or overbearing egotistical talk, I quickly begin to appreciate him.

He stands nearly six feet, his broad shoulders resting upon a slender but athletic body. High Indian cheekbones arch over his lightly pockmarked cheeks. His dark eyes, appearing narrow above those bones and almost becoming slits when he smiles, beam beneath his thick black hair. Despite his dark hair and eyes, his skin is light. He speaks in a soft voice with just a hint of a Mexican accent, acquired, he says, by speaking Spanish in his family.

As our troop train flashes by street lamps and the scattered lights of towns, we continue to chat, and I become more and more comfortable with him. Used to feeling a trifle shy and inadequate when I meet new people, I'm generally cautious about letting anyone into my personal territory. I'm apt to hold them at bay with a friendly smile rather than encouraging them to come any closer. I sometimes fend off their questions with short answers then glance away as though I want them to disappear. I fear they will crowd me, force me to do something I don't want to do or talk about a subject that I don't care about. I'm like a seagull standing on the sand that allows a beach stroller to approach only so close before lumbering off over the surf to resettle on the sand somewhere else at a safer distance.

But Carlo and I talk at an easy distance from each other, his kind smile and his interest in what I have to say sparkling in his eyes, melting my apprehensions. He listens well, giving me his full attention when I speak to him. He responds with thoughtful questions and short but adequate comments. As a person who's obviously at ease with himself, his conversation and actions are free of pretense. He neither brags nor varnishes his thoughts. He neither uses unnecessary vulgarity nor tells unlikely stories about his conquests of women, both tactics used by others I had met who were bent on exaggerating images of their manliness.

He beams with optimism, projecting a relaxed, pleasant aura. Like me, he looks forward to our training, confident that he will succeed. He also shares the excitement of new places and the changing scenes out of the train window.

*   *   *

Mexican children often scamper around the stations in Arizona and Texas where our train stops. Looking very poor with dark, mussed hair, dirt smeared faces and often barefoot, they shuffle along the tracks in the dust, looking up at the train windows. Carlo loves the little children, and they respond to him with their smiles when he speaks to them in Spanish. I try to talk to them in my meager high school Spanish, surprised when they actually appear to understand me.

"I have a girlfriend back home," says Carlo. "The trouble is she isn't Mexican-American, and her father doesn't like Mexicans."

"Oh. I'm sorry," I respond.

"We want to get married, but her father is set against it. He won't even discuss it."

"Both obstinate and prejudiced, eh?"

"Yeah. I'm determined to win my wings though. When he sees those silver wings on my officer's uniform, I think he'll change his mind."

"I hope so, Carlo."

I don't see how anyone could reject a nice guy like Carlo, but I know little about racial injustice.

* * *

I had never known a Mexican-American before. None ever lived in my neighborhood where surnames like Schaffer, Seymour, Hove, Homburg, Haw, Smith, Kelly and French, all Northern European names, were the rule. Only a very few of them sat in my junior high or high school classes, and somehow I had never made friends with them. I remember Jose Chavez who sat near the rear of my seventh-grade class with his mop of unruly black hair. Whitish spots paled the hollows of his dark cheeks, a sign, I thought, of poor health. Mrs. Peak, our teacher, whom I liked very much, once criticized him before the class for needlessly using too much paper, but he shot back defiantly, "This is my paper, and I can do anything I want with it!" The class remained silent for several minutes while she stared at him, obviously perplexed. I hated Jose for embarrassing our teacher, but I didn't know what fires smoldered within him.

Most of the Mexican-Americans in Inglewood lived in a dusty barrio spread out in a hollow away from everyone else. Their modest houses contrasted with our neat and orderly homes with their green lawns and deep backyards. Packed dirt ran between their houses. On Sundays some of them walked nearly a mile to St. John's Catholic Church while others worshipped in their own deteriorating Methodist church. I often saw the Mexican kids walking slowly home from school along the Santa Fe tracks. Near the old, barn-red Victorian station they disappeared over the sloping embankment into the hollow and their simple homes.

* * *

Carlo, like me, wants to be a bombardier, and I like him so much that I hope we'll have our training together. Later, at San Antonio, Carlo gets a pass into town then piques my interest by telling me about a river that flows right through the middle of it. He tells me that people can rent canoes, but I tell him that I tend to only row in circles. He talks to me about the little Mexican boys who dive for coins in the river. They stay underwater for a long time, suddenly bursting through the surface with wet, glistening faces, their cheeks full of coins bulging like chipmunks. When I get a pass, I intend to see San Antonio with him.

In a letter to my mother and father I pay him the highest of compliments from my limited vocabulary. I write that Carlo is *really a swell fellow.*

MEASLES AND MESS HALLS

The coarse army blanket scratches my bare neck as I lie idly on my bunk. I look up at the cream-colored rafters supporting the peaked roof of the barracks. There is nothing to do. We've had no work assigned to us since we arrived in San Antonio four days ago, a marked contrast to Fort MacArthur where digging trenches, picking up cigarette butts and other senseless details kept us busy. Even though we're inactive, we all sweat in the sauna-like atmosphere, our perspiration blotching our shirts. Upstairs, where I am, the hot air rises and collects in a steamy, stagnant pool. I, on the top bunk, am thrust even more into the tropic heat. The air conditioner, broken beyond repair, lies idle. Our only relief is to jump under the showerheads. Since the hot water system is inoperative the spray is always icy. I gasp for breath as I leap in and out of the chill showers with the others. Our spirited yelling and the slap of our bare feet on the wet cement floor resound in the small room. We are cool again--- for a while.

One man in our barracks has gone to the hospital with a case of German measles. Several of us become apprehensive because he had shared a berth on the troop train all the way from California with Henry Berman. Only the day before, I'd walked to the mess hall with the stricken man. I'd eaten with him. After we returned we sat facing each other on adjacent bunks, chatting for over an hour. Hopelessly exposed, I fear I must be next.

The hours pass slowly. I look forward to chow, not only to assuage my hunger but also to break the monotony.

36

We march in formation for a quarter mile to the mess hall, the orderly in charge clipping off a brisk cadence, our shoes clomping in rhythm. Despite the rumors about Army food—that the cooks often use goat meat instead of beef or that they dump saltpeter in the food to dampen our sexual appetites—I find it delicious. I don't understand the complainers. We help ourselves, loading as much on our plates as we want as long as we eat it all. A large intimidating sign reads, "TAKE ALL YOU WANT, BUT EAT ALL YOU TAKE." I never have a problem with this. The army serves meat at every meal, a contrast to the meager rations we were used to at home.

The next day another cadet succumbs to the measles and leaves immediately for the base infirmary. On several occasions I had long conversations with this man too. I'm sure now that I have no chance of escaping the disease. Both victims had noticed swelling in the glands behind their ears before they broke out in spots. Running my fingers behind my ears, I feel a small lump, like a pea under the skin.

Even with early symptoms I continue to eat voraciously. As I sit at the table for breakfast, I notice that I have far more food on my plate than any one else. I fill mine with an omelet full of sausage bits, a mound of fried potatoes, biscuits with butter, milk and the sweetest grapefruit I ever tasted. I note also that despite my prodigious helpings, I finish my breakfast before anyone else. I learn quickly that most men hardly eat any breakfast, preferring instead to pick at small portions as though they're not interested. I think to myself that they must have either poor appetites or sour stomachs.

Although I find no spots on my body, I dream that I break out in great rashes of them. So vivid is the nightmare that I'm convinced I actually have the disease. But except for a sniffle, I remain in good health.

As a way of restoring order to my directionless work-free days, I plan a regular personal routine. I exercise each morning, bask in the sun for an hour, brush my teeth twice a day, shave every two days, take a shower every night and eat an apple after breakfast to "keep the doctor away."

Still, without any suspicious marks anywhere on my body, I take general knowledge tests nearly all the next day. We learn that we'll undergo psychomotor tests next, then a two-day "64" physical, the general examination that investigates every aspect of our bodies. The hours of lounging in the barracks will soon be over.

I continue to savor military food. At dinner I consume corn, spinach, potatoes, hamburger with gravy, bun and butter, salad and peach pie so delicious that I have to have two large wedges. I'm what the army calls a chowhound.

* * *

During the last portion of the "64" physical, as I stand in a line of naked men waiting to be examined, one of the doctors sidles up to me.

"Have you been exposed to the measles lately? Look at you!" he exclaims.

" Yes I have sir. Two men in my barracks have it."

Frowning, he points out a growing number of red spots on my back and abdomen.

"Didn't you see that rash?" he asks.

"No. I just didn't notice it."

"Well, the damage has been done now," he says, half irritated and half smiling, "so you might as well finish your physical before you go to the hospital."

I pride myself on passing the rigorous examination despite my gradual surrender to the malady. I report to my squadron orderly room, then to the dispensary. A dull brown ambulance with a red cross on the side trundles me over to the base hospital where a bored medical attendant gives me a urinalysis and a blood test. Three times he attempts to shove the syringe into my puffing vein.

"Damn it! Why won't this lousy needle go in?"

I wince at his thrusts.

"Jesus Christ. You have the toughest skin I've ever seen."

Finally the point penetrates.

His remark fills me with pride. Tough skin. It sounds manly to me.

I slip easily into a luxurious stretch of life in the hospital. Even though red constellations spangle my body, I don't feel ill. I barely register a fever. I vegetate all day, and never have to stir before seven o'clock in the morning. Attendants deliver all our meals to our bedside and provide frosty pitchers of ice water. Attractive nurses bring us fruit juice every few hours, even during the night. Although the rooms are warm and stuffy, and I must swallow evil-tasting medicines, the luxury and pampering lulls me into a cocoon of contentment.

By the following day my rash begins to fade, but my swollen glands and lymph nodes around my head and neck still feel lumpy. All is well until the orderlies bring us our food. When they set the trays before us, we look at the meal, then glance at each other and burst out laughing. For breakfast we have scrambled eggs prepared from powder by an obvious novice, two cold overdone sausages that we can hardly cut and toast that had been dried to brick hardness. The cereal and milk are passable.

"My God! Do you call this a meal?" complains one cadet at next evening's dinner.

"Look at this! One piece of warm cheese, a thin slice of lunchmeat and this greasy round of salami."

"I guess they don't want us to eat very much," chimes in another.

"At least we have a hunk of bread and some butter to fill up on," says the man next to me.

I vow that when I return to my squadron, I'm going to stack my plate so high I won't be able to see over the top of it.

I had been the fourth cadet brought into the measles ward, but by that same evening five more men had joined our group. They tuck five additional new ones in beds the next day then two more the following day for a total of a dozen men, nearly filling the contagious disease ward. A camaraderie born out of our similar situations slowly grows among us. We share our spots, our idle time, our bed rest and our skimpy, ludicrous meals. Our similar conditions cut through our differences and put us at ease with each other.

We break out in laughter again at our meatball dinner served the following night.

"Hey," says one cadet. "We know there will never be a rubber shortage in the United States. The secret to synthetic rubber is right here in the hospital kitchen."

Another shouts, "I know these things would bounce if you dropped one of 'em on the floor."

Still another adds, "If anyone wants to know whatever happened to the horses in the U.S. Cavalry, you can tell them that the U.S. Army Air Corps is eating them."

Despite our easy life and good times, I eventually tire of lying in bed. I pledge that when I return to the barracks that I'll never idly lie on my bunk again. I'm also hungry. Meager portions of poorly prepared food have whetted my appetite for more substantial fare.

The same ambulance carts ten of us back to our respective barracks the following morning. I discover that I'm scheduled for a grass-cutting detail that afternoon, but I hope that my delicate condition and my recent release from the hospital will persuade them to excuse me.

Meanwhile I march to the mess hall in step once again with the familiar faces of barracks #1720. Now that my condition has passed and health again surges through my body, I generously pile my plate, then "eat like a demon."

VETERANS AMONG THE INNOCENT

"Their B-24 had engine trouble over Florida," says one of the men in our barracks. "The crew bailed out, but they had set the plane on automatic pilot so it would head for the Gulf of Mexico then crash into the sea. But after they jumped, the faulty engines sputtered back on, and the plane just kept flying. Eventually the damn thing was found in Mexico where it finally ran out of fuel. Naturally there was a mystery about the ship when it was discovered because no crew was found in the wreckage. Finally the Air Corps traced the number on the tail to their Florida field."

I listen to his story with a small group of other cadets, my attention riveted on him. Fascinated, I study the airman's face as he speaks, this special man who had actually trained as a gunner on a B-24 bomber and now is a cadet like us.

As he spins his tale, his nose and mouth become manlier, his chin more noble. I accept what he says without question. The oppressive heat of the barracks fades away as I focus on his every word.

I think about flying in a bomber. How might I react if I had to bail out? Could I pull the cord as I fell earthward through the freezing air? Would I blank out and suddenly not know what I was doing? That crew had to jump. So might I sometime in the months ahead. A tingling of fright and excitement ripples through my abdomen.

"Let me tell you about the engineer on our B-24," interjects one of the other veterans. "He was really depressed about something, so the guy commits suicide by jumping from ten thousand feet through the rear hatch. They haven't found him yet!"

The story appalls me. I had never thought much about suicide or understood it. My neighbor, Mr. McNichols, killed himself in his garage with a hose attached to his car's exhaust pipe. I was confused. Why would anyone want to take his own life?

A former gunner now training with us had not only flown but also had seen action in the South Pacific. We listen even more intently to him.

"Yeah," he says with a rather somber and serious expression on his face, "the Jap Zeros ran circles around our P-38s."

"If that's true, how come we're doing so well against them?" challenges one cadet.

"You've been reading those newspapers haven't you?" responds the veteran. "As long as you stick to the funny papers you're better off. We shoot down one of theirs for every one of ours, but sometimes they knock off two of ours for every one they lose. The only way we can win the war is by out-producing them."

I take all that he says as absolute truth. After all, a man who has been there ought to know. He shakes my faith in the accuracy of newspapers. Perhaps they only print American propaganda.

"The Japanese antiaircraft fire was 90% accurate," he adds. "The only way they could get away from it was by flying under the trees, not over them. Sometimes the flak is so thick you can get out and walk on it." The other men who had talked to returning crews agree with him.

I enshrine this knight. He becomes more than a man. He has been where I must go. He has faced the reality of combat, that dark, red business that exists only in my fantasies. Although military life is comfortable and exciting now, the end result of my training will lead to the hell that gunner grimly reveals.

In my bed at night, in the safety and quietness of my room at home, I had often thought about the war. I envisioned the bombing of London, intrepid firemen silhouetted against roaring flames, wailing air raid sirens and the rubble of leveled buildings, the scenes I had witnessed in newsreels from a comfortable theater seat. I wondered how I would have coped with the reality of it. I had always lived in a peaceful home on a peaceful street in a peaceful town. I had never seen any violence except an occasional fistfight on the school playgrounds or little destruction other than the 1933 earthquake, a few car collisions and a garage that burned down on the next block.

In my innocence the heroes touch me deeply. I no longer have to rely on third hand rumors or grainy newsreels about the war. I listen to real flesh and blood men whose eyes reflect the light from the barracks windows, who breathe softly, who have known the feel and smell of a bomber as well as the foul breath of death. In their presence I question myself again. How will I react? How will I behave when I encounter *flak so thick I can walk on it?*

THUNDERSTORMS

Sleep is impossible at first. Even though I lie uncovered and wear only a pair of loosely fitting shorts, I'm still uncomfortable. The day's heat, rising and accumulating in the second story of the barracks, lingers far into the night. I turn and twist, attempting to find any position that's cooler. Soft light shines in from the outside, touching the ghostly rows of double-decked bunks where other men also try to find sleep.

As I shift my body, random thoughts pass through my mind. I think about Easter and what a contrast this Easter Sunday had been to others in my life. Everyone would have been dressed in his finest clothes at home. The young girls would be dazzling in their bright orchid, yellow and peach pastels. Quarantined to the base for two weeks during classification testing, I see only ordinary sun tan uniforms and gray-green fatigue coveralls. Finally, during the latter part of the night, cool at last, I pull up my sheet.

Low clouds blanket the sky the next morning, their plain grayness reminding me of summer mornings in my hometown of Inglewood, California, where cooling "high fog" rolled in off of the Pacific every night and persisted until mid-morning. The misty deck here, though, suffocates us as it presses the humid heat close to the earth. The overcast burns off early, allowing the Texas sun to scorch the barracks roofs and the bare dust and gravel outside. We sweat profusely even though we don't exercise or work, all of us soiling our shirts with ugly wet blotches. Only the cold showers give us relief.

If we change into clean shirts, they soon become damp and mottled again.

The following day higher clouds obscure the sun, but no rain falls. I long for a good thunderstorm, a tempest to stir up the atmosphere, to loosen the stranglehold of the stagnant heat. Part of the thrill of traveling to a new part of the country is the anticipation of different weather. I expect the storms to be more violent than those I am used to in California. And I'm ready.

The days pass by, some with oven-like temperatures and others with clouds that temper the searing sun, but are too thin to bear a drop of rain. I would settle for even a sprinkle, a scattering of cold drops on the dust. Finally the weather cools, and a brisk wind breaths life into a clear sky dotted with clouds, but it doesn't rain. At least there is a change.

The next day a brief shower dampens the streets, but only increases the stickiness. It's even more unbearable. The steam bath persists into the night. Only the fireflies, which I still watch with a curious fascination, seem to enjoy it, their tiny lights wandering lazily in the dark like slow, white sparks.

Flickering blue light dances across the northwestern horizon four nights later. Only in the darkness away from the lights can I see the scintillations. I know that thunderstorms often move from northwest to southeast along cold fronts, so I feel sure that sometime during the night I'll meet my first Texas thunderstorm. At midnight the first rolls of thunder steal into my sleep. A continuous flashing pulses through the windows, flickering on the rows of bunks and sleeping men. I'm fully awake as the storm envelopes us, the unending thunder booming and shaking our barracks and the constant lightning bolts transforming the sky into an electric-blue convulsion. Several jagged streaks rip to the ground nearby, the deafening cannon-like thunder exploding across the base. Rain roars on the roof, sweeps by the windows in waves and streams noisily off the eaves.

I watch the whole wondrous show. Never have I experienced such a raging storm. For over an hour it shudders and shimmers unceasingly, fascinating me and frightening me at the same time. I marvel at its power and awesome energy, thrill to its powerful drama and novelty.

*   *   *

At home, my father's excitement about the changing weather had been contagious. We parked one night near a sea cliff to watch a lightning storm out over the Pacific. "It's over Catalina," he said as we gasped and sighed at the infinite electric patterns in the clouds. In heavy storms he often drove happily and probably foolishly through the rain, splashing along the slick streets and fording flooded intersections where brownish waters lapped at our running boards. From our windows at home, we often watched the rain slant down. He particularly enjoyed the time just before an impending storm, those looming forces somehow energizing him. We chatted about how much rain we might receive from each system. We constructed a beautiful mercury barometer and an accurate rain gauge, recording the rainfall amounts in a little notebook. We bought a good thermometer then looked for record heat and cold. He fashioned a wooden arrow with a propeller on it to find the direction of the wind. For my birthday he bought me a heavy, slick book all about cloud types, the dynamics of weather and plans for simple weather instruments. I learned how to find the air's dew point anytime, using a thermometer and a glass of ice water.

He subscribed to the weather map published each day, bringing it home to me every night after work. We studied the patterns of isobars that looked like giant thumbprints and the mysterious movements of the "Highs" and "Lows," hoping for the possibility of a storm, some meteorological excitement.

He, having grown up on a farm in Indiana, where the vagaries of the weather determined the successes or failures of crops, had always cast his eyes toward the sky. He had seen ball lightning roll across the farmhouse floor, had been knocked flat near an open barn door with a close blast of lightning reeking of ozone. His family had been forced to move to California when a late spring blizzard devastated their clover fields. I was caught up in the infectious thrill that ran through his voice, his keen interest in the weather and his unspoken love for me. He and I always waited anxiously for the intoxication of the rain. And I wait for it still.

*   *   *

The following night I pull up my blanket against the chill air, the one that had been folded at my feet for so long. But the heat returns all too soon, sending its anesthesia coursing through my limbs, paralyzing me into inaction. I can only step under a bracing shower, letting the stream-cold water rake me for ten minutes. I dress in fresh clothes, but as before, rivulets of perspiration soon trickle down my back. The steamy air boils off of the Gulf of Mexico, enveloping Texas and the entire South.

Several days later the muggy air spawns yet another storm at night. One lightning strike zaps into an adjacent field, setting off an explosive thunder crack that jars the barracks. Furious winds drive the heavy rain almost horizontally, tremble the barracks and rattle the windows. Even while we wait for chow the following morning, lightning still splits the air and snakes in bright streamers through the gray clouds. As a gentle rain falls on our orderly formation lined up before the mess hall door, I think about how much stormy weather delights me. Later, back in the barracks, a cool breeze billows through the open window, and I reflect about how much I like to be cool and how I welcome it after the scorching days. My father and I had always wilted in the heat.

After a brief respite, the tropical weather soon returns with its moist numbing heat. I can only hope for another tempest to cool us off. I find myself wishing that my father were here so that we could enjoy the show together.

LITTLE RED LIGHTS

Flickering at first, the small red light in front of me suddenly glows continuously before I can extinguish it again. I try to relax, regain my poise. I grasp the wooden handle at the end of a long, stiff wire that rests upon a support. The wire projects into a little hole in a metal plate. If I don't hold my arm and hand perfectly steady, the wire will touch the side of the hole, complete an electrical circuit and light up the lamp. I tell myself to be calm. I hold my hand as still as possible, but the slightest movement sets it aglow again. Each blink tells me that I have failed. I have added numbers on a counter, raising the score against me.

As I struggle, the sergeant in charge shouts in his penetrating voice.

"Some of you are not doing very well. Your lights are on too much. Some of you are getting more and more tense. I can see it in the lights. How do you ever expect to be pilots if you can't be steadier than this?"

Is he talking about me? I can't check the performance of others without taking my eyes off what I'm doing. I must not lose my concentration. The sergeant's threatening voice tightens my muscles. I see that mocking red light as the possible end of my training. I could be grounded or "washed out," the most feared of all phrases. .The sadistic non-com again bellows over the hushed but apprehensive room of cadets.

"Okay. While you hold your hand absolutely steady, I want you to remember these numbers 1--6--12--2--4. Got that? And while you're at it memorize these letters H--S--W--B—P."

I concentrate on the numbers and letters, losing precious seconds of attention and setting the light fluttering like a defective tail light, running up my score.

"Okay. Stop now. Relax!" yells the taskmaster, the room filling with nervous voices and futile laughs.

Gasping with relief that the excruciating test is over, I shake my head, turn to the guy next to me. "Oh my God". I suppose we all feel in our hearts that we've performed poorly.

Before we can completely recover, we're directed to another room where we sit before large boards with squat pegs stuck in holes. Our task is to pull them out, turn them clockwise, exactly half way around, then place them in the hole again. As we wait to begin the test, I relax. I feel this one will be much easier than the last. How difficult can it be to turn around a peg in a hole? The tester explains that we'll be given only a short time to complete the exercise, and that we must insert the pegs precisely.

At his signal, we all begin, the room alive with the clicking and clacking of the pegs. Over the din he shouts at us.

"Hurry! Hurry! You're falling behind. You have only a few minutes left! Come on! You can turn those things faster than that!"

Very quickly I discover that the peg fits only if it's turned a certain way, any deviation preventing it from sliding into the hole. I try to jam some of them in three or four times before I find the exact position. I have to slow down to adjust them while he screams. "Faster! Faster!" A few cadets drop their pegs, and I hear them skitter across the floor. "Stop!" blasts the sergeant. I hadn't turned nearly as many as I thought I could, again feeling that I'd not performed well. As we file out of the room, I glance at the boards of others. Some had more success than I, but others less.

All morning long we move from one room to another, from one psychomotor test to the next. The doctors and psychologists attempt to determine how well our hands, eyes and feet work with our brain. As the day wears on, I become discouraged about my coordination, but so do many others.

In another room we sit before turntables that look like record players. A tiny metal disk is fixed to it on top near one edge. We hold a stylus in our hand and attempt to keep it in contact with it as the turntable spins. We find our rhythm only with difficulty then lose it again, resuming the chase for the elusive dime-sized spot. The officer in charge harasses us unmercifully. We laugh out of frustration when we finish.

I pursue game-like artificial planes pulling artificial targets then continue to shuffle from one stressful task to another. By lunchtime I've finished the battery of tests, the nervous strain mercifully over for a while. On our way to the mess hall, I'm relieved to be out in the open again, moving, marching away my tension and filling my lungs with pure air. At the same time, I carry the weight of a peculiar sadness, a dull lump somewhere inside, a residue of a shoddy performance on the psychomotor tests and its possible consequences. I try to suppress rising fantasies of "washing out." After lunch we must face the first part of our two-day physical examination, the infamous "64" physical.

* * *

The day before, we had taken written examinations from early morning until evening. We sat at plain wooden tables in a room of bare roof rafters and unshaded light bulbs that hung from the ceiling. They tested our general knowledge of the world then became more specific with examinations on mathematics, mechanical aptitude, vocabulary, map reading and dial and instrument reading. Some of the tests determined our aptitude for flying while others measured our ability to identify aircraft and naval ships from silhouettes and our skill at locating objectives from aerial photographs.

Limp with fatigue from the sheer volume and pace of the tests, I'd come away feeling relaxed and satisfied. Although my high school grades had not reflected it, words and reading had always been my strength. I had a good general knowledge of the world because I had many natural interests, and I'd studied aircraft and ship identification on my own because it excited me. Mathematics had always been my Achilles heel, but I found that I knew a passable amount.

*   *   *

Although we had taken thorough medical examinations at our draft boards and again when we qualified for cadet training, we must undergo a final "64" physical, which determines our fitness for the rigors of flying and the performance of tasks at high altitude. We hear about the ordeal long before we take it. Rumors abound that the Army doctors will find even the slightest defect, and, of course, that many men never pass the exam. I know of nothing physically wrong with me, but I become apprehensive that the medics will discover an obscure, unknown problem.

We strip to our shorts, padding barefooted from one test to another. We line up to have blood extracted, stand in queues holding warm jars of yellow urine and wait for the doctors to examine our bodies from our hair to our toenails. Every orifice of our body is rigorously examined. The doctors check our reflexes, determine our blood pressure, listen to our hearts and x-ray our chests.

Finally we face the eye examination, the most critical and the most feared of all. Having worn glasses briefly for astigmatism as a child (I wore them only in the presence of my mother, taking them off as soon as our house was out of sight), I am concerned they will say my problem is too severe for flying. In a dark room they probe my eyes with a tiny light, have me read charts from across the room then test my depth perception. By means of handles on strings we try to align two tall black pegs that are twenty feet away from us.

Despite succumbing to a case of measles during the physical, I pass. My eyes test 20/20, my astigmatism has disappeared and my depth perception is the best in my barracks. I align the pegs only 1mm apart while the average is 10mm. My good friend, Henry Berman, who wants to be a pilot, places the pegs 17mm apart. I feel proud enough to write home about it.

I cease to worry about my eyes, my body or any of the written examinations, although I still harbor doubts about the psychomotor tests. All of us, having been through the same procedures, discuss the tests ad nauseam, and in doing so we build camaraderie. Our uniforms, our sleeping, eating and marching together form a bond which helps us bear the anxieties, doubts and fears that we all share. I still see that red light blinking, however, and wonder why I could not have been cooler and more collected at the time. If I had only one more chance at turning those pegs! Coordination is essential for pilots, but for a bombardier perhaps it is not so important. Or is it?

THE PSYCHIATRIST

The doctor glares at me, his lips drawn into a sneer. I don't know whether he curses his bad luck at being stuck in San Antonio as an Army psychiatrist or that in some peculiar way the very sight of me annoys him. His scowl, his silver first lieutenant's bars and his thick black moustache present a menacing figure. He intimidates me before he utters a word. I look back at him with a blend of fear and anger.

Without any introduction or effort to put me at ease, he snaps, "Describe a P-38. Quickly!"

I sit on the edge of my chair, searching my memory for all I have read about it.

It's an interceptor made by Lockheed, and it has twin booms and two Allison engines of over 1000 horsepower each. It's called the 'Lightning.' It carries a cannon and four machine guns in its nose. It has a maximum speed of 400 miles per hour and a range of 1000 miles.

He watches me intently, never changing his grim expression. He raises his eyes and turns his head slightly, either surprised at how much I know about the plane or dumbfounded that anyone would want to tell him that much. I know that I blurt out the statistics rapidly, and probably, to him, nervously or childishly.

He stops my description of the P-38 and asks, "How does a P-38 differ from a P-39?" Again I rattle off facts as fast as I can, thinking that if I should hesitate he will think less about what I know.

"The P-39 has a single Allison 1100 horsepower engine, and it is built around a large cannon which fires through the propeller hub. It also has machine guns in its wings. It's called the 'Airacobra.' It can fly at 375 miles per hour."

Looking straight at me, the doctor says, "Stop! That's enough."

I detect a slight twinkle in his eye, thinking he will confound me on the next question. "Describe a P-61," he commands.

As the plane is new and not in service yet, I feel he doesn't expect me to know about it.

"The P-61 is a twin-boomed night interceptor called the 'Black Widow' and is made by Northrop." I suspect that I have impressed him.

Becoming more personal, he asks me if I had ever walked in my sleep. I hesitate then recall an instance when I was a child.

"Only once when I was seven years old," I tell him. "I walked down the street at night then turned back when a couple in a car asked me what I was doing out there so late at night in my pajamas. When I walked back home, I tried to wake up my parents by ringing the bell and knocking on the door, but they didn't hear me. I yelled at their window, but they still didn't wake up."

"Go on," he says, very interested.

"Well, I looked down the street to see if any of the neighbors were up, and I spotted one lighted window about three doors down. The woman there took me back home, and we finally woke my surprised mom and dad who got up to let me in."

The doctor jots a few notes on his interview form then looks at me again with the same hard expression.

"Did you ever faint?" he asks.

"The only time I ever felt like it," I said "was when I had my shots at Fort MacArthur, but I sat down on the floor and lowered my head and nothing happened."

He again averts his eyes, writing comments on my evaluation form. "Ever get seasick?"

"Just once. I was on a small boat with a dead engine. The wallowing in the swells made me queasy."

"When did you last masturbate?" he suddenly asks.

I had been told by others who had already had their psychiatric interview that they would ask this question and inwardly laughed at one cadet's response when he asked the examiner in return, "Well. What time is it now?"

I hesitate then answer sheepishly, "I don't know."

"I notice you have a sister just a few years younger than you," he says. "When was the last time you had sexual relations with her?"

"Never!" I blurt. "I never have!"

He squints at me incredulously, and asks again in a mocking voice, "Oh, come on now. Don't tell me you never have. When was the last time?"

"I've never touched my sister!" I snap back at him, anger tightening my voice. The question annoys me. Not only had I not done this, I had never even thought about it. Why would he think I had? Was he only trying to stir me up, check my reactions? Did most men who had sisters do that? He scribbles more notes on his forms.

Appearing tired and becoming even more agitated and annoyed, he asks," What would you say is your main goal in life?" In an angry, supercilious tone he adds, "And don't tell me your main goal in life is to be a pilot!"

I pause a moment then tell him, "My main goal in life is to marry someone that I love and have a family. I want to be a good father and want the family to be as happy as the one I grew up in."

At this, he slams the folder shut, squirms in his chair, looks at me accusingly and says in a most mocking tone, "My God! You really are a mama's boy aren't you?"

"I am not!" I fire back.

Frowning, he reopens the folder and quickly jots down a few final notes, hands me a form and says, "Here. Take this down to room 202 and sit and wait until your name's called."

As I walk down the narrow hall with the form clutched in my hand, I still smolder. Hot coals flare in my firebox. Of all that the wretched psychiatrist said to me, the most infuriating was "mama's boy!" He had pulled my psyche's master switch, setting off all of my emotional alarms. I'm quite conscious that at eighteen years old I still look boyish compared to the majority of the men. I shave only every two days while others who are more genetically rugged, their shadowed cheeks and chins dark even when they are shaved, must use a razor twice a day to pass inspection.

I recall standing before a mirror in a bare-walled latrine, my face encased in lather, drawing my safety razor across my cheek. In the mirror I see another cadet behind me, his blond sunburned hair rippling from his tanned forehead, his amused grin revealing small even teeth.

"Hey," he said, "Isn't that razor supposed to make some noise when you drag it across your face?" He chuckled in a mocking way, and I grinned in recognition of his joke.

I remember too how a sergeant stared at me as I as I walked in to pick up my uniforms. "How old are you?" he asked, looking at my face with an expression of disbelief. "Eighteen," I answered. He turned to the other enlisted men who were preparing the bundles of uniforms and mumbled loud enough that I could hear, "My God! What's happening to the Army Air Corps? They're letting young boys into it now". I felt the sting, gathered my uniforms and walked out.

I sit with others in chairs lined against the wall in the room where the psychiatrist directed me. Presently an orderly shouts my name. I walk into a large office where a lieutenant I assume to be in his forties sits behind a massive desk. His dark hair is combed loosely back from his longish but handsome face. With the door closed his office is silent. He greets me with a relaxed smile, his eyes friendly and warm, then ruffles through the papers on his desk.

"Well lad, the psychiatrist that interviewed you recommends a G.D.O., ground duty only for you."

I gasp, stunned, momentarily feeling suspended in my chair, unable to cope with the enormity of what he has just said.

"You know, small things like walking in your sleep even as a child and feeling faint with your shots could be a sign of nervous instability. You might complete your training but then when you were in combat you could become tense and be unable to perform your job."

My eyes are wide, my heart flip-flopping. He can't be saying these words.

"Extend your arms toward me with your palms down and your fingers spread, lad", he says.

No one has ever called me "lad" before. Is he looking at me as a boy from his exalted position of age? Is the term complimentary or derogatory? He looks carefully at my spread fingers then grasps my wrist to check my pulse.

"Right now your fingers are trembling slightly, and your pulse indicates that your heart is pounding."

"I'm shocked by what you just said. I never expected to be grounded, and that's why I'm upset."

In his soothing voice he begins to ask me questions.

"Where is Algeria and what country formerly protected it?"

"It's a country in North Africa. The French used to protect it."

"What are the French possessions in the Western Hemisphere?"

I can think of only two.

"There is one more, French Guiana," he says.

"I know about it. It's in South America," I respond.

"What notorious place is near there?" he continues.

"Devil's Island."

"Where is Luzon?"

Feeling much more relaxed now and more confident, I answer, "It is the largest and most northern island in the Philippines."

He congratulates me on my responses, but at the same time I wonder why he asks me these questions. Did the other psychiatrist tell him I was stupid?

He goes on with his questioning,

"Have you ever heard of Alexander DeSeversky?"

"Yes."

"Who is he?"

"He is the president of Republic Aircraft and has recently written a book."

"Do you know the name of the book, lad?"

"*Victory Through Air Power*," I answer.

He again asks me to extend my arms, and takes my pulse.

"You don't seem to be trembling now, and your pulse is normal. You impress me as being very intelligent, and you seem stable enough to me. After your physical examination today, come back and see me. I think maybe we can lift that G.D.O."

I leave his office heavy with the burden of possible grounding, but with a beginning surge of confidence, especially after his final words.

*   *   *

Back in the barracks, lying disconsolately on my bunk, still smarting from the sentencing by the "crazy psychiatrist"

I cope with my sadness. Turbulent thoughts tumble around in my mind. A bowling ball-sized tumor of depression weighs heavily in my psyche. Did I misunderstand? Did he ask me about a P-51 rather than the P-61 that I described? If I misheard him, he must think me an ignorant fool. Maybe that is why the second officer asked me all of those questions.

Knowing that an examiner would ask me questions about airplanes, I had studied aircraft booklets, until I knew almost every detail about them. Obviously I had told the psychiatrist too much and spit out the facts too rapidly and nervously. He could see my discomfort and my tension as I tried to remember every fact crammed in my head. It must have been evident to him that I had prepared myself so thoroughly because I feared failing the interview. I think all he wanted to know were generalities expressed in a relaxed manner rather than the rapid-fire barrage of statistics I spewed at him.

Why did I have to tell him about sleepwalking, faintness and seasickness when each had only happened once in my life before? Others told me that they had suffered all of those conditions then simply lied to the examiner.

"Why in hell did you tell him all of that crap? Get with it, Stevens."

They think I'm a fool for revealing all that to the psychiatrist. He no doubt thought me incredibly naive and innocent for telling him. As Don Olson had warned me several times before, "The trouble with you Stevens is that you are too damned honest."

Mama's boy! No one on the high school track team had ever thought of me that way. Didn't the sportswriter in the local paper call me "Iron Man?" Didn't my friends compliment me on my physique? Didn't the salesgirls at Newberry's call me "Muscles" when I reported for stock work in T-shirts? I would say that I'm more of a "papa's boy."

Why would he call me "mama's boy" just because my goal in life is to be a father in a good family? What is the matter with that?

The psychiatrist obviously had not liked me from the moment I entered his cubicle. Instead of a potential intrepid airman, tall, rugged, square-jawed with an intense, faraway look in his eyes, he saw a baby-faced high school kid. He must have said in his heart, "I'll not let him fly." I knew that I was as much of a man as anyone else and possessed the same kind of courage that they did, but I also knew I was younger, had had less worldly experience and was less physically mature than they. I had an abiding faith that I would grow in every way.

Why had he said so much about nervousness? During track meets I had learned to relax and calm the tensions of competition. Runners that were too tense lost races. I had seen others fighting their dry mouths, the paleness that spread over their lips and faces, the trembling in the starting blocks, but I had overcome them all.

One of our cadet manuals had stated, "Should a cadet be classified for ground duty only, he should not be discouraged. In the ground services of the Army Air Forces the grounded man will find ample opportunities for service and advancement." I would have none of it. My sights had been set on flying, to become a combat bombardier. My parents knew what I wanted and so did all of my friends back home. If I failed to reach my goal, I would not only be a failure to myself but also to others.

Near the end of the physical, even after one of the doctors discovered my measles rash, my confidence rose.

*   *   *

Feeling much better about myself, and with red spots beginning to creep over my body, I return to the lieutenant I had last seen. I feel that I must know his final decision before I report to the dispensary and move on for a stay in the hospital. He again greets me calmly and, with a friendly manner, says, "Hold out your hands to me again." I extend my hands that are now relaxed and steady. "Okay," he says, "We're going to give you a crack at it."

THE ALAMO

Crumbling walls still maintain their scalloped outline at the Alamo, the mission fortress where 187 brave Texas defenders fought to the last man against the siege of 5,000 Mexican soldiers. Carlo and I stand in front of its old arched entrance and massive spiraled columns, looking up at the bells and the deteriorating but sturdy walls. Davy Crockett and Jim Bowie, heroes that I had heard about as a child, had died here. The place still stands as a monument to their courage. It is a special place for me too because it's the first significant historical structure that I've ever seen on my own, without tagging along after my parents. It's Carlo's first experience too.

I had wanted to see the Alamo ever since the Texans moved into our neighborhood at home, just before I entered high school. Their twangy drawls and their double names--- Billy Joe and Winnie Lou, initials like C.J. and nicknames like "Sweet Thing" fascinated me. C. J. Fletcher taught me about Texas metaphors. He puzzled me at first by telling me he had "high-tailed it to the store." I appreciated the impact of the image, the added vision of a wild horse galloping over a grassy Texas field, its mane ruffling in its own wind and its tail streaming high out behind. A new and potent dimension was added to the dull word, "hurried."

C. J., who became my good friend, also taught me the Texas state song.

> *"Beautiful, beautiful Texas,*
> *The land where the bluebonnets grow,*
> *The land of our forefathers,*
> *Who fought at the Alamo."*

I had never heard of the Alamo until then, the old fortress existing only as a word in a song. C. J. knew about what had happened there.

Now I stand before it, making that wonderful, satisfying leap from the abstract to the specific, from my imagination to reality. We walk through the ponderous arch to the inside where the men had held out for so long. A squat, heavy mortar actually used by the defenders to fight off Santa Anna's men is still poised at a high angle. Carlo and I tarry at the museum, learning more about what happened here in 1836.

* * *

After being denied a pass because of illness, K.P. and guard duty, the commanding officer finally issues me one, giving me my first opportunity to see downtown San Antonio. I like going into town with Carlo because we enjoy the same activities.

An old bus picks us up conveniently near the squadron barracks. It's identical to the type used on the Inglewood line at home. It makes me feel comfortable, and kindles thoughts of being back there. The driver charges us 25 cents each! I think the fare a little high. We rumble into the city, getting off at the Gunter Hotel, the best in the area and the only one that provides a special center for cadets.

Hungry, we hustle into the hotel's grand, air-conditioned restaurant, enjoying being cool for a change. We both order breaded veal cutlets. Delicious! With the meal they serve a small bowl of beans that they call black-eyed peas, a vegetable I'd never tried before. Warm and steaming in a broth, they taste wonderfully different, a kind of earthy flavor that I immediately like. Rolls with butter and potatoes round out the main dish. We also order malted milks to accompany the meal then a slice of raisin pie to top it off. Comfortably full, we relax in the icy luxury of the artificial air.

Back out on the warm street again, we walk to the Moffet Studios to have our pictures taken. I bemoan the shocking price of $3.75 for a half dozen photographs to be placed in special Army Air Corps frames.

Once again facing the heat, we walk into the air-cooled Majestic Theater to see, fittingly enough, a film called "Bombardier." We enjoy it, but the theater itself delights us more. The very high ceiling, black with a purplish haze, resembles the night sky, and somehow stars twinkle and realistic clouds sweep slowly across the firmament. The crisp air and the expanse of the sky above make us feel as though we're out on the open prairie at night.

Outside, we again walk down the sun-baked streets, our eyes squinting and struggling to adjust to the bright sunlight. At the river we turn off onto a special walk that follows its banks, ambling along the pathways, enjoying the green comfort of the grass and the shade of the trees. Having come from Southern California where rivers run only when it rained, the pleasant, slow-flowing water winding its way through the tall city buildings captivates us. Near one of the bridges two other cadets in a canoe, their laughter spilling out over the sun-speckled surface, row in helpless circles, occasionally banging the little boat into the sides of the canal. I laugh at them because their plight reminds me of a time when my sister and I tried to row on Crystal Lake. Unable to make the boat move forward, we only floundered in ridiculous spirals.

*   *   *

After touring the Alamo, we mosey around town, looking in at shop windows and restaurants before we decide to take in another movie, this time at the Aztec Theater where we see "Crystal Ball" with Paulette Goddard and Ray Milland. When we emerge from our second movie of the day with the hour growing late, we trace our way back to the Gunter Hotel and its tempting restaurant. This time I launch into a chicken pie, backing it up with rolls and butter. I order both milk and Coca-Cola then sink my fork into a thick, soft slab of cream pie for dessert. Carlo cannot resist a T-bone steak with a mound of French fried potatoes.

Satiated and weary, we wait for the bus in the comfort of the hotel lobby. Several of the other cadets, having spent the afternoon drinking, walk unsteadily, a few of them barely able to stand up. Since, in my innocence, I don't either drink or smoke, I have trouble understanding those that do. Their erratic, unpredictable actions, loudness and being out of control make me uneasy. The guy next to me tells me that the stairs leading up to the service men's lounge on the mezzanine floor is lined all the way up with vomit from a series of drunken cadets.

Hard-looking young women sit around on benches and chairs in the lobby waiting to be picked up. Intoxicated cadets and other soldiers stagger by, take one of the girls by the hand and walk off. I think about my high school track coach whose every word I believed to be absolutely correct and morally right, telling us how girlfriends wreck athletes and how they can in general ruin a good man's life.

As a member of the high school track team I used to sit around on the lawn on the inside oval of the track listening to instructions, our bodies smelling of stale sweat and the sweet odor of wintergreen lotion that we rubbed into our sore muscles.

The coach always wore a hat and closed one eye as he talked to us. "Yeah. Copeland's not out for track any more. He'd rather be with his little floozy than come out here and work to be his best."

I can also hear my mother saying that sex was always wrong before marriage and that some girls are "not all they should be."

The spectacle interests me, actually captivates me. It's new, different and tantalizing. But I can think only about how these loose women are ruining the lives of the young soldiers. Other groups of prostitutes stand on the street corner near the hotel, leering at us as we walk by. They make me uneasy.

We rumble back to the base, a few cadets alcohol-loud, a few dozing, but most talking softly with each other. My head is full of San Antonio images. I think about the Alamo again, wondering if I as a soldier would ever be able to fight to the last man. I wonder too if I will have the courage someday soon to fly a combat mission as a bombardier as we had seen in the film that afternoon.

BOMBARDIER

The British bombardier bends over his bombsight, his fingers working with the precision of a surgeon on its sensitive dials. Close bursts of antiaircraft fire flash in the German night sky, jostling the bomber. He bravely stays with his task. Bundled in his thick flying suit, encumbered with a helmet and oxygen mask, his trained eye never leaves his instrument. More explosions briefly light up the inside of the plane, reflecting eerily off his helmet. An enemy night interceptor rips a volley of machine gun bullets through the fuselage. The gunners retaliate with a clatter of rapid-fire bursts. The bombardier holds a thumb switch in one hand. He presses the button at the precise moment, releasing his load, sending his bombs screaming toward the dark target. Moments later, dull thuds and thunderous explosions erupt from below as they find their mark in the Ruhr Valley. Another Nazi factory destroyed. The bombardier turns, his eyes squinty as though he smiles beneath his oxygen mask, his hand raised in victory, a job well done.

As I sat comfortably in the Newsreel Theater in downtown Los Angeles, I watched the film with awe and fascination. The combination of the bombardier's skill and courage impressed me. As a high school student, I knew that I would have to join one of the services soon, and this film, along with others, convinced me that I wanted to sign up for the Army Air Corps and become a bombardier.

A Hollywood film about the development of the top-secret Norden bombsight reinforced my interest. A bombardier, in a demonstration of its incredible accuracy, dropped a bomb from high altitude directly into the center of a pickle barrel floating on a small raft at sea. The wonders of the sight were magical to me. In another war film, a bomber crew streaked over a tall-stacked enemy factory. The pilot, cheering on the bombardier over the intercom said, "Okay. Let's see you put your bombs right down the stacks!" He answered, "Which stack?" The pilot chuckled. The uncanny accuracy of the sight and the man's skill were established.

*   *   *

At the classification center in San Antonio a board of officers examines our qualifications, basing their decisions on the results of our tests and personal choices. Would we be pilots, bombardiers or navigators? Most of the cadets want to be pilots as that's where most of the real action and glory are, but some of us actually want to be bombardiers or navigators.

I lay in the hospital with a case of measles still not knowing whether I have been classified. Restless, I yearn to get back to my squadron so I can find out. I finally return to the barracks to find that only two men have been told what they will be, both pilots, their first choice.

By the following day most of the men know how they have been rated, a good number of them bombardiers, but because of my time in the hospital, the decision about me is delayed. I must wait, irritated by the tension of not knowing. Many of the men who passionately want to be pilots are told they will be bombardiers instead. The sour news hits them hard. Some sink into a gray gloom, their eyes cast down, their mouths a sad slit while others rage and fume across the wooden barracks floors, threatening that they will fight the decision. Some who use sarcasm to vent their discouragement stand at the top of the stairs, lean over the railing and yell, "Bombs Away! Bombs Away!" then laugh in a mocking way, smoldering at the same time. Although I sympathize with them, I can't help laughing at their antics.

Even by the next day I have no word about my status. I worry that I've again become a victim of army errors, another colossal mix-up. Since the threat of grounding was made, I agonize over whether that order might still stand. I don't handle "not knowing" very well, especially when knowing is so vital to my future and what I think of myself.

The following day as I relax on my bunk a raspy voice over the loudspeaker announces, "All cadets not classified report to the orderly room at once!" I bounce from my bed, clatter down the stairs and sprint over to report, taking a place in line at the lieutenant's door. We approach his desk one at a time. My turn at last, I walk in, cut a sharp square right turn, salute and say, "Aviation Cadet Charles N. Stevens reporting, sir." The lieutenant runs his finger down a list on his desk, stops then says, "You've been classified as a bombardier this morning."

"Thank you, sir!"

I salute smartly, turn and march out, my head up, my back proudly straight. .

All the way to the barracks I walk buoyantly, whistling to myself. Inflated with joy, I want to share the good news with my parents who care most about my good fortune. Miraculously my cold begins to vanish, my athlete's foot is clearing up, my boil has broken and will now heal and my strength returns after my bout with the measles.

I officially belong to the brotherhood of bombardiers. I dash off a letter home

If I am one of the top men in my bombardier class, I may have a chance to become a bombardier-navigator. They fly on attack bombers. They navigate to the target, bomb when they reach it then navigate back home again. Did you know that a bombardier is a gunner too? He takes the nose guns, twin .50 calibers. We get five and a half weeks of gunnery and turret training.

Carlo Zuniga, my good friend, will be a bombardier too, and we both hope to ship out together. The following day most of the men leave for preflight school, but I remain as I was classified late. I'm delighted that Carlo doesn't ship out either, so our chances of training together are very good.

I finally find out my qualification ratings for pilot, bombardier and navigator. Cadets must score a "3" to have a chance at any one of them. I qualify with a "6" for bombardier, "6" for navigator and "5" for pilot. I could have had my pick.

I am ecstatic at having at last passed through the first gate toward my goal, that I have now overcome two major hurdles. Perhaps I'll yet take my place in the pantheon along side that British bombardier I so admired in the newsreel.

THOUGHTS OF HOME

"Mail call!" shouts the sergeant at one end of the dimly lit barracks. Clutching a pack of letters in one hand, he sets several packages down at his feet while the cadets cluster around him. Waiting until most of the men have arrived, he smiles benignly as though he senses he's the bearer of good news. He shouts the first name in his deep, authoritarian voice.

"Smith!"

"Hyo!" yells the happy cadet, dashing forward, tearing open the envelope.

"Spence!"

"Hyo!"

"Stern!"

"Hyo!"

We listen attentively, almost painfully, for our names. I, like most of them, have been away only a month, but we all yearn for news from home. I have a passion for knowing what's happening there, even about the most mundane activities. I long to hear from my parents because they represent home, but I also look forward to the latest about the neighborhood, the "kids" on the block that I grew up with, my home town and my friends from church. I hope for letters from my relatives, schoolmates, a thin sprinkling of girlfriends and even the high school track coach. I treasure them all. They are the ones who know me well and care about me. The army thinks of us only as names and numbers, the essential facts embossed on the metal dog tags dangling from my neck, "Charles N. Stevens, 39569857, Blood Type O."

"Hyo!" I shout as the electric sound of my name rolls off the sergeant's tongue. A thrill flashes through my body like a jolt of sudden fear. I snatch my letter. I recognize my mother's distinctive handwriting. On the airmail stamp in the corner a red airplane speeds across a red sky. I sit on the nearest bunk, slide my finger under the envelope flap and unfold the thin paper. I scan the letter at first then savor it more as I reread, absorbing the essence of home.

*   *   *

My mother and father were soft-spoken people. Not prone to emotional outbursts, they seldom yelled at my sister or me and never at each other. Calmness and quietness reigned in our house, the radio on only in the evening for the regular programs---Jack Benny, Fibber McGee and Molly, Lum and Abner, the Lux Radio Theater or Amos and Andy. On weekends, during the season, my father listened to football games. When I became a teenager, I bought records that filled the house with the music of Glenn Miller, Tommy Dorsey, Kay Keyser and rarely Guy Lombardo--but usually when my parents were gone.

On a typical evening my father sat in his soft upholstered chair near the radio, alternately listening and glancing at the newspaper. My mother sewed on buttons or mended socks stretched over a black darning egg. If she were drying dishes in the kitchen, my father would beg her to come in and listen to our favorite programs. She would saunter in reluctantly, carrying the damp dishtowel with her then sit on his lap. The dog lay asleep on the rug, quivering in his dreams, and my sister and I relaxed on the couch or dabbled at our homework.

My sister and I felt secure in their love, even during the Depression. Although my father had to swallow cuts in pay, he always had a job. They never burdened us with worries about money. We often had to wear the same clothes several days or more, and our simple meals sometimes did not include meat. My frugal father, mechanically gifted, fixed everything.

Like a majority of the neighbors we kept chickens and always had cats, often watching the birth of new litters with fascination. A dog, Pal, adopted us and became a part of our family. I included his name in the salutation of my letters home.

After the war began, my father organized a shop in our garage as an adjunct to his regular job in Los Angeles. He brought in tanks of oxygen and acetylene along with welding equipment to silver-solder brass fittings onto flexible metal hoses designed to be part of aircraft engines. My mother also learned the skill, both laboring in the garage, wearing thick gloves and engineer-like caps to keep the sparks out of their hair. Wisps of white smoke drifted up toward the fluorescent lights as they worked. They produced hundreds of shiny flexible lines, feeling they were a vital part of the war effort.

* * *

I receive another letter from my mother, one from my sister, Charline, and one from a neighbor girl. The letters are like caresses, and I bask in them.

At my first opportunity I attempt to answer all their questions and comment on their news.

Yes, my sty and my red eyes from staring out of the open train window have cleared up. No, you don't need to send me any more socks or underwear. I will be issued five more pairs of each in a few days. The army gives you everything. Thanks for the pictures. They are swell. Yes, I still have the same uniform, but I will have Army Air Force insignia on it in a few days. Charline,

I didn't know your handwriting was so beautiful. I sat staring at it, too thrilled and amazed to move when I opened it. It sure is easy to read.

Please tell Pal that I'm sorry he cut his foot. I hope it doesn't hurt him too much. No, I didn't hear anything about a blackout in Los Angeles. San Antonio does not get very much news from California. It's always a bunch of Texas jabber. The money situation was grave, but the two bucks you sent helped a lot. I should be paid soon, and that will relieve the situation immensely. There are lots of little things you have to buy, and that keeps adding up.

Before I left home I planted a Victory Garden, but the shoots had just begun to push through the soil when I left. Many of our neighbors had them too as vegetables were in short supply in the markets.

My mother reports that the garden is growing well. I picture it in my mind---even rows of radishes and lacy carrot tops, red-veined beet leaves and thick-stemmed squash vines. I can also see the rising corn stalks, the pale lettuce leaves and the slow-growing turnips.

My mother writes that she plans to set Snowball, one of our plump white hens. I think about the mystery of setting hens, how all of a sudden they stay on the nest and won't get off. I think about the incredible warmth beneath a hen, how I warmed my cold hands beneath them on a chilly day.

I'm glad you're going to set Snowball. We haven't had little chicks in a long time. I hear that chicks are only 12 cents each here in Texas.

I learn from the letter that my parents plan to store some boxes in my room. I caution them to not wreck my bed, that I would hate to have anything happen to it. My father and I had built the room out of one-half of the garage so that I would have a quiet place to study away from the distractions of the house and the nightly radio programs. I slept in the room and considered it my house. I see my room clearly in my imagination---My bed takes up most of the space, a desk and chair occupying part of the rest. On one wall hangs a gigantic map of the United States, while color portraits of Veronica Lake and Alexis Smith smile down on me from the back wall. Above the bed, fastened to the ceiling is a weather bureau poster of all the cloud types.

Each letter brings another glimmer from home. For a few moments, at least, I live there again.

You have my consent to buy a new mattress for my room, but please save the one you have now so that I can sleep on it when I get home. Don't renovate my lovely hard mattress. I love it! So you are having another salad out of my garden. That is swell.

Mama, I didn't get you a Mother's Day card, but I just didn't have time. I think of you and love you with all my heart everyday of the world. I constantly look forward to the day when I will see you all again. One appreciates his folks and friends more and more as the days wear on, and he doesn't see them.

THE KELLY CLIP

Fluffy tufts of hair, remnants of the soft waves I had combed back for so long, fall to my shoulders, drop to the floor. The barber's clicking scissors hover over my head as though making decisions before swooping down to shear off another lock. Piles of black, brown and blond hair accumulate on the linoleum as a dozen of us submit to the Kelly Clip, a special haircut leaving us nearly bare at the sides with a half-inch stubble on top. The white-jacketed barber runs the buzzing electric clippers over my head, perfecting an even trim. His hands smell of lotion, the razor of machine oil. Although I don't mind the short cut as I have always wanted a "butch", I have no choice. They require us to undergo the trimming, named after Kelly Field adjacent to our base.

My enterprising sheep shearer, senses he has an innocent cadet in his chair.

"You know, you have a little dandruff there. Dandruff is nothin' but dead skin flakes, but the germ that causes it is very contagious. You can get it by just putting your head down on someone's bunk."

I listen as he continues his pitch.

"I notice that your hair's getting a little thin in back. I have something that'll get rid of your flaking problem and help you from losing any more."

He holds up a bottle of beetle-dark liquid he calls Dixol.

"You see this stuff. I've been putting this on my scalp, and my hair's starting to grow back. See!"

I look at his pinkish pate, dully mirroring the lights of the barbershop in its waxy shine. Sure enough, a thin streak of fine, blondish hair flourishes there.

"Would you like me to try it on you?" he asks.

"Sure. Go ahead."

As he anoints me with the inky potion, a powerful odor envelopes me, reminding me of Lysol, creosote and carbolic acid mixed together. After working it in, he wraps a hot, damp towel around my head, the turban transforming me into a Turkish potentate. The steamy heat, in combination with the caustic chemicals burns my scalp so fiercely that I can hardly bear it. No germ could possibly survive under such conditions. My discomfort reminds me of our neighbor's cat at home. They bathed him in coal oil to rid him of fleas. No wonder the unfortunate thing screeched and bounded around the yard as if he were on fire. I feel the same.

Mercifully the man removes the towel and shampoos the vile stuff out of my hair. He applies sweet-smelling oil, and I'm finished. I pay him $1.35 for the haircut, treatment and shampoo and now have only $4.00. We leave the shop with our new haircuts, my scalp still tingling, all of us now looking alike. We sleep in the same barracks in identical bunks, wear the same uniforms, rise and eat together at the same time---now our heads all look alike. We are required to visit the barbershop each week to maintain our clean-cut, military look.

We are quarantined to our barracks and the immediate vicinity for fifteen days, until we are classified. During this period doctors examine us briefly every day at 12:30. I don't mind being confined since we're all together, but I long to have a pass to San Antonio which, in my imagination, looms as some mysterious paradise.

Rules and regulations govern all our activities. We have to march to the mess hall in formation then, when we arrive, file through the door and take our place behind one of eighteen chairs at the table, remaining at attention until all eighteen men are present. Only then can we sit down. We dish food from bowls and platters on to our plates ourselves, but when we eat we must place the hand we are not using in our laps. We can't leave the table until every cadet finishes. Even then we can't wander back to our barracks alone, but are required to march back in groups.

We learn that the clock has twenty-four hours, AM and PM becoming irrelevant. 1500 hours is 3 o'clock in the afternoon. It is as though I were now privy to a military secret that separates me from the rest of society.

*   *   *

The fifteen-day quarantine finally ends, and we're relatively free men again. Henry Berman and I walk to the base theater where we see "Sherlock Holmes in Washington" and "Desert Victory", a film that follows the British advance from El Alamein to Tripoli in North Africa. Light hearted and buoyant after shedding our restrictions, we stroll to the Service Club where we each order huge strawberry sundaes. Although a dance had been arranged there, we don't participate. With an ugly boil on my jaw, I fear no woman would feel comfortable dancing with me.

The end of the quarantine, although giving us more latitude, does nothing to soften the regulation of our lives. Our overseers, equating idleness with sin, provide us with a multitude of tasks to keep us busy. When a group of cadets ship out, some of us are selected to load their stuffed barracks bags onto old Railway Express cars. We perspire in the heat as we lift, throw and drag their baggage.

I rise in the dark at 0400 hours. Still sleepy, I pass beneath the dim outside barracks lights, on my way to the mess hall where I've been assigned three days of kitchen police duty. Lights shine brightly from the kitchen windows in contrast to the darkened barracks where cadets still sleep soundly. Preparations for the day begin early. I carry plates to the long tables, turning each upside down in front of a chair. I distribute salt and pepper shakers then silverware. When the orderly squadrons of cadets march to the mess hall door, file in and take their seats, I tote pitchers of milk, decanters of coffee and steaming platters and bowls to the tables, refilling each when they clean them out. Discouraged, I feel like I'll never get into San Antonio.

Now that we have warm water, I indulge in long, drenching showers. Feeling especially clean and good about myself, I slip into my sharply pressed class A uniform. I look forward to a tasty meal in the mess hall followed by an exciting movie at the base theater, "Crash Dive" in Technicolor with Tyrone Power. As I float contentedly in a mild euphoria, the crackly, always intrusive loudspeaker blares out my name and the names of three other cadets, directing us to report to the orderly room immediately.

"We're sorry. We know it's a raw deal," the orderly tells us when we arrive, "but you four will have to report to Mess Hall C right away for K.P. duty."

Unhappy and mumbling epithets under my breath, I slouch out of the orderly room with the others, my pleasant glow suddenly stripped away. I rarely mind regulations or routines as long as I know when they are going to occur. I had never liked abrupt changes in plans. When I design my day, I strongly fantasize the events ahead of me and so, in a sense, have them. Changing shatters my fantasies.

Back in the barracks, still fuming, I carefully remove my uniform and slide into my gray-green fatigue suit. The four of us walk to Mess Hall C where a mountain of fresh string beans waits for us. Taking only time off to eat dinner, we attack them one at a time, pulling off the ends and snapping them into inch sections. Two of us snap far into the night, completing two bushels of them.

*   *   *

Mops, brooms, brushes, soap, buckets of water and dust rags are ironically the implements of a G.I. Party, a misnomer used to describe the scouring of the barracks. After sweeping the floors and dusting every surface and object in sight including the rafters and wall structures, we scrub the floor with wet brushes and soap, their pungent smell pervading the room. We finish by slopping mops across them until they're immaculate. We straighten our footlockers and tidy our wooden closet, the finishing touch in our preparations for Saturday's inspection.

On Saturday morning we stand at attention in front of our barracks for personal inspection. Dressed in our class A uniforms, suntan shirts, trousers, ties, silk stockings and cadet caps, our polished brass belt buckles gleaming, our heavy brown shoes glistening, we wait. A small spring-loaded collar stay keeps our collars stiff at the points. Spotless white gloves cover our hands. A captain and a lieutenant, their bars shining, walk slowly along the rows, pausing to scrutinize each man. They look for soiled uniforms, sloppiness or poor positions. They peer grimly at my face, their eyes small and squinty beneath the leather bills of their officer's caps, checking my shave. Their eyes rove down my body as I stare straight ahead at a fixed point.

"Your feet are a few degrees off. Move 'em! Let's see that 45-degree angle. Your hands turn out a trifle too much. Okay, that's better."

They move on to the next man.

After our barracks and personal inspection, we fill the morning by marching and drilling before the officers.

If any of the barracks don't pass inspection, they must be checked again. This occurs the following Saturday as we stand inside for personal review due to a steady light rain. Ours passes, but others do not, so we must clean the rest of the morning to prepare for another checkup after lunch. This time the officers examine more closely, one of them discovering a trace of dust on a board on the wall behind me. I'm caught. I'm gigged. I must walk the ramp for an hour wearing my class A uniform with white gloves as punishment.

*   *   *

I'm ordered to report to the guardhouse for duty at noon, and I must stay there on call until 1000 hours the next morning. Because my name is fourteen on the list, I'm a supernumerary guard, only being called in case another becomes ill or is called away. The cadet officer in charge tries to teach me the Manual of Arms, to raise or lower or position a rifle through a series of snappy manipulations. He performs the movements quickly and smoothly, but he expects me to be as accomplished after only twenty minutes of training. I, of course, disappoint him and myself by not being able to approximate his routine. I can't handle the rifle any better than I can keep time to music, dance well or row a boat in a straight line. The gun simply doesn't make the correct moves at the correct time. Essentially believing the flourishes are stupid, I have little motivation to master them other than to get the duty behind me. I don't see why I can't place the rifle on my shoulder any way I want.

During the long, tedious hours of being on call, my only task is to relieve one person for twenty minutes, at a post where I don't even have to carry a rifle. The place I "guard" swarms with officers, and I salute them until my arm aches. Guard duty seems senseless. Although we carry a rifle, it's not loaded, and we're not really guarding anything.

*   *   *

As I write a letter home, I study the letterhead of the stationery I'd purchased at the P.X. In a small photograph at one edge of the top, white-gloved cadets stand at attention bearing squadron flags while four others stand in front of them, one carrying the American flag snapping in the wind, another with the eagle emblem. The other two balance rifles on their shoulders. Across the right hand top of the page a fierce-looking eagle spreads its wings and reaches out with his sharp, curved talons as though ready to pounce on his prey. Beneath the menacing bird are the words:

"From the sidewalks and countryside of every part of the nation, young men come to the San Antonio Aviation Cadet Center to learn to be not only pilots but officers as well. In order to instill the importance of strict discipline as a fundamental of good soldiering, everything the cadet does must be executed with exaggerated precision. Cadet life at the San Antonio Aviation Cadet Center is comparable to a college campus camouflaged with war paint---a campus on which men are taught to fly and fight, to command and obey."

Discipline, duty and obedience. I understand their necessity. I tolerate loading barracks bags on trucks, fanaticism about cleanliness, gas mask drills, sweaty retreats, picking up rocks and weeds, and even the Kelly Clip as part of what I must endure to reach my goal, but I don't have to like it.

RUMORS AND RESOLVE

While we dress in the morning or shave in front of the latrine mirrors, we chat with each other. We even talk while we sit in rows on open toilets. It's a fertile field for the sowing of half-truths, hearsay, and rumors.

"They say that Preflight is pretty tough. A bunch of the guys wash out there."
"Some of my friends told me that Preflight was just too damn much for them, so they just plain quit."

We hear endless stories, most of them no doubt nurtured by our unspoken fears of failure, of washing out. Preflight School, the next step in our training, gradually becomes a frightening place where the regimen and the demands of study seem so severe that they verge on the impossible. Ruthless, exacting officers scrutinize each cadet for the slightest shortcoming. The main purpose of Preflight School, according to the wild tales, is to eliminate men rather than train them.

I sense an amorphous trembling inside, begin to doubt myself, become anxious and uncertain about my abilities. If Preflight School is all they say it is, will it grind me down? Will they expose my flaws? Will they pry into my imperfections, my inadequacies? Will the authorities, discovering that I'm unfit after all, send me away with the other failures? Fortunately, my apprehensions are tempered by waves of confidence that come and go. I write to my parents on stationery imprinted at the top with a golden pair of Air Corps wings, the type I intend to wear some day.

I have made up my mind that I am going through with the whole deal until I have my wings on my chest and gold bars on my shoulders. I am going to study as I never have before. If I wash out, it will be no fault of mine. I must succeed, and that's all there is to it.

The tempo of the rumors increases as we near the end of our classification at San Antonio.

"They say if you drop your pencil in class, you get so far behind that you like to never catch up."

"I hear that they start you out with two plus two and end with advanced physics."

Having barely survived high school physics and with only average grades in mathematics, the remarks concern me, temporarily dampening my resolve. I blame my high school grades on my lack of effort and motivation, the distractions of running on the track team and a lackadaisical attitude toward homework. When I vow that these defects will never dominate me again, I feel my spirits warm.

During our final days at San Antonio, more second hand "facts" revolve around when we'll ship out and where. The captain in charge tells us only that we're to remain in the squadron area and wait for announcements. The army never informs us about anything until the final moment, if then. The tactic keeps the underlings out of all decisions and teaches us to follow when officers give their commands.

Having been in Texas less than a month, I still find myself longing for home. The rumble bouncing around the orderly room is that we might be sent to Santa Ana, California, only fifty miles from home. I know that going there is unlikely, but the outside chance is appealing. I'm torn between the exciting possibilities of new places and experiences and nestling in the security of my family, friends and the familiar in California.

The captain orders us to sign the pay book in the finance office before nightfall, a sure sign we're about to leave. Not knowing the location of our Preflight School is annoying, but on the other hand the mystery of it is stimulating.

Even though our departure could occur at any time, the officers allow us no idle moments as they firmly believe that it leads to discontent and laziness. After taking another series of shots in both arms, I report to retreat, the ritual of lowering the flag in the late afternoon. We stand at attention in the scorching slant of the sun, the sweet, wavering notes of the bugle mingling with the flapping of the Stars and Stripes. We follow the ceremony with a march of a mile to a dusty drill field where we again stand at attention for nearly a half hour while officers review us. Sweat soaks through our formerly crisp uniforms, wilting their creases and mottling the cloth clinging to our backs.

That night my arms throb from the inoculations. I can't find any position in bed that will relieve the dull aching. I'm probably running a slight fever, but the heat of the room is so like an inferno that I can't tell whether I have one or not. I don't feel woozy from the shots the way I did at Fort MacArthur. I decided beforehand that they wouldn't affect me, that I would go about my business and not think about them.

On the following day our commander tells us that our squadron, even though we are on the verge of leaving, "must keep doing something." In the searing heat we bend to the ground pulling weeds and picking up small rocks, sweat dripping from our faces. I stop often to wipe my forehead with my sleeve.

The cadet pilots all leave, merely marching across the street to their Preflight School. Only thirty-six of us, those classified as navigators and bombardiers remain. A silence and emptiness settles over the barracks, and I realize how many friends I had made among the pilots and how I miss them.

Casual information circulating among us is that our trip will begin in two days and that it will be a three-day journey. In what direction we don't know. The suspense eats at me.

We sign forms that all cadets must complete before leaving, and the lieutenant now in charge orders that we all move into the same barracks. The entire morning we move our clothes, barracks bags, and personal belongings---letters from home, toilet articles, writing materials and magazines---from our footlockers into our new quarters. Still no word on when or where we'll ship.

At last we learn that we'll leave in the evening, the destination still remaining a "military secret," especially to us. I still hold a slim hope for Santa Ana, but I know that Ellington Field in Houston, Texas is more likely. I write my parents, warning them that *from now on it's one mass of studying* and that I'll probably not have time to write everyday. At least my weekends will be free, and Houston is an even larger city than San Antonio, an exciting prospect. We all pack our bags and anticipate the adventures that lie ahead.

NIGHT TRAIN TO SOMEWHERE

Hurtling through the rain-soaked night, the troop train rushes toward an unknown destination. Over the tops of the plush green seats the cadets' heads lurch and sway with the movement of the coach. In the dim light several men who have given up trying to sleep light up cigarettes, the smoke curling upward to the plain brown ceiling. Small groups at one end bend over cards. Now and then, above the hollow roar of the train wheels and their rhythmic clicking, the deep, melodic tones of the locomotive whistle flow out into the night. We streak through small towns where people have long been asleep.

Except for the quick, occasional lights of these places, the world outside the train windows is a moist, black void. In the rain-streaked window I see my own dull reflection, my short-cropped hair, my head leaning against the back of the seat, my shirt open at the collar. I can't sleep. I squirm and twist, seeking any comfortable position. A dull headache creeps down toward my neck, and my stomach is sour. The blinking lights at a grade crossing momentarily flash a pale ruby glow inside the coach, the clanging of the warning bells muffled by the din of the train. Towns are only scattered streetlights and, here and there, a lighted window. I miss seeing these isolated hamlets as well as the hills and rivers now swallowed by darkness. I glance at my watch. After midnight. Aside from a few brief moments when the sound of the train seems strange and far away, I haven't been close to dreaming.

Annoyed at not knowing where the train is headed, I tumble the rumors and bits of information around in my head again. We appear to be traveling east towards Ellington Field near Houston, Texas, our most likely destination, but in all the blackness I could have confused directions. The train may race toward the west, perhaps to the preflight school at Santa Ana, California, near where I could bask in the warmth of my family and friends. No, I sense that the train is eastbound.

Why all the secrecy anyway? Surely the railroad authorities know where we're going. The train crew and the locomotive engineer would also. The officers in charge have their orders. I can't understand why the cadets are not told. During wartime all military moves remain secret, but the transporting of green cadets on their way to preflight school seems innocent enough. Perhaps they reason that blowing up a few hundred potential bombardiers all at once now would be better than picking off fully trained men, one at a time, later over Germany or Japan.

As I shift to another posture, a freight train thunders by in the opposite direction, its compression momentarily rocking our coach. I wish that Carlo Zuniga were sitting with me so that we could talk and bolster each other a little, but by order of the officers we're seated alphabetically. Sachs, Senter, Shields, Smith, Southwell, Stewart, Spano and all of the other "S"s are my traveling companions. Carlo with his "Zu" is always last, the story of his life he tells me, and sits or luckily sleeps in his seat several coaches back.

I think about preflight school again with the same blend of apprehension and confidence. Knowing that they will throw physics and mathematics at me, I fear they will cut to the heart of my weaknesses. I also worry about the iron-fisted discipline and the severity of the training. I tell myself that I've scored higher on tests than many of my fellow cadets and that I've withstood the strict discipline at San Antonio. We pass the yellow headlight of a locomotive waiting on a siding, streaks of rain slanting down through its light beam.

*   *   *

Anxious about shipping out in the evening, we had eaten our last meal at San Antonio in the late afternoon. The scraping of forks on our tin plates and the musical tinkling of silverware penetrated the required silence in the mess hall. We sat rigidly, our unused hand in our laps, finishing up our dessert. With our short hair and suntan uniforms we looked like multiple mirror images of each other. Those who had finished sat silently and patiently, waiting for the slower eaters. No one could leave the table until all were ready. Cadets on KP duty, wearing gray-green fatigues, removed the bowls and platters from the table, carrying them on trays to the dishwashers.

We marched back to our squadron area, hut...hut... hut..., our heavy shoes clomping in unison. I gathered my rolled raincoat, gas mask and bag of personal belongings, placing some of the equipment in a special carrying kit my grandfather had sent me. I had last seen him in Indiana when I was three or four years old, and had only a vague idea about what he looked like from photographs.

By number, the numbers based on the initial of our last name, we scrambled on to the railway coaches, our clumsy shoes scraping on the steel steps. The troop train had conveniently backed into the cadet center only a short march away. We fumbled into our assigned seats, stowed our bags and sat back for our trip to an unknown destination to be reached at an unknown time. At 1730 hours the train chugged out of the cadet center, the sweet smell of the black smoke wafting through the partially opened windows.

We stopped at the main railroad station in San Antonio where we waited for what seemed like hours. Clouds that had gathered all day began to give up their moisture. Rain streaks etched the train windows as the drops softly slanted down. The passenger car on the track next to us became shiny wet, bringing out the essence of its olive color the way dull rocks become beautiful under water. The rain failed to temper the heat. I pulled at my collar and loosened another button. I watched people rushing on the platform. A glistening patina of wetness mirrored the station and reflected the lights as I settled back, ready for the journey to somewhere.

*   *   *

Nearly punch drunk from the lack of sleep, we file off the troop train with our belongings then line up according to our numbers. A warm overcast sky that nearly stifles me, combined with my sleepless night, adds to the surreal quality of the morning. We're where most thought we'd be, at Ellington Field. We'd arrived in Houston at 3:30 in the morning, remained at the station for two hours, then were finally pulled to the airbase, 20 miles from town on the Missouri Pacific Lines. Dazed but functional, we troop off to our assigned barracks.

Through our half-open eyes we behold our first pleasant surprise. Even though our barracks are two-storied as they were in San Antonio, these are much roomier. Instead of bunk beds jammed into the space, comfortable-looking steel spring cots lie evenly down each side of the floor with ample room in between them. On each floor stand ten desks with drawers in them and a fluorescent study lamp on top, each desk pushed against the wall between the cots. The sight opens our eyes a little, even regenerates us.

No sooner do we glance at our new barracks and jettison our luggage, than the cadet officers command us to fall out on the double. Our tired feet rumble over the floor and down the few wooden steps to the street where we line up at attention. None of us having eaten since the afternoon before, we're glad to know that we're on our way to chow.

I stand in awe at the mess hall. Before us lies a great stainless steel griddle that looks just like the one in Sally's, the most popular restaurant in Inglewood. All across the gleaming griddle ranks of fried eggs bubble and sputter. We can have them sunny side-up, over easy or any other way. Pleasant fry cooks scoop them up with steel spatulas two at a time, sliding them gently on to our trays. I help myself to potatoes, bacon and grapefruit. White cloths soften the tables, and our silverware nestles in a rolled linen napkin. I can't believe the luxury, the contrast to our meals in San Antonio. I don't even have to take my tray back; we leave them on the table for someone else to bus. The freedom of being able to talk as we eat and get up from the table and sit down when we please is a great relief.

Lunch proves just as exciting. I take chicken a la king with peas, salad, iced tea, Jello and apple pie with ice cream. We have our choice of three or four desserts and four different salads at every lunch and dinner. Seasoned cadets tell us that Ellington Field is the country club of the Army Air Corps. Skeptics that we are, however, we suspect that lurking behind the spacious barracks, the endless griddle and the four kinds of desserts must be something more sinister, something diabolical to compensate for it all.

A glimmer of the whole truth appears when we learn that the class system will be strictly enforced. The upper classmen have complete control over us. We lower classmen cannot attend a movie or visit the base PX except on Saturday or Sunday, and then only if we have an open post pass. We must also stand guard duty on some of our "free" days. We must stand at attention at all formations or briefly at parade rest, with our feet exactly twelve inches apart, our left thumb lying in our right palm behind our back. We must look straight ahead, remain silent and maintain perfect posture.

At ten o'clock the lights are out, and I nestle into my cot for the first time. Outside, the rain falls gently again. I'm still in Texas. I can forget about being near home. I'll be at Ellington for ten weeks followed by six weeks in gunnery school. Most of the advanced bombardier training schools are in Texas too, another twelve weeks. In the sticky heat of Houston I dream of inhaling some nice, cool, foggy California air fresh off the ocean.

TOUCHING AIRPLANES

Swinging slowly around at the end of the runway, the B-24 Liberator taxies along the tire-stained concrete, its four propellers flickering silver discs. Menacing stinger guns protrude from its squat abdomen. The oscillating roar of the engines blends with the flat slapping of the propellers as they slice the air. Waist gunners lean out of their bays, as they relax on their backs. Appearing blasé and superior in their exalted positions, they squint into the glaring sun, gawking at the field. Standing near the hangars on my first day at Ellington Field, I watch the bomber rolling low to the concrete, rocking slightly but gliding smoothly on its great tires. I have never been so close to a military plane. At San Antonio the sound of training planes had often drifted over from the nearby pilot schools, and we frequently saw the two-winged Stearman training planes circling high like pale buzzards. But to behold a combat bomber at such close range sends a pleasant chill through my body. For the first time I feel, in my boyish pride, as though I belong to the brotherhood of airmen. But I realize that months of training lie ahead before I would ever be their equal.

Even from my barracks window I often see military planes landing and taking off. Most are Curtiss AT-9s or silver Beechcraft AT-10s, twin-engine craft used for advanced pilot training, but occasionally more exotic ones glide silently past my window. As I sit at my desk, a silver B-17, a Flying Fortress, whispers in for a landing, its star insignia bright, its ball turret clearly visible beneath. A Curtiss P-40 in war paint, its wheels lowered, finds the runway. A Lockheed B-34 medium bomber and a C-78 cargo plane settle in. They land where I'm stationed, and I feel that somehow I'm connected with them.

Several days later we march at a parade on the grease-dappled airfield ramp, the brassy beat of the band drifting among the airplanes parked in the hot sun. Our line of march takes us beneath their wings, through their sanctified shadows and several times nearly close enough to brush their tails. Although I must look straight ahead, my eyes stray to capture quick images of Douglas B-18 bombers and a covey of Martin B-26 medium bombers, all much larger than I ever imagined. Beyond a trim Douglas A-29 attack bomber lay rows of twin-engine trainers and a gleaming AT-6 single-engine pilot trainer.

Reveling in my newfound kinship with military planes, I buy some special stationery in the PX with photographs from Ellington Field along the top border. A Beechcraft AT-10 "Wichita" banks casually to the left over a fluffy layer of white clouds. A flight of three Curtiss AT-9 "Jeeps" fly in formation, the sun gleaming off of their wings. An AT-10 climbs sharply, its propellers a wispy blur. Beneath the photographs part of the caption reads, "Here aviation cadets learn how to handle the big jobs by flying AT-9s and AT-10s---and well, for soon after graduation they will be piloting our Flying Fortresses and Liberators, the sluggers of Uncle Sam which are blazing trails of destruction among our enemies the world over." The people at home will now understand the new world that I've entered.

The trainers zoom over our barracks as they take off, vibrating the windows and trembling the rafters. The buzz of their straining engines penetrates our classrooms, causing momentary halts in lectures. At our parades on the flight ramp a flight of six AT-10s "scalp" us, first streaking over our heads at 100 feet then lowering to 50 feet on a second pass. As a test of our discipline, we must not look up at them, even as we are enveloped in their deafening crescendo and their quick shadows. Being caught in their sound, feeling their vibrations in my muscles and on my skin only intensifies my intimacy with them.

Several days later, Walter Kelson, a fellow cadet, and I walk down to the flight line to ogle the planes, to be even closer to them. Much shorter than I, he walks ramrod straight to pull up his height and stand as tall as possible. His eyes always look sleepy to me. He rarely smiles, and when he speaks he does so with a sophisticated New York dialect. He has the same love affair with airplanes that I have. Down on the ramp we examine an AT-11, a standard training plane for bombardiers. We touch its warm aluminum skin and trace our fingers along its body. We caress it, slap it softly, listen to its metal hollowness. If all goes well, we'll both become much more acquainted with this plane later in advanced bombardier training. We look over two twin-engine Vega Venturas, stroking them wherever we desire.

Beyond the ramp a Martin B-26 "Marauder" sits poised on its tricycle landing gear. Two lieutenants, each clutching a pretty girl, walk happily across the tarmac towards it. The girls giggle as the officers, the pilots of the plane, wrap their arms around their slender waists and pull them playfully toward them. They stand talking beneath the plane enjoying its cool shadow. The girls laugh as a light wind plays with their hair. As they walk back toward us, we summon our courage and salute smartly.

"Sir. Do you mind if we walk out to look at your plane?" I ask.

"I really have no authority here," one lieutenant says, "but as pilot of the plane it's okay with me. If anybody stops you, just tell them that Lieutenant Lee sent you."

"Thank you sir."

We stride out to the magnificent airplane with its clean, sharp lines. We scrutinize every rivet on its skin then concentrate on the bombardier's compartment, peering in through the Plexiglas. We wonder how it would be to sit up there, racing at low altitude toward a target.

Still excited by viewing a combat plane, we stroll off the ramp on the way back towards our barracks. Just before we clear the flight line, a soldier with an MP armband pulls up beside us in his jeep.

"Hey!" he shouts, "Didn't you know you weren't supposed to be out here?"

"No, sir, we didn't know. We thought it was okay."

"Only authorized personnel are allowed on the ramp. Remember that."

"Yes, sir."

Several days later our cadet squadron parades the entire length of the airfield, finally coming to a halt on the ramp. While we stand, AT-10 training planes take off one at a time, each one disappearing quickly into a low, threatening overcast. Even before the last one takes off we feel the first cold drops of rain and watch from the corners of our eyes the growing speckling of the concrete ramp. The smell of it is in the air as the tempo picks up. Rushing the ceremony, the officers order us to march off the field. Just after we clear the ramp nearly fifty planes in groups of twelve skim across where we had just stood at only 30 to 50 feet off of the ground. Again we were to be "scalped" by them, to be tested, to not look up or flinch. I miss the thrill of being wrapped in their trembling thunder. As we duck inside of our quarters, the weather collapses into a blinding downpour that masks all but the closest barracks.

One afternoon near the end of our stay at Ellington Field, despite the warning Kelson and I had from the MP, several of us who are the most interested in airplanes make one last trip to the ramp to see what might be lurking there. The heat ripples across the field, distorting some of the more distant training planes. We discover a B-24, two B-17s, a B-26 and four blue Navy SBD dive bombers. Stopping first at the B-24 curiously named "Stud Duck," we hoist ourselves up through the belly gunner's position midway between the wing and tail. The stagnant oven heat of the day locked in the fuselage smells of aluminum, grease and rubber. At our first experience inside a warplane we're amazed at how large it is, like being inside a gigantic whale with aluminum ribs. We prowl toward the tail to look at the roomy tail gunner's position then retrace our steps and file one at a time over the narrow catwalk that spans the bomb bays to the claustrophobic bombardier's compartment. Parachutes, uniforms and papers lie scattered throughout the plane as though operated by a slipshod crew, but we envy them. We can hardly believe that we tread where they have, that we step reverently through a real combat bomber.

As yet I had not flown, but airplanes gradually become less abstract to me and more touchable. Photographs and silhouettes become warm aluminum machines that smell and snarl and feel sensuous under the fingers.

THE FACE AT THE LATRINE WINDOW

Flames of anger erupt from the latrine window.

"You God-damned son of a bitch!" screams the man inside.

From where I stand outside, the screened rectangle frames his profile as though it were a live painting of raw rage.

"Who the hell do you think you are?" he yells.

The screen softens the fire in his eyes, his unruly blond hair. Still in his underwear, he remains in the dim light, hurling another epithet.

"You chicken shit bastard!"

We have just fallen out on the double as usual, fully dressed and bed made. I stand at parade rest a precise distance from the other men, my eyes focused on the neck of the man in front of me. But my eyes instinctively wander to where the venom spews from the window. The object of the abuse, our cadet officer, stands uncomfortably in front of us.

"You lousy fucker!" the indignant cadet shouts from the opening.

I'm embarrassed and stunned. I've never seen such an outrageous loss of self-control. I don't know why the guy is so angry. It's an inexcusable breach of discipline in front of the officer's men. The sting of the cadet's curses is visible in the officer's eyes and the rigidity of his bloodless lips. Unlike most cadet officers who are tall, slender and clean-cut, he's short and stocky. Finally, struggling with his composure, he shouts in a quavering voice, "Right face! For-ward harch! Hut...hut... hut", as we leave the insubordinate in the window and march to breakfast.

Our ranks are quiet except for the rhythmic thudding of our heavy shoes on the street and the soft rustling of our uniforms. My mind is full of what I've just witnessed. What will happen to the man? I can't understand how a cadet can become irate enough to jeopardize his chances of becoming a bombardier and an officer. Having rarely expressed anger in my own life, I find it difficult to fathom the depth of the cadet's rage.

As we file past the great silver griddle in the mess hall, the yellow eyes of eggs peeping out of their whites, I learn more about why the man was so upset. According to the men assigned to his barracks, the angry cadet initiated a prank to get even with the cadet officer for his excessive authoritarianism. With the help of others he lifted the officer's bed, placed it in the open barracks rafters, and hooked its legs over the two-by-fours. When the cadet officer returned in the evening to the darkened quarters, he discovered he had no bed.

"Okay you guys," he had said, turning on the lights. "Very funny! Some of you men help me get the damn thing down."

No one moved.

"I said get the damn bed down! You, Parker, Potter, Russell! Move it!"

Afraid not to obey his command, they went to work.

The cadet officer saw it not as a prank, but as a challenge to his authority. Threatening disciplinary action for everyone in the barracks, the perpetrator reluctantly confessed. He immediately suspended him from training for an unspecified time, with the blessing of the lieutenant in charge. My fork bursting through the yoke of an over-easy egg, I again try to comprehend the situation, but I don't have the personal experience to understand it.

Some men seek to be cadet officers, vying for leadership positions so that they can exert their influence over others, and feel the satisfaction of commanding men and earning their respect. Most feel that becoming cadet officers will give them an edge in their military careers, particularly for advancement in rank. Many have prior experience in another branch of the service, R.O.T.C. or military schools. To distinguish them from the rest of us they wear silver brass on their epaulets, three diamond shapes for squadron commander, two for adjutant and one for first sergeant. They walk about with a commanding air, their bodies always at attention as though they had broomsticks down their backs, their heads always slightly raised as though peering over something we can't see. Very conscious of their rank, they gather by themselves to chat rather than fraternizing with the men. One day I hear a cadet officer say to another, "What I like more than anything else is to see men hop to when I give an order." I know they're necessary, and I tolerate them, even respect some of them, but I would never think of crossing one or even being one.

Being under the thumb of cadet officers eases us into the vast hierarchy of the military system and the absolutes of rank. The cadet class system also emphasizes the differences among cadets according to how long they have been in training. Middle classmen no longer stand guard duty or miss passes into town. Upper classmen eat before the lower classmen and are given haircuts on Fridays and Saturdays just before inspection so they'll look sharp. Being in the upper class gives the men a sense of smugness, superiority and pride.

Upper classmen can, as a cruel demonstration of their superiority, put lower classmen in a brace, an exaggerated posture of attention.

"Okay, Mister," they say, accosting some hapless lower classmen. " Suck in that gut! Throw out that chest! Farther!

Get those arms up and shoulders back! Come on. Let's see a wrinkle in that chin! Another!"

The unfortunate victim can only comply, standing at rigid attention with his upper torso raised, his arms drawn to the side then back and up, his chin tucked in.

"What's your name, Mister? What's your outfit, Mister? What do you do for a living, Mister?" they shout.

For the answer to the last question, the standard reply that we all wish we had the guts to use is, "I saw toilet seats in half for half-assed cadets like you."

* * *

Sloshing through a thin layer of soapy water, the bristles of my brush dig down into the pores of the wooden floor. The muffled scraping of it and those of the others fills the barracks. Sometimes I work on my hands and knees, but when my knees begin to ache, I squat on the balls of my feet. The broom crew has swept the floor, buckets of water with suds from large, ugly bars of brownish GI soap have been spilled, and now we attack the floor with brushes. The mop crew follows behind us. I inhale the smell of the soap and the wet wood as I swing my brush in arcs across the floor. Outside, a sudden shower falls, the rain dripping off the eaves. The bluish flicker of faraway lightning barely penetrates the lighted barracks.

"My God," exclaims one cadet. "It's only an hour before midnight and here we are down on this smelly floor working our butts off."

"If they'd just give us time during the day, we wouldn't have to stay up so damn late," says another.

"Yeah. We'd be in bed by now. I'm so tired I can hardly move this friggin brush."

"Why do we have to scour the barracks three times a week? Once ought to be enough. These officers are fanatics."

"We do it because they say so."

Exhausted, we all long for sleep, but we must also polish our shoes and buff our brass, especially our belt buckle as even a moist fingerprint will mar its brilliance. Pungent Blitz cloths purchased at the PX magically restore the mirror-like finish. The Army's uncompromising attitude toward cleanliness and our being sharp at all times tests our obedience, tolerance and level of frustration.

In the morning we jump out of bed, leap into the latrine to brush our teeth, shave and smooth down our short hair. We straighten our belongings then make our beds. The main blanket must be so tight that a flick of the thumb and finger sends a ripple from one end of the bed to the other. Around the pillow the blanket must be taut enough that a dropped quarter bounces on it. In ten minutes from the sound of reveille we must accomplish all this and be standing at attention in the street in front of the barracks, our shoes polished and our brass gleaming. The first morning I rush out a few seconds late, and the officer takes my name. Embarrassed, I vow to try harder. The following morning I'm the first one out and am never late again. I believe the discipline is good for me, good for all of us, at least I convince myself of that.

*   *   *

Crunching and popping gravel under my shoes, I walk briskly on the athletic field, several other cadets with me. We stride nearly 150 yards in one direction, then stop, execute a sharp "about face", then march 150 yards back We repeat the routine over and over. We have been at it nearly an hour, back and forth without a word to each other, the only sounds being the whisper of our trouser legs and the grating of our footsteps. Spotless white gloves cover our hands, and billed hats rest perfectly on our heads. Our suntan ties, knotted tightly at our necks, keep our body heat from escaping. Sweat trickles down the groove in the small of my back. Dressed in our class A uniforms, we appear to be marching in a parade, but actually we suffer our punishment, tread the ramp, walk tours.

Tours, one tour equaling one hour of walking, are assigned for negligence or breaking rules, no matter how slight. Moving our eyeballs or letting our eyes rove from the neck of the cadet in front of us while we stand in formation can cost us three tours, all to be done during our free time on the weekends. I'm walking because I've been caught or "gigged" twice. During one inspection the officer reported that the chair at my desk was tipped on its side. When I left the barracks prior to the inspection it had been upright and perfectly aligned. No excuses are allowed, so I swallow the accusation. At a later inspection a fastidious officer found dust on top of a door I was in charge of. I couldn't reach the top of it. Whirling around in my mind as I walk is the humiliation of having to endure punishment for trivial offenses that I consider not totally my fault. Tumbling with it is the resolve to always check everything again just before the inspection. I could have stood on a chair to reach that dust. It's all a game, a scattering of stumbling blocks to trip up cadets and test their will, endurance and patience.

Lesser punishments correct minor errors. The officers in charge think that the men in our group swing our arms too much when we march. As a remedy, we must hold our arms straight down at our sides, grasping our trouser seams with our thumbs and forefingers. We must use the technique everywhere we march, even to the mess hall. We appear sissified and ridiculous marching this way, bringing taunting laughs from middle and upper classmen.

One of the cadets in our barracks fails to return after his weekend pass.

"Hey. Did you hear that Sullivan never came back from his pass? The son of a bitch is AWOL."

"No. Where the hell is he? He either got drunk or found some babe he couldn't leave I suppose."

"The worst thing about it is that the chicken shit officer in charge of us is going to cancel all our passes for the coming weekend."

"We didn't do anything. Why the hell should we be penalized?"

"I guess he thinks we'll put pressure on the guy so he won't do it again."

"It's not fair!"

"Aren't you used to the army yet?"

Squadron competitions at least give us incentives to practice good discipline, the reward being to leave on pass before the others, being able to jump on the first trucks leaving for town. Each squadron begins the week with sixty points. Officers deduct points for sloppy marching, dirty latrines, arriving late to the mess hall or not turning the lights off on time at night. They add points for winning "March on-s" and barracks inspections. When our squadron wins the Wing marching competition and has no deductions, we scramble into the covered army trucks first, waving at the others who must wait.

On rare occasions the officers mercifully relax the rules. Due to the extreme heat and humidity, we are no longer required to wear ties except at retreat, the evening mess and anywhere off the base. I, who don't like to wear strangling ties under any conditions, even in cool weather, am especially grateful.

*   *   *

When we return to our barracks after breakfast, the cursing cadet and all his equipment is gone. No one can tell us what happened to him or where he was taken. He simply disappeared.

I don't feel sorry for him, as any man who has been so blatantly insubordinate and out of control would never make a good bombardier. In my innocence I'm deeply puzzled by him, but think he should be punished. He brought his troubles on himself. I'm relieved that he's gone. Deep down I believe that discipline is necessary even though its demands chafe me at times. As long as it's reasonable, just and fair, I like the sense of order it brings.

BREATH OF THE GULF

The glowing dust of the Milky Way traces a pale path across the moonless sky, the scattered stars crisp pinpoints of light. Late at night the air is cool and refreshing, a welcome relief from the searing daytime sun. I enjoy the night and the infinite depth of the firmament as I walk in the dark, an unloaded rifle on my shoulder. The starlight is bright enough that the black silhouettes of the barracks loom against it. I like being alone with the heavens and my own thoughts. During normal waking hours we cadets are always together and have little time to think about ourselves. The rifle grows heavy as I walk my two-block beat, and I have yet to fulfill one hour of my four-hour guard duty. Except for my own footsteps the night is quiet, and no one stirs.

After pacing the street for nearly an hour, bluish light begins to flicker in the southeast, momentarily joining the starlight. The flashes gradually grow in brilliance, and yet the stars still rule the sky. Having no raincoat, I feel vulnerable and hope that the faraway storm's path will veer away from Ellington Field.

Just before the first light of dawn, towering clouds begin to erase the stars in the southern quadrant. Lightning lights up the approaching cloud turrets like strange cosmic lamps. Muted drum rolls of thunder rumble over the flat land as the gathering storm clouds, like vaporous bullies, crowd out the stars. Quickening breezes carry the musty smell of rain. I remember from memorizing the General Orders before we marched to guard duty that the fifth order reads that I am,

"To quit my post only when properly relieved," and I see no relief in sight.

The deluge begins abruptly as thick curtains of rain sweep down the street, the lightning casting brief, eerie scenes in its glow through the mist. Wave chases wave of rain down the street, races across the sparse lawns and beats against the barracks. I walk in a frenzy of water as the drops dance on the street. I hang my rifle over my shoulder by its strap so that the barrel points down, a much more comfortable position. Rain trickles into my eyes and drips off my nose. It quickly soaks through my light suntan uniform. It invades my shoes, saturating my socks so that my feet squish inside of them at every step. The clammy uniform sticks to my skin, and the gusty winds chill my bones. No one rushes out with a raincoat. The cadets sleep soundly in their soft, warm beds.

At last the storm tapers off then suddenly ceases, allowing the streets and my uniform to begin to dry. Early in the morning I notice someone walking up the damp street through the last of the night's shadows.

I shout, "Halt!"

He stops.

"Identify yourself!"

"Lieutenant Sigman," he replies as he resumes his quick officer-like stride.

He undoubtedly tests me to see if I'm on duty and if I'm alert and correct with my challenge. I salute as he passes. He returns it, but is as silent and grim as ever, inquiring not at all about my condition even though I stand before him in my pathetic rain-soaked uniform. I'm sure he believes that experiences like this one toughen me and make me a better soldier.

Before another cadet relieves me, two more showers prolong my dampness, but that's the nature of the weather in the moist breath from the Gulf of Mexico. The blue waters of the gulf bake under intense tropical sun, creating masses of sauna-like air that stream northward over the southern states, bearing torrid heat, a heavy burden of moisture and a fickle menu of weather. Although it wilts me, it also fascinates me. Back in the barracks, I shower then slip deliciously into my dry clothes before breakfast.

*   *   *

Despite my exhaustion, I can't sleep in the heat. If I throw off my covers, the mosquitoes will attack me. I've already slapped my face, my ear and my pillow, flailing vainly at their shrill quavering sounds. Mosquitoes lurk in the shadowed barracks rafters during the day then feed on the cadets at night. The insects breed in astronomical numbers in the humid climate then seek flesh. They're so large that we call them bombers or four-engine mosquitoes. When we're lucky enough to smash them, their frail but bloated bodies burst with blood, the cadets' blood, leaving a gory smear on our hands, the sheets or the walls.

If I pull the covers around my neck for protection, I'm too hot, and, what's worse, my "prickly heat" begins to irritate me. The "prickly heat" rash began several days ago when the weather turned especially hot and humid. Most of us have it to some degree. The nettle-like pain is acute when I'm warm or if I sweat, but especially when I move any part of the skin where the rash is. The nuisance especially affects my back. If I move any muscle there, the sharp, prickly pain irritates my skin. Despite the mosquitoes and the prickly heat, I drift off to sleep.

As July melts into August, the mosquitoes become more numerous and bolder, assaulting us during the daytime as well as at night. Heavier rains bring out more of them, and they begin to chew me up at night, leaving their bites all over my face, neck and arms. I think black thoughts about ways of ridding them from the face of the earth.

My prickly heat becomes more severe, every movement pushing thousands of little pins into my flesh. Most of us sprinkle medicated drying powder on the tender areas, but the relief is only temporary and never reduces the rash. Our only hope is to move somewhere dryer and cooler, but that's impossible because we'll be kept in Texas for many weeks yet. We endure.

We are often out in the withering heat for physical training, marching drills and parades. The hottest days bring no leniency from our superiors who feel that the tougher they are, the better we'll be able to withstand combat conditions. We march in parades with the temperature hovering near 100-degrees, then stand at attention on the oven-like ramp, hoping not to pass out. A few do. Sweat seeps into our uniforms, aggravating our rashes. My nose, already sunburned, becomes redder.

Some men perspire so profusely that their drying shirts leave distorted rings of salt on the cloth. When they wear them like this, they are good men to stay away from. We drink gallons of water, iced tea, Coca-Cola or any other liquid to counteract our dehydration. We think of several designs for medals to be awarded to cadets who serve in Texas. One design depicts two crossed empty Coca-Cola bottles with a long, parched tongue hanging between them. In the background of the design is a Coca-Cola machine that says "empty." For over a year's service in Texas the cadet will receive a medal portraying four massive cockroaches holding up a footlocker by each corner. A sign on top of it reads, "Gigs, Tours, Names."

Due to the high heat and humidity, we have to buy extra towels, as we must take a minimum of two showers a day. The air is so humid that towels take twenty-four hours to dry. The same happens to our soggy uniforms. I buy a package of envelopes only to find that a combination of humidity and a book resting on top of them has neatly sealed them all. Even though I like the meteorological excitement of tropical weather, I decide I would never want to live in it.

* * *

Walter Southwell and I bump along in one of four buses packed with cadets on their way from downtown Houston to the Plantation Club, a trip of nearly five miles. We had heard that a regular corps of girls went out there and that service men were admitted free. After arriving, much to our surprise, we find that five cadets exist for every girl. Discouraged and somewhat relieved, we slide into a booth for a root beer and watch the few dancers on the floor.

Outside, the sky darkens, the deepening shadows creeping into the Plantation Club along the dance floor and between the tables. Suddenly lightning strikes the field next to the club, setting off an explosive report louder than any I had ever heard. In rapid succession one strike follows another, each one like the deafening firing of close cannons. The thunder doesn't roll or reverberate but detonates in a single blast, each bolt with only seconds between. A blinding, gray downpour obscures all of the fields around the club as lightning arcs down all around us. Having never experienced anything this severe before, I'm excited, astounded and somewhat concerned for my safety, but most of the cadets pay little attention to it. They go on talking, dancing and drinking as though nothing is happening. Their blasé attitude amazes me almost as much as the storm itself. Even when a brilliant flash followed by an explosive clap of thunder knocks out the electricity in the club, hardly a stir ripples through the happy crowd. The ends of our fingers tingle with static electricity. Another close strike crackles all over the ground, sounding like crumpling cellophane. Then, as quickly as it had begun, the spasm ends, the skies lighten and the electricity is restored. I had waited years to experience a genuine thunderstorm, and, in a way, I'm sorry to see it end.

Southwell doesn't know how to dance, and I, considering the ratio of cadets to girls, lose interest in the Plantation Club. With the skies clearing, we hitchhike back to Houston.

THE SWEET SMELL OF GRASS

Easing myself down from the rear of an army truck, I catch the scent again, stronger this time. I had smelled it faintly as I rode in with Carlo Zuniga and several other cadets. The truck leaves us near Harrisburg, a small town just outside of Houston. Bright orange city buses will take us the remainder of the way. As we wait, we stand in the brilliant sunlight of a sparkling day with fluffy white cloud towers ballooning up into the blue. Each breeze brings us the fragrance again, a subtle perfume exuded by tall grasses that cover the fields around us. The scent of the grasses, the dazzling sun, and the lush green fields fill me with a kind of joy, an almost sensual feeling deep in my abdomen. Just the prospect of seeing a new city is seductive.

The fragrance rolls into the open windows of the pumpkin-colored bus as we grind our way toward Houston. I'd never been where green dominates the summer. The color bursts out of the fields, the verdant shrubs and trees. In California, wild oats, weeds and grasses would be straw-tan dead by now. Trim colonial-style houses built partly of brick and white-painted wood sit back from luxuriant lawns. I occasionally talk to Carlo, but I float in a dream and want to keep it.

After the bus drops us off downtown, Carlo and I walk the streets with no particular destination in mind. The city surprises us with its towering buildings and its wide, clean streets. We both agree that it's far superior to San Antonio. Our walking and the excitement of seeing the new city kindle a keen appetite. We make our way to the Rice Hotel, the largest and most luxurious one in town, where we both down a steak dinner in their air-conditioned coffee shop.

Following lunch we resume our aimlessness, peering in shop windows and restaurants, noting anything unusual. We end up on a bridge over a shallow, muddy river, its banks softened with a thick copse of trees and shrubs. We pause, looking down into the murky water as passing cloud shadows dim the sun. Turtles swim in the water, their dark heads contrasting with the coffee-and-cream color of the river. Several others bask in muddy clearings along the bank. One large one floats on a board, going anywhere the slow current takes him, much the way that Carlo and I drift around town. Baby turtles scamper through the water after a larger one.

Before we return to the base, we stop at the Lowe's State Theater where we see "The Human Comedy" with Mickey Rooney and Frank Morgan. Based on William Saroyan's story about a young man who must deliver telegrams during the war, sometimes about the death of a soldier, it relates to our lives. Despite the film's sadness, we enjoy it.

*   *   *

Thundering down the slick hardwood alley, the bowling ball curves to the right, too far to the right, clunking into only three outer pins. Most of them still stand, laughing at me. I'm out of practice. Joe Stewart is rusty too. He's a gentle, rather soft-spoken Texan from Port Arthur. Slender and of medium height, he appears frail at times. His friendly eyes sag slightly at the outside edges. Although he speaks with an accent, his words are not twangy, nasal or harsh. I finally hit a strike, the pins exploding in a satisfying wooden blast.

After our workout, stretching muscles we had not used for a while, we sit in a malt shop, slurping thick chocolate concoctions through paper straws barely strong enough to withstand the pressure.

Just after a draw on his straw hollows his cheeks, Stewart says, "My grandmother lives here in Houston. We'll go out and visit her sometime, okay?"

"Yeah, I'd like that. I really miss my family. It'd be neat to be around anyone's family again."

Later in the day we plan to meet Stewart's brother, a pilot who had earned his wings just two weeks before. He's coming through Houston on his way to Austin.

Stewart drags again on his straw, swallows and says, "My brother's very proud now that he's a lieutenant and has his wings. He really tried hard to prove himself because our dad didn't think he could do it. He wasn't mean to him. He just belittled him in subtle ways, letting him know that his chances of ever making it were slim. Winning his wings made him feel a hell of a lot more confident."

Stewart radiates a concern for people, reaching out in his quiet way to everyone as though they all belong to his family.

We stroll down to the Rice Hotel after stopping at a theater to see a movie based on the life of Amelia Earhart. We sit in the plush hotel lobby waiting for Stewart's brother. A second lieutenant strides in, looks for a seat, then sits on the couch beside us. Stewart strikes up a conversation with him.

"Where did you get your cadet training?" he asks.

"I didn't win my commission by coming up through the cadets," he replies. "I flew with the R.A.F. in England. I flew Spitfires in combat for seven months before I returned to the states to join the Army Air Corps."

Fascinated to be talking to such a hero, I ask, "Did you shoot down any enemy planes?"

"A few", he answers, "one Messerschmitt 109 fighter and two Junkers 88 light bombers."

"How did you feel when you were about to tangle with the Germans?"

"When you take off, you're scared, but it's no disgrace because there's not a fighter pilot who isn't. When you sight the enemy, you get even more scared, but when you rush in, the fear turns into a kind of excitement. You figure that the German pilots are just as frightened as you are, and that helps some. When you get in a dogfight, you're so busy you don't have time to think. When you get back though, you're so shaky that you can hardly light a cigarette. Some pilots crack under the strain."

We're spellbound.

I had seen his P-51 Mustang land at Ellington Field then patrolled near it during guard duty, never remotely thinking that I would ever meet its pilot. I also recall his name, O'Brien, as one of the two or three pilots left from the American Eagle Squadron in England.

He says, "The Mustang is the best fighter plane in the world."

"Yeah, that's what we've heard."

"Why don't you have dinner with us," asks Stewart.

"I'd like to, but I've got to get back to Ellington Field. I've got to fly on to another base."

"Okay. Good luck to you."

Stewart's brother, Jack, finally walks in with a Marine lieutenant, a fighter pilot who is an instructor at Corpus Christie. Jack bears the same affable manner that Stewart does. Small and slender, he's trim in his new officer's uniform, his pilot's wings gleaming on his tunic. He accepts me immediately, inviting me into his life as though he'd known me for years. As Stewart and I walk into the Rice Hotel Coffee Shop with the two lieutenants, I feel conspicuous. Associating with officers that up to now I had only saluted is an awkward situation for me, but Stewart is completely at ease.

He and his brother have much catching up to do over the steak dinner, but we all share in the relaxed conversation. The Marine lieutenant dashes off right after supper as he has a train to catch. The three of us walk off the meal by strolling the evening streets. Jack's arm works like a machine as the many cadets still on the street individually salute him. As his arm is about to fall off, we slip back into the Rice Hotel, walking to the mezzanine where we can sit quietly and talk. Shortly after 11 pm we accompany him to the Southern Pacific station where he boards his train for Austin.

I admire Jack. I place him among my growing gallery of role models, my pantheon of heroes. To me, he's a perfect example of a fellow who really wants to fly, then, with persistence and motivation, stays "on the ball" until he makes it through his training and wins his wings. I want to be like him.

Back uptown, Stewart and I can't find the Ellington Field bus. We frantically search all the logical street corners to no avail. My watch reads 11:30, and we must be back to the field by 12:30, and it's twenty miles away. We begin to worry, even panic, but suddenly a taxi with two cadets in back pulls up at the curb.

"Hey! You guys going back to Ellington Field?" they ask.

"Yeah! You going there?"

"Sure. Come on. Get in!"

"Thanks a lot you guys. We were really stuck."

We sprint for the open door, tumbling in beside them. The taxi driver picks up two more stranded cadets, charging each of us one dollar for the trip, a high price but well worth it.

On our fast trip back, I think about Stewart and the kind of day we've had. Although I liked going to town with Carlo Zuniga, we were very much the same, not having much to give the other except pleasant company. Stewart was not only more active but also reached out to people, his gregariousness carrying me along in its energy. Without him I might never have talked to the R.A.F. fighter pilot, met the

Marine lieutenant or certainly wouldn't have had the pleasure of meeting his brother.

* * *

Pellets ping when they strike the white metal ducks parading across the back of the shooting gallery. The identical, untiring drakes chase one another in a perpetual procession. I line up one of them in my rifle sights, follow its predictable motion, take the proper lead then squeeze the trigger. Following the rap of the rifle and the ping of the pellet, the tin bird falls on its side, only to be resurrected by a mechanism close to the conveyor belt. John Sacks aims his rifle and "ping", down goes another. Feeling smug about our accuracy, we stroll through the noisy aisles of Playmore, a kind of glorified penny arcade. We stop at a stand for a hot dog. After slathering mustard on it, we enjoy the first either of us has tasted since leaving home.

We walk back to the now-familiar Rice Hotel with its three-towers, air-conditioning and one thousand rooms, where we have engaged one of them for Saturday night with two other cadets. Enjoying our freedom and privacy, we stay up until 1:30 am. It's the first hotel room I have ever stayed in other than with my parents. I feel adult, proud and independent.

We don't stir until after 9:30 the following morning. Two of us write letters, proudly mailing them in envelopes bearing the name of the hotel below an engraving of the magnificent building. I'm sorry that Carlo Zuniga who is ill on the base can't be here, but John Sacks is a good substitute. Nearly as short as I am, he is huskier and more solid. He combs his wavy, almost kinky, hair straight back. White teeth and a bright smile light up his round face. When he sleeps, his rosy cheeks, slightly puckered lips, and the halo of his pillow surrounding his head make him look like a little cherub.

Although Sacks is amiable, he is very sure of himself and is used to having his own way.

Near downtown we enter the First Methodist Church for their Sunday morning service. The large gothic sanctuary surpasses the size of the one I attended at home. The congregation is very friendly, providing a much-needed respite from our harsh, impersonal military life. It's also like being at home--the people dressed in Sunday clothes, the familiar pews and altar, the same hymns we sing at home, organ chords rolling around among the arches. Being here massages the stiff, sore backs of our loneliness, our longing for home. The minister speaks well, his words penetrating and relevant.

Following a steak lunch at Scholl's, we see a film, our standard entertainment. The movie "White Savage", starring Jon Hall, Maria Montez, Sabu and Turhan Bey, a new film in Technicolor, is only fair. It was something about hunting sharks in the tropics for the vitamin A in their livers. Making good use of our hotel room, we walk back for a lengthy afternoon nap. Despite our sizeable lunch, we wake up hungry. At the Rice Hotel we tackle a huge shrimp dinner, ten plump, succulent gulf shrimp arranged on a great white platter.

* * *

With only a few more days left at Ellington Field, the commander gives our entire squadron overnight passes. Carlo and I have a comfortable double room in the fully air-conditioned Texas State Hotel. From the fourteenth floor the whole city of Houston lies before us. Past the buildings and houses, the deep green fields and the darker green of trees paint a soothing backdrop. We peer down at the rooftops, the boulevards crowded with tiny cars and beyond where cumulus clouds blossom far over the countryside. Gazing at the gleaming buildings nestled in their rich rural surroundings is a fitting climax before parting.

We spend our time as always---walking the streets, eating at every opportunity (especially shrimp dinners) and ducking into theaters. We see "Coney Island" then laugh ourselves silly at Laurel and Hardy in "Air Raid Wardens."

On the way back to Ellington Field, I smell the sweet fragrance of the wild grasses of Houston for the last time, savoring every breath. Something sensuous, almost mystical rides the scent. It bears the excitement of new places and new experiences, of some stirring deep inside of me.

THE SUNSHINE SPECIAL

Leaving a white plume of steam in the moist air, the short passenger train rumbles by Ellington Field not a quarter mile from my barracks window. As I sit at my desk looking outside to rest my eyes after studying physics---quantitative heat, pressure and volume problems, and coefficient of linear expansion---I see it passing. I don't know where it goes, but I suspect it's Galveston. I notice it puffing south on the Missouri Pacific tracks nearly every afternoon as I study in the barracks, march on the ramp or hurdle a mud puddle on the obstacle course. The train intrigues me. I imagine myself in one of its old coaches, discovering new vistas in the lush east Texas countryside as I nestle in one of its worn seats and gaze out of the window, the train whisking me away from the pressures and demands of cadet training. I want the fun of riding it no matter where it goes.

Even as a cadet I'm still enamored of trains, watching them whenever I have a chance. Within me is the same boy who met the noon freight every day in my hometown of Inglewood. Pedaling over to the tracks several miles away, I would wait for the turbulent wreath of black smoke over the brow of the hill as the locomotive engineer poured on fuel to pull the heavy train up the grade. Finally, out of the sooty halo, the locomotive would appear. I wondered what its number would be this time, what kinds of freight cars made it up and how many. Once over the hill, the train rolled down the slope, its bell clanging, its great driving rods clanking, little wisps and geysers of steam escaping everywhere. The steam smelled sweet and the oil smoke like an exciting perfume. On most days I watched the train alone, rarely finding anyone else who was as thrilled about them as I was.

At the Missouri Pacific station in Houston, I discover that the diminutive train I see everyday is a remnant of the Sunshine Special that originates in Little Rock, Arkansas and arrives in Houston with a dozen or more cars. Only the baggage car and two coaches go on to Galveston with a different locomotive. Having always liked to plan trips, I design the railroad journey in my head.

* * *

Clicking smoothly over the rails, the Sunshine Special lumbers through the flat lowlands between Houston and Galveston, Texas. Only a few passengers slouch in their coach seats as the train sways gently over the uneven roadbed. The engineer blasts his shrill whistle at each grade crossing, most of them lonely roads knifing through the level countryside. The saturated green of the rice fields fills the coach with an unnatural light. Here and there, cloud shadows drift across their velvety surface. They're even greener than the alfalfa fields back home in California.

I travel the fifty-mile journey alone. I had thought I might ask Carlo Zuniga to go with me. In fact, I stopped by his barracks to invite him just before I left the base, but he was out. Like the cloud shadows that wander over the rice fields, shadows of guilt pass through my conscience. That Carlo or at least some other cadet is not with me weighs on my mind. On the other hand I sometimes need to be alone in a place where I don't have to attend to anyone, where I can cherish the moment or think in peace. I had planned exactly how I wanted to make the trip---to travel by this special train to Galveston, to explore the country through the train window, to check out Galveston then return to Houston by bus. If I had asked someone to go with me, I would have worried about whether he liked what I had chosen to do. I also feared he might offer alternate suggestions that would destroy my intricate plan.

He might say, "Naw. Let's not take that damn slow train down there. Let's hitchhike" Or,"Galveston's just a dump. Let's go to Beaumont instead."

If I traveled with a companion, I'd have to talk to him or listen to him---about his family, his girlfriend, his way with women, his hometown, his life plans---all worthy subjects in the barracks but not when I would rather succumb to the spell of the passing scene.

Eventually the tracks lead out of the rice fields and the swamps to a long causeway over open water to Galveston Island. Automobiles travel a separate one nearby. For two miles the train crawls over the open water, the structure so narrow I can barely see it beneath us. We seem to float over the water, only the hollow sound of the wheels on the trestle giving the illusion away. Once on Galveston Island, the station is not far away.

Having no plan, I stroll the empty streets of Galveston. Dead buildings constructed at the turn of the century line the streets. Galveston's wrist is without a pulse. Dust and dullness dominate. I begin to feel lifeless and uncomfortable, and within minutes I decide to return to Houston as soon as possible. The destination was never as important as the trip anyway, especially not as meaningful as that great train ride.

I find an early bus bound for Houston that stops at Ellington Field. On the way back I sit with a man who's only a year older than I am. I notice that he's slightly crippled. We soon begin talking.

"When I worked on the rigs, I jumped off an oil derrick from 25 feet up," he says. "I broke my leg and shattered the ball socket in my hip."

"My god. That's terrible. Why did you have to jump?"

"A section of drill pipe got loose and was coming right for me. I had to leap for my life."

"So your condition is permanent."

"Yeah. I'll always have this limp, but so what. Everybody's got some burden they're carrying around."

Conversing with this mature young man tempers my loneliness and the pangs of guilt I feel at taking the trip alone. Raindrops from a light shower streak the bus windows as we approach Ellington Field. I bid my traveling companion goodbye and wish him well.

Back on the base, I find Carlo in his barracks. I tell him about my taking the train trip to Galveston. With a disappointed look, his mouth drops open.

"Gee. I really would have liked that trip," he says. "Why didn't you tell me about it?"

"I don't know. I didn't know whether you would have wanted to go. I did stop by before I went, but you weren't here."

I should have been more aggressive about asking him. I was wrongly afraid that he wouldn't like my trip. Well, Carlo and I plan to stay in a Houston hotel on our last pass, and we both look forward to the good time we'll have together.

TAIL GUNNER VANIGLIA

Frank "Tail Gunner" Vaniglia sits on his bed, his eyes straight ahead, mouth open, lower lip sagging. His empty stare and slack jaw distort his Italian handsomeness. He runs his fingers through his thick, curly hair. We, who scurry around him or stretch out on our beds for a few minutes rest, must be only vague shapes and shadows to him. The babble of the men, the door slamming, the chairs scraping on the wooden floor fail to break his mood. I imagine our actions must sound hollow or distant to him as though he's under water or at the edge of a dream.

We know where his thoughts center. They are two thousand miles away in the small town of New Dorp on Staten Island in New York. Most of us suffer in some degree from homesickness. A majority of the men have been away only a few months, but Tail Gunner Vaniglia has not seen his house, his neighborhood, his parents or his friends for a year.

He had washed out as a pilot after completing much of his training. His commanding officers then offered him gunnery school. Graduating from there, he became a tail gunner on a bomber crew. After a short time they gave him a chance to re-enter cadet training as a bombardier. Disappointment about washing out and the paralyzing grip of his homesickness dulled the keen edge of his excitement about flying.

Suddenly, one day, his attitude changes. His eyes focus and light dances in them again. Smiles and laughter replace his drooping mouth, and his good looks leap back into his face. He greets other cadets and strides about with energy and purpose.

He has heard that the Army Air Force is awarding furloughs to men who have not been home for a year. He wisecracks and smiles wherever he is---on his bunk, in the latrine, at the mess hall--- even purchases new luggage at the PX for $17.

He secures the proper furlough application then fills it out. His enthusiasm sweeping him along, he rushes the completed form to the squadron commander. He and two other officers must sign it. The squadron commander writes his name on the proper line, and the group commander, Lieutenant Fogg, scrawls his signature without hesitation. The application moves then to First Lieutenant Arthur A. Cadorette, the commandant. He, who has the distinction of having been at Schofield Barracks in Hawaii the day the Japanese bombed Pearl Harbor, and claims "his energy is now devoted to training bombardiers to avenge Pearl Harbor" refuses to sign the application. He points out that Tail Gunner is a week shy of having served a full year. Lieutenant Cadorette, a career officer, believes that rules are rules.

Tail gunner is a broken man again, even worse than before. He's been allowed to taste the sweet fruit of freedom, to imagine the joy of going home, then has them withdrawn. More than emptiness now dulls his face; bitterness creeps into his features, tightening his lips, creasing his brow. At times we see the clear seeds of tears in the corners of his eyes. We feel his sadness and share his anger because he's any one of us longing for home.

*   *   *

Thumbing through the photographs from home again, I scrutinize each one. I don't know how many times I've studied them since I received them in the mail. Four photographs show the views from our house in each direction. The one to the east down Brett Street shows the pine-like casuarina trees, a single tall one in everyone's parkway. I see

125

Ben Seymour's house plainly and Bob Schaffer's yard by the overhanging street lamp beneath which we all played kick-the-can on warm summer evenings. The south view is taken from the old wooden observation tower my father and I built behind the garage. Beyond our roof and its vents stands our casuarina tree. I hear it whining with the others in winter winds. Beyond is a muted scene of rooftops with date palms and fan palms tucked in between the houses. To the north is a more modern house built on the vacant lot where we once threw mud balls at each other, high jumped into a sawdust pit, floated boards in large rain-filled puddles and made sweet-smelling huts out of wet, discarded cypress boughs. The west is only a silhouette of trees and telephone wires. The memories that cling to our house and street rush back to me. I haven't been away from home nearly as long as Tail Gunner Vaniglia, but I feel the beginnings of that longing.

I pull my desk chair back, glancing at the two-storied barracks next door. I know where I am. I flick on the fluorescent lamp and look again at the rest of the photographs. My sister, Charline, sits on the grass looking beautiful, one of her hands resting on Pal's back, the dog looking content, his tail out straight. Another shows my mother in a sweet pose at one of the tablet-arm chairs in the barbeque enclosure that my father built. Pal sits beside her in the next seat. In another my father also stands by a tablet arm, Pal posing with his feet up on the arm itself. I look a long time at the next photograph of my mother and father sitting at the dining room table. I think about all the meals I enjoyed there---my favorite foods---Italian delight, porcupines, potato salad, fried potatoes with creamed tomatoes, baked beans and apple pie. The Dutch oven rests on the table and so does the wooden napkin holder that Charline made at school, the one depicting the stereotypical Mexican in a huge sombrero dozing by a towering saguaro cactus. The same salt and peppershakers are there and the oblong tin where my mother kept her icebox cookies. Beyond my father sits the old bell-shaped clock, the one I wound so many times and sent its chimes resounding through our house even in the middle of the night. Above it hangs an oil painting of flowers that I never appreciated until now.

In a final photograph Charline and my mother stand in the narrow kitchen, Charline at the sink and my mother at the high-legged Acorn stove. My mother, draped in a print apron, grasps a frying pan handle in one hand and stirs with the other as she turns her head slightly, her lips pressed into a Mona Lisa smile. The cooking smells can only be imagined. Beneath the Acorn stove the cat used to bask in its warmth, nodding, closing his green eyes.

The scenes that were so ordinary to me then now loom large and lovely in my mind. The commonplace clock, napkin holder, and the old stove---how precious they've become. I look down the even rows of beds with their identical wool blankets, the sterile walls of the barracks, the bare wooden floors---all starkly contrasting to the images of home that now move so tenderly through my mind. I recognize the first symptoms of the sickness that now holds Tail Gunner Vaniglia in its grasp.

*   *   *

Gliding smoothly down the highway in Franklin Smith's father's 1942 Chevrolet, we speed almost silently toward Beaumont, Texas. Smith, a cadet from our barracks, sits in front with his father, his girlfriend nestled between them. Stewart and I, who are on our way to Port Arthur to visit his parents, sit in the back. Mr. Smith speaks gently, and is kind to his son and to us. I think about Smith and how lucky he is to be with his father. I remember I had missed sending my dad a Father's Day card.

I forgot to get a Father's Day card for you, Pop. No card could quite express the way I feel about you anyway. You're the best Pop a fellow could ever wish for or hope for. You will always be the best fellow I know. The sooner I can see you again, the better.

Despite my wandering thoughts and our conversations, I observe the passing green beauty of East Texas through the side window. We stop at the San Jacinto River, where a car ferry takes us across. I'm surprised that the ferry operator is a woman, a rugged, sun-browned blond wearing an old dress and a great floppy bonnet. Across the river lies the San Jacinto Battlefield where Texas finally won its independence from Mexico. A tall obelisk like the Washington Monument with a star on top marks the site. Mr. Smith, obviously the proud Texan, relates all the details of the battle.

Near the Neches River we stop at the town of Liberty for a Coke. The highway bridge spans the river there as well as the swamps that flank it. Trees grow green and thick down to the water's edge, and lavender water hyacinth flowers cover the swampy water in the quieter parts. I have never seen anything like it before. The scene steals away the thoughts of home, replacing them with new sights, sounds and smells, new experiences. We pass miles of pinewoods, a lush, green underbrush growing among the trees. Everywhere, it seems, I can almost see the vegetation growing and sense the sharp smell of fertility in the air.

The Smiths bid us goodbye at Beaumont, a thriving center of oil refineries and ship- building. The pungent smell of the refineries pulls my thoughts toward home again. I remember during rainstorms how the south wind carried the oily breath of the refineries from El Segundo, so that I thought rain smelled that way.

After hitchhiking, we arrive at Stewart's house shortly before noon, surprising his parents. They're close to the same age as my own, and their kind, interested manner reminds me of them. Entering the house is like stepping into a dream. I hadn't been inside a home since I'd left nearly four months ago. I'm soothed by its array of familiar objects--- the carpets, the comfortable furniture, the radio and the sheet music on the piano the way it was at home. I watch Stewart melt like a little boy into his natural surroundings.

Stewart's mother and father take us into town for a nice, sixty-nine cent chicken dinner at a cafeteria. It's comforting to be with them, to be with people who care about us. The sharp smell of butadiene hangs in the air as five synthetic rubber plants operate to help the war effort and make up for the shortage of natural rubber. The sight of a fully armed merchant ship traveling along the ground astounds me until I learn it plies a narrow canal not visible from the road.

After some homemade sandwiches in Stewart's kitchen, we begin the long trek back to Ellington Field. I'm sad about leaving because I enjoy being with his parents and relaxing in that quiet house. It's a sanctuary to me, like being in my own home again.

As we hitchhike just outside Port Arthur I'm amazed to see people fishing in the large ditches at the side of the road. In places where the water hyacinths have not covered the surface, fishermen pull out two and three-pound bass as well as perch and catfish.

At Beaumont the Stewarts drop us off, and Mr. Smith drives us back to the base where we sign in just an hour before midnight. We walk across the empty, dimly lit grounds, step up to the bare barracks porch and into our dull dormitory. At least we had sampled, if only briefly, the warmth and tenderness of fathers and mothers. I think again about my own home where my parents wonder about me and of Tail Gunner Vaniglia's home far across the country on Staten Island where his parents no doubt sleep in their darkened house and dream about their son.

THE WORLD'S ON FIRE

Their piercing voices echo through the streets and between the dimly lit barracks. Their babble, fractured with volleys of raucous laughter, becomes louder and closer. I knew the cadets that had gone to town would return late, but I hoped I would be asleep and miss their clumsy entrance. I rest uneasily in the dark, not knowing what to expect, but my heart beats faster as I listen to their boisterous shouts.

Unsteady footsteps drum on the porch as the revelers burst through the door into the hushed barracks of sleeping and half-sleeping cadets.

"Okay! Everybody up!" they yell. "Come on! Everybody up and piss. The world's on fire! Come on, we need everybody. Everybody up and piss! The world's on fire!"

One of the drunken cadets sits on my bed. He leans over me with his withering whiskey breath, shakes my shoulders and says, "Stevens! Stevens! Are you awake? Are you awake?"

"Yeah", I answer in a small, annoyed voice.

"Okay", he says, "I just wanna be sure you're not asleep. You sure? Ya gotta get up and piss, Stevens. The whole damn world's on fire out there!"

I try to humor him. "I just got back from the latrine and can't possibly do what you want."

He moves on to another bed. "Hey Stewart! Wake up! Ya gotta piss. The world's on fire!"

I'm relieved he's left me and hasn't collapsed the legs of my cot the way some cadets did. I always took the prank as a joke, but rolling out on the floor and righting the bed again was a nuisance in the middle of the night.

Desk lights flicker on here and there, revealing the disheveled, unsteady cadets trying to struggle out of their clothes, a few still laughing at nothing. Some wear their badges of honor, red prints on their cheeks and brows or lips so crimson with smeared lipstick they look like little children who have been mouthing cherry popsicles. Finally, with a last few distorted words about the women they'd kissed and some uneasy comments about how fast their beds are spinning, they settle down into heavy-breathed sleep and drunken snores.

*　*　*

When I read in a letter from home that my sister Charline is interested in going out with a cadet, I become apprehensive. Although I know many fine cadets, I worry about her being drawn to the ones who think of a weekend pass only as an opportunity to find a woman and drink themselves senseless. Like some of them in my barracks.

I suppose it's all right for Charline to go with the cadet although I do know quite a bit about them. When Mrs. Kiefer says that he doesn't drink, she really doesn't have the slightest idea. There are fellows here that go out sometimes and get slaphappy drunk, who have admitted to me that their own folks don't even know they look at the stuff. If their mothers ever saw them, they would be shocked. So how could a cousin be sure?

Even if he does drink and Charline finds it out later, she doesn't have to do anything to be a so-called 'good sport.' She doesn't even have to take a sip of beer. That's not what a 'good sport' is---that's just following the black sheep over the cliff. Every time she or anyone else passes up something like that, it's another victory for their will power. Anyone who will not like another person just because he doesn't 'dissipate' as he himself does is not worth having as a friend. I suppose he is a fine, upstanding cadet, but I say these things just in case.

* * *

A Trolley Ride Downtown

Hissing, the bus doors unfolded, letting us out at the curb. Across the street the old yellow "8" car waited at the end of the line for the return trip downtown. The Los Angeles Railway Company never modernized this line, so the trolley's paint faded on its ancient sides. A derelict in need of a shave hoisted himself up the trolley steps then walked unsteadily to a seat, dropping carelessly into it. My mother held on to my sister's hand and mine. She didn't trust the man. She kept a wary eye on him.

"I hope he doesn't get up and sit near to us", she said. "Men who have been drinking sometimes throw up. They heave all over anyone around them." I sat on my hard, wooden seat, the trolley motor growling and the bell clanging, hoping that the disheveled man would get off soon or move father away from us. I gripped the wooden seat with my other hand and watched the bum. I imagined the vile stench of his vomiting.

Grandma

"I don't know where the can of beer came from," I had said to Grandma. "It was just in our icebox. I think an auto parts dealer gave it to him. They have only one can. I think they just want to taste it to see what it's like."

I didn't know that I was not supposed to say anything about it, especially to her. Despite my youth, I should have known, since my grandfather and grandmother, both devout followers of Herbert Hoover, often extolled the virtues of prohibition.

Her raised eyebrows were enough to tell me I had said the wrong thing.

"Well they shouldn't have it. It's wrong to drink alcohol in any form!"

I had gotten my parents in trouble. My mother scolded me later for having told her.

My grandmother who is so proper that she tried to persuade my mother to remain indoors and hide when she was pregnant with me and who would not let me continue watering the lawn after I held the hose between my legs, was not the one to tell about the beer.

Joe the Barber

First nodding his head, and then closing his eyes, Joe the barber, Cousin Grace's new boyfriend, seemed to be dropping off to sleep in his chair at the dining room table. I couldn't understand why anyone would want to sleep at the table. I had never seen anyone do it before.

"Why is he sleeping?" I asked my mother in a soft voice.

In a near-whisper she answered," Well, I think he has had too much wine to drink."

No wine or alcoholic drink of any kind was ever served at our family dinners, but this meal was at Joe's house. As any good, fun-loving Italian would do, he served wine in his home. My mother and father took only a few courteous sips to avoid insulting the host and to show respect to a different culture. Joe swilled the deep red wine as was his habit, gradually easing into slumber at the table, his chin down on his chest.

I never saw Joe again.

Coach Arnett

Coaching the track team was only a sideline for Coach "Tricky Dick" Arnett. His real joy was lecturing about morals and virtues. Each afternoon the track team assembled on the infield grass, all of us sitting or slouching on the lawn as we listened to his instructions. The smell of wintergreen lotion rubbed on our sore muscles leaked out of our gray sweat suits, and the spikes on our track shoes gleamed in the afternoon sun.

Coach Arnett stood in the middle of us, his left foot planted ahead of his right, his head turning from time to time so that we could all hear him. He squinted one eye beneath his Stetson hat when he talked, and used his hands to make his points. He always wore his cream-colored poplin windbreaker.

He spun off a hat full of examples to support his moral ideals, particularly of the virtuous athlete and gentleman who shunned loose women, tobacco and alcohol, the competitor who respected his profession, his name and his own body. He had no patience with "dissipaters" who ruined body and soul by cavorting with the wrong kind of women, drinking, smoking, being lazy, having no morals and succumbing to poor eating habits. While many of the boys on the team thought he was full of crap, I hung on his every word. I believed him implicitly, silently vowing that I would never chase after indecent women, drink or smoke or "dissipate" in any way. While competing on the track team I refused to eat ice cream, pie, cake or anything that might injure my good health or sap my energy.

Coach Arnett accentuated all I had learned about morals from my parents and from the Methodist church. Coach Arnett is God wearing a Stetson hat and poplin jacket.

The J. J. Newberry Department Store

Joining the crowds on the sidewalk among the sounds of accelerating automobiles and the hollow roar of the red trolleys, I walked along Hollywood Boulevard. On my dinner break from working as a stock boy at the J. J. Newberry Department Store, I clutched my rumpled lunch sack in my hand. I liked to eat at the bowling alley several doors down so that I could sit in a comfortable seat and watch people bowl as I ate my sandwich.

"Hey Muscles!" someone shouted as I passed near the entrance to the bowling alley. Two of the salesgirls from Newberry's sat at a small table outside, beckoning me to come over.

"Hi, Muscles," said the prettier of the two. "We're each having a drink. Would you like to join us?"

"Thanks, but I don't drink. I'm just on my way to the bowling alley to have lunch."

"One little drink never hurt anybody. What's wrong with it?" asks the same woman.

"Well, I just don't drink," I say. "A lot of people can't control it."

"Well we are. We're just having one little drink. Come on."

Picking on my shyness and innocence, they teased me about drinking, their lips curved into impish smiles. Finally one of them said, "You've seen drink do harm, haven't you?"

"Yes," I answered, although I couldn't think of a direct example. But it was a good excuse to use for passing up the drink and being on my way again.

Leaving them, I thought about the man who answered the door that night when I was selling Liberty magazines. He pushed the door open halfway, filled the space with his rumpled form, and said, his voice gruff and slurry, "I'm drunk now, and I can't drink no more. I don't want no magazines." Before he shut the door and I wheeled quickly off the porch, I saw his little dog lying on the floor as though nothing was happening. I thought about Dave, the salesman at my father's shop. We had shaken hands, and I felt his trembling grip and looked up at his quivering lips, his bloodshot nose and cheeks. My father explained that he had DT's from drinking too much. When I thought of these two examples, I believed I'd answered the woman truthfully.

Glad to be away from the women, I walked into the bowling alley, sitting in the same row of seats as always. Only a few bowlers used the lanes. The rumble of the ball down the alley, the hollow wooden scattering of the pins and the curses erupting when errant pins hit the pin boys, echoed through the building.

As I finished my sandwich, a thick, hard hand slapped the side of my head. Startled, I turned around. Behind me stood one of the "pin boys", a burly man in his forties with a flattened nose like Slapsy Maxie Rosenbloom's. He stared at me drunkenly, wavering. Frightened, I had no idea what he planned next. Mercifully the manager called him away from me. The bowling alley would never be the same again.

* * *

The blast of the CQ's shrill whistle at five-thirty in the morning shatters the silence. We have five minutes to get up, dress, partially make our bed, tumble out of the door on the double and line up at parade rest. The revelers of the previous night who had so rudely disturbed us can't shake the sleep out of their fuzzy heads, and it's our turn to rouse them. As we line up in the fresh scents of the morning, last night's celebrants are grim. One rubs a lipstick print off his cheek with his handkerchief. Next to me, tall, gangly John Simon has difficulty standing straight, even at parade rest. With his heavy eyelids refusing to open all the way, his jutting blade of a nose, his prominent front teeth, his protruding Adam's apple, he musters all his strength to stand steadily. His hat askew, he straightens it just before roll call.

He appears comical to me. I have an urge to laugh at him and all the rest who struggle to maintain their soldierly composure. I find their suffering satisfying. They pay dearly now for what they had done. Their sour expressions must match their sour stomachs. I imagine their heads pounding and throbbing beneath their caps.

After roll we march to a small reveille ceremony with the entire squadron. A trumpet sounds as cadets raise the flag. "All present and accounted for, sir!" yells each flight commander in turn. The shaky cadets regain a part of their equilibrium in the fresh morning air.

Back in the barracks where we have fifteen minutes to finish making our beds, hang up our towels and sweep and mop the floor before we march to the mess hall, the night-howlers mope and hang their heads. I feel another sense of satisfaction when I see how they agonize. Coach Arnett was right. When a man dissipates, he must pay for it. It's as simple as that. Maybe they'll not roar into the barracks at midnight again, proclaiming that "the world's on fire". Maybe they'll let us alone.

OBSTACLES

Milling around on the gravelly soil, babbling to each other, we wait for our turn on the obstacle course. I worry about completing it. Even before we start we sweat in the oppressive heat despite being stripped down to our shorts and gym shoes. The instructors remind us we have to run for another mile after we complete the course. Not being a distance runner, I'm uneasy, especially when I look ahead at the forbidding walls and pits.

The training instructor shouts in his booming voice "Okay, let's go! Don't stop for anything! Take those obstacles as fast as you can, and remember to keep on running afterwards until you cross the finish line on the track! Come on! Let's go! Faster! Faster! Hustle there!"

I dash with all the rest towards a four-foot fence, a herd-like pounding of shoes and panting breaths around me. I scale the barricade easily, only to see a twelve-foot wide ditch filled with water in front of me. Without much room to run, I sprint as fast as I can, spring from the edge and clear all the stagnant water and mud, landing on dry soil. I'm glad I was a broad jumper in high school. Several other cadets falter, splashing into the quagmire, a ragged chorus of "shits," "damns" and "Christs" rising out of them.

Safely past the water ditch, I reach a netting of chicken wire built so low to the ground that I have to slither under it. I grunt, groan and wallow in the dirt with the rest, finally emerging from the other end, the pungent smell of dust in my nostrils. Next I scoot under a series of wire fences. After I clear the last one, I face a twenty-foot high wooden wall. Boards crossways on the front of it form a precarious ladder that we all scramble up together, our shoes kicking and squeaking against the wall, the agonized grunts of straining on both sides of me. The back of the wall is slick and flat, the only way down being a series of thick ropes. I grab one of them, lower myself hand over hand, my feet walking down the face of the wall.

After two more formidable walls, we run between zigzagging wire fences, cutting first one way then the other. We attempt to run sideways on a tilted wooden embankment then over the tops of logs placed at angles to each other, having to turn sharply at the end of each one without falling off. I pant like a St. Bernard on a hot day and so do the rest as we push our bodies along with our arms and hands on long, cruel parallel bars.

Three trenches loom ahead of us, each one five feet deep. I jump into the first one, scramble out, then the second and the third, each one taxing my flagging energy. I jog with the other men towards another twenty-foot wall, this one like a gigantic ladder. We climb up one side then down the other. I grasp a thick rope, and swing my body over the ground, scurry over one more hurdle, and I'm done.

"Okay, now run the cross country track!" yells an assistant stationed at the end. " Come on now! Get moving! Don't stop!"

Already exhausted, I start down the track, conscious only of my own footsteps hammering the dirt, my labored breathing and a distorted vision of straggly weeds at the edge of the path. I push myself, hoping for a second wind. The finish line seems miles away.

Closer to the end now, I'm only a disembodied pair of lungs, swollen like great balloons frantic for air. The raspy sound of my breath rushing in and out of my throat is all that I can hear. What I see of the field ahead of me is a fuzzy whiteness softly edged with darkness. I struggle past the finish line, walk with my hands on my hips, trying to come back down to earth. The cadets around me breathe like steam engines, none of us able to talk to each other. Our bodies glisten with sweat. In a short time, the field restores itself, our lungs lapse back into normal breathing, our hearts stop pounding, and we begin to laugh and joke again.

Only the day before we ran three-quarters of a mile. Halfway through the race my calves tied up. I peeled away from the others, grabbing my legs. The cadets streamed past me like stampeding wildebeests as I worked my fingers into my tight muscles. By the time I was ready to run again, they had all passed me. Not wanting to finish last, I chased after them. The guys ahead, some tiring and others not trying, were easy prey. I closed the gap quickly, passing up dozens of them before I crossed the finish line, preserving my dignity and preventing the shame of trailing the end of the pack.

Each day the training officers try to whip us into shape, and my muscles respond to their efforts with a mixture of dull aches and sharp pains that I try to ignore, as there is no respite. In addition to obstacle courses and cross-country running, we often stand in orderly rows in the wet heat performing every calisthenic exercise known to the instructors---from simple push ups and sit ups to the intricacies of the Randolph Shuffle. They are determined to mold us into perfect specimens even if they have to kill us.

*   *   *

Ducking and bobbing, Stewart and I approach each other, our boxing gloves raised to guard our faces. All around us cadet pairs challenge each other. Their athletic shoes scuffle on the hardwood floor and the dull slap of boxing gloves against bare skin resounds in the echoing gym. Stewart winces as I land a right to his body, but his counterpunch has little sting. I hit him several more times, one time near his face. His taut lips already pale and drawn become grimmer and the skin around his eyes sags downward as though he's about to cry. But there are no tears. I realize he's afraid, and isn't used to fighting any more than I am. I realize that I could, if I chose, whip him easily. Even though I feel the power of that thought, I have no urge to hurt my friend. We spar cautiously until the instructor stops us.

At his direction, I place my head on Stewart's shoulder. At close range we pound each other's chest and abdomen as hard and as fast as we can. We don't stop until our wilting arms won't move any more. After a brief rest, I raise my arms, place my gloved hands behind my neck and head, and allow Stewart to pummel me again. It feels strange to let him batter me as though I'm a punching bag. At a signal from the instructor, we reverse, and I repay the blows.

Learning the art of boxing is another way that the officers attempt to transform us into "fighting men." Newspapers, cadet brochures and slogans often refer to us as "fighting men" which always seems ludicrous to me. I want to become a bombardier, but the idea of my becoming a "fighting man" is very different from the way I feel about myself. I'd never been aggressive. I'd never picked on anyone, and I'd always tried to avoid the bullies that did. Having been raised in a loving family, I never developed any hatreds or dark passions. I felt good about my life.

I had only one fight in my life. That was a long time ago. Ben Seymour, a neighbor boy, and I, for no reason, began punching each other. I threw a playful fist at his arm. He returned a jab to my shoulder, harder. Each blow we traded landed with more force until both of us were out of control. It was as though we slipped into a spell, each of us whaling into the other, unable to stop, a fuzzy, dream-like whirling of blows and counter blows. Ben's mother finally rushed out and mercifully separated us. Blood streamed from Ben's nose, and I walked home with an already-swollen eye that soon turned as blue-black as the underside of a thunderstorm. I wasn't angry at Ben, or he with me. We apologized to each other and remained fast friends.

Following several days of boxing, we practice the rudiments of Judo, slamming each other to the matted floor as we "attack" one another. Days of wrestling test our strength and stamina as we try to hone our "fighting" skills.

* * *

His whistle shrieking, the instructor sends us on another short sprint. We dig our shoes into the dirt, struggling to hurtle forward. Another blast of his whistle brings us to a complete stop; the next one starts us off again. Wind sprints, the instructor explains, builds up our wind and endurance. Frozen like puffing statues, we prepare to dash forward again. Finally finished, we stand gasping for air, each cadet seeking some position to restore his breathing.

After a brief rest, the sergeant in charge lines us up on the field.

"This is a race," he shouts. "You have 100 yards to run as fast as you can. I want to see every cadet try his best. Okay! Get set! Go!"

In a noisy scuffling of shoes the long line of cadets streaks across the gravely field. I have a good start, and it's exhilarating to sprint without stopping. I pull away from those around me, but notice several others out of the corner of my eye who also shoot out ahead of the pack. I push my legs to the limit. To my surprise I flash over the finish line first.

Even though the effort destroys me physically for the rest of the day, I feel a keen sense of satisfaction. Although I don't shave every day or appear as rugged or manly as many of them, I'm physically able to hold my own against them. In a sense I become what they are---men.

Our Preflight School yearbook attempts to explain why the instructors drive us so hard.

"Ah-h-h--that's it, Mister, smile! Smile so that tired but hardening body can taste the sweet weariness of a well-earned rest. Flex those new, sweaty, aching muscles in the sun. Let the air pour into those expanding lungs. Listen to your heart pounding hard and steady. That body you're building today is your weapon for tomorrow.

Store all the strength and stamina you can, for a dangerous game and a cruel enemy lie ahead. Death's game of war has no time-outs for tired men. The man wins who can give and take the longest .

Come on! Drive those legs harder! Swing those arms faster! Work, man, work! You're winning or losing your battle now. But, don't forget to smile!"

Another portion states, "Although cadets grunt and groan as the instructors put them through some new type of 'torture', each one knows that his condition, and the physical condition of the men with him, must be perfect to endure the long flying hours of a bombing mission. Physical fitness is also necessary to secure the perfect coordination so essential in the performance of that mission."

At least these officers did not justify physical training as a method to turn us into "fighting men", but rather men who could endure and perform.

Near the end of our training I breeze over the obstacle course, and cruise the cross-country track with ease. I feel like a coiled spring, like the inner workings of a fine watch. My legs feel like machined pistons. I float just off the ground as I walk, my heels clicking rhythmically. I think about Coach Arnett's vision of the finely tuned athlete as a young stallion. "He whinnies and kicks in the barn, and when they open the gate, he gallops and prances and farts, and, holding his head high, he frisks across the meadow, his tail and mane flying in the wind."

HURRICANE

Belting out all the songs we know, we march down the rain-dampened street. Our raincoats crackle over our fatigues, and our heavy GI shoes clomp in a steady rhythm. The wet composition shingles on the barracks roofs ruffle like papery scales in the strengthening wind, flashing dull silver on their undersides. With my cap turned inside out and pulled down over my ears, I glance at the glistening roofs with their flapping shingles and the ominous push of lowering gray clouds. We'll all be down on the flight ramp soon. Before the full force of the storm strikes, each cadet will be at his place, grasping a rope, a wing or a tail. We'll pit our strength against the rippling muscles of the wind for the possession of the airplanes.

As the storm intensifies, the officers command that we run to the ramp. Still in formation, we trot in double time toward the moored training planes. A cadet officer shouts in the slanting rain.

"Okay Stevens. You and Sacks hang on tight to the wing rope, and don't let go!"

We grab the wet line and brace ourselves. If we turn our heads into the rain, the wind-driven drops sting our faces like volleys of rice.

The rising wind rakes the airplane, fluttering and lifting its tail. The two cadets assigned to that section can't control it. Sacks and I leave the wing, stagger to the tail to help them. The four of us apply all our energy to holding it down, but, despite our weight and our strength, it rises in each strong gust. I try to keep wooden blocks wedged against the tail wheel, but the plane shimmies and wiggles in the gale like a caught fish. I can't keep the blocks in place.

I'd never seen such torrents of rain or felt such overwhelming strength in the wind. The horizontal deluge blasts the airplane and rattles against our thin raincoats like an unholy static. When I think that the rain can't pour any harder or the wind become more severe, they both increase. The accumulating water beneath us streams over the high tops of our shoes and washes away the tail blocks. Rain froths the surface of the turbulent runoff. Driving wind whips the surface into white caps, as though the sea has moved into the airport. The quivering, rising tail sometimes pulls us out of the water. We hang on to prevent being blown away.

As we desperately hold on, Sacks works one hand free, nudges me on the shoulder. In the din of the storm, the wind blows our voices away. He points to the outer ramp where an AT-10 training plane rolls backwards out toward the field. A dozen men chase after it. Scrambling through the wind-whipped water, they desperately try to stay on their feet. Suddenly a blinding torrent obscures them. When we see them again, half are on the ground, some on their knees, a few on their backs. They appear like frolicking ghosts cavorting in a graveyard fog. As the airplane finally bogs down in the mud, the Keystone Cop-like cadets slog after it, eventually entangling it in ropes like a runaway animal.

Another plane blows past us, its fuselage buckled in the center like a badly fractured arm, its nose and tail pointing skyward. It disappears in the rain. Another plane tumbles end over end, like a loose wad of paper on a city street. Ripped off sections of tarpaper, shingles, boards, tree branches, and small pieces of airplanes fly through the air, tumbling and twisting and riding the vagaries of the gusts. We can't watch out for them because it's impossible to turn our heads toward the wind. A piece of roofing jabs my leg, flips in the wind and lands in the water. The airplane propellers, difficult to move by hand, turn like slow windmills.

For five hours we endure the hurricane's fury, rain soaking us to our bones, wind threatening to tear us loose. I think about being flung into the air with the rest of the debris. Only my fascination with the storm prevents me from succumbing to the terror of it. I'm humbled by its violence. I realize how insignificant I am compared to its raw force. More airplanes break loose, colliding with others, damaging them all. I worry about the nervous, wind-buffeted craft we cling to---whether it might tear loose like the others.

Finally other men replace us, and the officers give us permission to go to the mess hall. We release our grip on the tail, our stiff hands almost fixed in the clinging position. Sacks' face is blue and so are his hands. I look down at my own fingers that are also numb and bluish. The storm has slackened, but the wind is still so strong we can barely stand. Four of us lock our arms, lean at a low angle into the gale then push our way slowly to the mess hall. At times the heavier gusts stop us, but we proceed when they taper off. We struggle through water and mud up to our ankles. Exposure has chilled us all to our very centers.

Once inside the candle-lit mess hall, we begin to feel the storm's toll on our bodies. Sacks and I both ache in our arms and groins. I can hardly lift my legs over the mess hall bench. I savor my food. Our chow had never tasted so good. The warmth of the hot food sliding down into my chilled body is comforting. I thaw out my fingers around a mug of coffee. Outside, the wind still rips more shingles from the roofs.

An assortment of rumors circulates around the mess hall. The wind's velocity had hit 96 mph with gusts of 113. One cadet hit by a rudder, then treated at the infirmary reports that the doctor there has just set his fourth broken back. The infirmary is full of bruised and injured cadets. The cowling from an aircraft engine had blown off, striking a cadet on the head, killing him. A flying board killed another by knocking him down in the water where he drowned. A collapsing airplane crushed another.

After eating and resting in the mess hall, we make our way back to the barracks, the calmer eye of the hurricane now giving us some respite. Telephone poles lean at odd angles, their severed wires drooping to the ground. The few trees growing on the base lie twisted and broken in the mud. Tangled sheet metal and crumpled ventilators rest far from their original locations. We pass our day room, now punched full of holes by flying debris. Finally reaching our barracks, we discover that the entire, 25-foot front eave is missing. It had blown over the top of our roof then struck the next barracks, gouging two large chunks out of the roof and smashing out an entire window frame. Shattered glass, remnants of screen and splintered wood litter the inside of their barracks. A long 1 x 6 board sticks like a knife through the side of the same barracks. Protruding three feet inside, it had stopped only inches from a resting cadet's head.

Water covers the floor of our darkened quarters, two inches deep in places, soaking into our footlockers. Exhausted, I peel off my wet clothes, dry myself the best I can and slither into bed.

Their shoes fumbling on the soaked floor, men carrying flashlights roust us out after we had been in bed for only two hours. Behind the beam of the flashlight a voice shouts, "Come on. Get up! We need you out there again. The second part of the storm is about to hit!" In the glare of his flashlight I check my watch. It is 2200. Still drugged with fatigue and lack of sleep, I march back with the others to the ramp where we take up positions around the planes again. Trucks with floodlights and noisy generators light up the rainy gloom so that we can at least partially see what we're doing. Lightning bolts light up the night sky, casting an eerie blue glow in the driving rain and a ghostly scene of bone-weary cadets struggling to protect the airplanes. The rain and wind, although fiercer than any I had seen up until today, is not quite as severe as the withering, wind-whipped deluge we had experienced earlier. One hour after midnight, three hours after we had been routed out of our comfortable beds, shadowy men grab our arms and shout, "The worst is over. Return to your barracks now."

* * *

As early as Monday morning, meteorologists had warned that a hurricane was centered south of Port Arthur, Texas, moving on a northerly course. The airplanes at Ellington Field, usually flown to safer havens in northern Texas and Oklahoma during hurricane threats, remained at the base. Mechanics had worked through the night to service and fuel them for the evacuation to the north. Tuesday morning, the officer in charge of the base decided to keep the planes at Ellington Field to avoid the expense of flying them out, hoping that the storm would only graze the Houston area. When it rapidly approached, bearing directly down on Houston, they had to come up with a plan. That's when they decided that the cadets would help hold the planes down.

An orderly had burst into our first-aid class, demanding that we immediately return to our barracks, change into fatigues and rain coats and stand by. In less than one-half hour officers ordered us to fall out of the barracks and line up in formation in the street. I stood with the rest, properly dressed, even wearing my fancy green garters to hold up my stockings as the officers explained what we were about to do.

* * *

Bending and stooping constantly the next day, we pick up scraps on the debris-littered base as though we're kids forced to clean up our own mess. Tatters of everything lie strewn down the streets, between the barracks and in the fields. Thousands of shingles are scattered everywhere like fallen leaves. A large truck lies on its side, its undercarriage tipped to the sunlight. We have no electricity, and our water is polluted.

We can't even brush our teeth with it. When we're thirsty, we must join a long line in front of the mess hall where we wait for a dipper of boiled water. After years of sanitary training, I wince when we all use the same dipper. At the morning mess we eat by candlelight.

Several days later, the electricity and water restored, our base returns to near normal. We read with both amusement and concern an account of our experience in a Riverside, California newspaper sent to Carlo Zuniga. The paper reports that only slight damage was done to Ellington Field whereas we were informed that destruction of airplanes alone would amount to at least a half million dollars. The article states that the cadets sang songs throughout the storm. What a joke! Even if a few cadets were singing, no one could possibly have heard them. The article further states that we were well prepared for such an emergency---a flat lie. The paper reports that we had adequate and proper clothing to withstand the storm. We all laugh at this nonsense. We wore only thin raincoats and fatigues. My fatigues weighed a ton when I took them off. I wrung about a gallon of water out of one pair, and it took them two days to dry out. The last printed falsehood is that no cadet was hospitalized. I knew of one cadet who had broken his back and was to remain immobilized in the hospital. Another smashed his collarbone and suffered a concussion. One fellow was unconscious for three days. A strong rumor still persists that three were taken to the morgue rather than the hospital. As the veteran had told me in San Antonio, "If you read the newspapers, you're better off sticking to the funny papers." I see myself slowly sliding toward his cynicism.

Stewart reports when he returns from Port Arthur to see how his parents weathered the storm that all of Port Arthur "stinks". Over 19 inches of rain drowned thousands of chickens as well as cats and dogs, all of which rot everywhere. The standing water turned stagnant then began to reek in the humid heat. Stewart's mother thought that the roof would cave in from the heavy rains.

We learn that 12 inches of rain had fallen from the storm and that the barometric pressure had dropped to 28.80 inches. Galveston is off limits to cadets because of unsafe water.

I was able to stand up to the hurricane. I let it pummel me the way I allowed Stewart to pound my chest and abdomen with his gloved fists. I had taken its wild, shrieking beating as well as any other man, but I had also been humbled by its awesome power. I feel a quiet pride now that it's all over.

ACADEMICS

Beeping in my ears, the high staccato of the Morse code speaks a language I'm just beginning to understand. What at first was electric gibberish now becomes a series of distinct forms that spell out letters. We sit at long tables, earphones fixed to our heads, listening intently to the dots and dashes and jotting the letters on paper. Thunder rumbles outside, the deep reverberations rolling through the shrill chirping in our earphones. Rain streaks the windows as a heavy shower drums on the roof. The room's inner walls are bare, the wooden studs exposed like fragile ribs. A corporal sits at a table in front of the room where he can operate the code tapes and control the circuits to our earphones. This is the first of our classes. They tell us that, *"The ultimate purpose of Preflight academics is the destruction of the enemy."*

Learning code is like being let in on a secret. Meaningless bits of sound become intelligible, at least to the privileged few. I soon surprise myself by taking 100 characters at 5 words per minute and not missing any. When the beeps fly by at 7 words per minute, I still don't miss any. Only 6 cadets out of 80 do as well. Not used to being at the top of the class, I'm giddy in this rarified atmosphere.

Ground forces classes teach us about Army organization and combat strategies. Our maps and charts class, practical but difficult, opens up the fields of map projections, aerial photography and target recognition. Mathematics, my old nemesis, takes us through a review of basic math, algebra and finally vectors that will help us later with dead

151

reckoning navigation. Physics begins with acceleration and deceleration problems, the foundation of bombardier physics. We concentrate on velocity problems, meteorology and force vectors. We study confidential aerial photographs and plan bombing missions.

My expectations rise. I had never cared about high grades before, but now they're a means to an end, my bombardier's wings. I study every spare moment, hoping for high scores on all my examinations. I become very serious about my courses, listening intently in all my classes, filling reams of paper with meticulous notes, poring over my books and guides. I study under the glow of my fluorescent desk lamp or with my friends in the day room, and run the concepts through my mind during calisthenics, even as I pant over the obstacle course. The will is there, the attention is there and the direction of my energy is there, but my skills lack a sharp edge due to years of a relaxed attitude toward academics.

I expect 95% on my next mathematics test, but I receive only 65%. Carelessness drags me down the way it always did. Even though I know better, in the heat of an examination, I commit inexcusable mistakes. For multiplying 3 times 12 and getting 24 I lose 10 points because this error at the first part of a complex problem distorts my final answer. For another similar miscalculation I lose 15 points, and finally, using a "plus" sign when I should have used a "minus" sign, drops my score 10 more points.

The low grade frightens me. I slide into the quiet darkness of disappointment. I see the result as a monumental failure that could lead, if compounded, to washing out in Preflight School. Teetering on the edge of a shadowy depression, I finally decide that's no way to be. With new resolve I launch myself into studying for the next test on aeronautical charts and aerial photography. I'm the only one in my flight who passes the 6 words per minute code check, a little boost that restores my confidence.

* * *

Mrs. Glenn, my high school geometry teacher, sits on her desk as she usually does, unconsciously kicking one of her dangling legs back and forth as she talks to the class. Even though the serious Mrs. Glenn is no beauty and seems ancient to me, I think it's sexy when she swings her leg like that.

The second-story classroom with its large windows on two sides not only lets in volumes of light but also provides fascinating views of the traffic on Manchester Boulevard and the swaying trees and soothing grass of Grevillea Park. As I gaze out of the window, watching the cars and trucks accelerate up the boulevard, I hear a voice that sounds as though it comes from outer space. "What do you think about that, Norman?" she asks. I can only stare blankly at Mrs. Glenn as the class looks at me, and she waits for an answer that she knows I can't give. Saying nothing, feeling the heat of my own embarrassment in my cheeks and suffering the amused looks of the other students, I can only look at her. "I suggest you pay attention from now on, Norman." I agree and, for a while, listen to what she has to say about axioms and postulates.

The abstract world of geometry can't touch the concrete world I behold out of those windows. The cars that stream by carry people who are going places---to shop, to work, to the grocery---anywhere. They move and have purpose while I sit in my assigned seat listening to concepts I don't fully understand or want to. Outside, trucks carry boulders, sand, cement, lumber and pipes, real objects a person can touch. Wind bends the trees in the park. A heavy shower suddenly obscures them, turning them into wet tree ghosts. Cars with their headlights reflecting in the slick streets, slosh through the puddles. People scurry with raised umbrellas while parents in cars pick up their sons or daughters. The real excitement lies outside the windows.

My mother tells me after her conference with Mrs. Glenn that I look out of the windows too much. "He just looks at the trucks all of the time instead of listening to me," says Mrs. Glenn. My mother relays the comments, but doesn't threaten me. She knows that all she can do is tell me, that I must do the rest on my own.

Basic mathematics seems practical to me, but all of the other phases of it seem of little use. Who cares how much older Jim is than Bob at one age compared to another? Who cares about lines being tangent to circles? I study enough to pass the courses, but that's all.

English classes interest me least of all. I fill out endless blanks in grammar workbooks with out ever learning much from them. Despite the workbooks, my writing and my way of talking never change. I never see the remotest connection between what I'm exposed to in class and the way I talk. My sentences are full of questionable grammar and Midwesternisms, all ingrained in me from listening to my parents and relatives.

My mother who reads novels during her afternoon rests suggests that I also read them so that I shall, "have a better understanding of life and love." I tell her that novels are just a pack of lies. They're a bunch of words about things that never happened. I prefer reading non-fiction books about real people who are active, like Father Hubbard's book, *The Land of Ten Thousand Smokes*, about his adventures exploring the Aleutian Islands.

School stifles me with its confinement. I had always yearned for the outdoors. At home, most of my waking hours were spent out of the house. Forced to take afternoon rests by my mother when I was younger, I rebelled by never closing my eyes. I squirmed and listened longingly to the other children playing outside or leafed through an old picture book on World War I or played with a pencil pretending it's a rocket ship. Even movies with indoor scenes bored me. I liked outdoor action films with airplanes or cowboy films with guns, horses, cattle, mountains, boulder-strewn landscapes and thundering locomotives.

Striving to excel in all my courses, as a matter of principle is alien to me. Study and academic discipline for its own sake as a key to success is incomprehensible. I participate in the classes I like, and I merely pass the ones that don't interest me. General science, biology and, strangely, Latin excite me to action while all the English, social studies and mathematics courses are tepid water. The beginning sciences with their emphasis on the tangible engage me, but chemistry, which I drop, and physics, which I barely pass, lose me in their mathematical abstractness.

I have no academic goals, feeling somehow that the future will take care of itself. I go about my business from day to day blindly following my own interests and doing only what I feel like doing. For the most part my teachers are very good, but there is little they can do with me. I, having little insight into my situation, believe I'm just not as smart as those who make good grades. I don't even consider my lack of effort and poor concentration as contributing to my mediocre grades. My mother, having just come from a special conference with the school counselor, tries to talk seriously to me.

"The counselor showed me your record", she says. "She claims you have a very high IQ, but your grades are far below what you are capable of."

* * *

Bluish light from my fluorescent desk lamp pours over my class notes and manuals as I try to understand the formulas that will explain the mysteries of acceleration, force vectors and centrifugal force. Many of us sit at the desks between the heads of our beds, making use of the precious time between supper and "lights out." All around the barracks pools of light glow like small phosphorescent islands over separate desks.

I still ache from the obstacle course, the slamming of my body to the mats during jujitsu practice and the boxing

155

bouts. My brain hums with a kind of static after the day's class work. Although the days and nights have cooled slightly, the humidity remains the same. The papers and pages of the manuals are damp and sticky, the papers sometimes clinging to my forearm when I lean on them.

I float on a strange sea of success. Hard study finally brings results, and I'm intoxicated with the taste of it. I can send 10 code words per minute, and I can understand the blinking of a red code light as though it speaks to me. I can identify the silhouette of any airplane as it flashes for an instant on the screen. I help others at night to learn the shapes. I score a 96% on a maps and charts test and 98% on a physics test after "studying like a demon." I pass the vector test in mathematics with an 80% grade when the class average is 50%. My average grade for all of my courses is 90%, and surprisingly I find myself wanting to raise my scores.

Being at the top of the class rather than at the center or even below as I had been in high school is wonderfully different. I feel a new pride in myself, a growing confidence that I can succeed. I also begin to feel anxious that somehow I'm in for a fall, that my grades are a fluke, that they will soon begin to tumble. I write home to my parents.

If I had studied half as much in high school as I do here, I would have been in the Scholarship Society.

After scoring 98% on all of my physics tests and bringing my overall academic average up to 94%, I again write.

I'm telling you I really had to work for that average. I have learned more here in Preflight than I learned in all four years of high school.

I also reflect at the end of my fourth month in the Army that not only have I opened up academically, but also I have greatly expanded my experiences. It's like a rheostat in my mind that gradually turns up the intensity of the light, reaching recesses that up until now had lain in shadow.

I have been in the Army one-third of a year. It sure seems like a long time since I have seen you, but I wouldn't trade this experience and the education for anything. It's surprising how much I have learned about people and places since I have been in. All of the men have different ideas about things, and we sure learn to see other people's views.

I can feel myself changing, growing.

GAS MASKS AND PRESSURE
CHAMBERS

"Okay men. Turn your backs to the wind," shouts an officer over a loudspeaker. "It's time to start our tests."

Two hundred of us in an open field obey the command, shift our positions. I look down at the gravel and the clumps of weeds, waiting, not knowing what else to do. I'd heard the ugly rumors about these tests. I'm tense thinking about them.

"You'll only detect a tiny amount of gas," claims a sergeant. "It's very important that you learn to distinguish between the different types of poisonous gases. You never know when you'll have to use this information." Our gas masks hang at our side in their cases. Most of us have inked in the places we've been stationed on the coarse khaki cloth of the holder. I run my fingers over its roughness. We're not allowed to use our masks during the drills.

Upwind, the chemical warfare unit sets off a vial of chloropicrin, the foul gas floating towards us on a light breeze. It smells like flypaper, an evil odor I associate with insects and filth. I take only a cautious whiff as it drifts by. We babble to each other after it passes. I'm relieved that I've withstood the first "attack" without any ill effects.

"Remember now! When you hear the detonation of the vial, take a deep breath," yells the sergeant. "Let your breath out very slowly. When the gas gets to you, just barely sniff it then walk quickly out of the area."

After a dose of Lewisite that's nearly odorless, a creeping cloud of mustard gas envelops us, its pungent odor like a just-opened bottle of horseradish. I inhale more of the noxious stuff than I'd planned, then scurry away with the crowd before I have to breathe again. The sour odor stays with me like foul perfume.

Still recovering from our snort of mustard gas, we again assemble with our backs to the wind for the last demonstration gas, phosgene. It reaches us quickly. Again I sniff too much. It gets in my eyes. They burn and water so much that I can hardly see where I'm going. I try to scramble out of its irritating path. I gasp and blink as I tramp off with the others, their trousers and shoes distorted through my tears. We had all heard the stories about these exercises ---that earlier two cadets had breathed too much phosgene, causing them to collapse and become sick at their stomachs---that one cadet had spit up blood for two days. I dash for the clear air.

Finally finished with the mock gas attacks, the ordinance crews demonstrate the action of incendiary bombs. A magnesium airplane part as a substitute for the bomb burns vigorously with a white-hot flame, so bright that we can't look at it directly, clouds of dense white smoke billowing from it. As part of the demonstration one of the crew directs a stream of water at the fire, causing the magnesium to explode, scattering hot blobs everywhere. We duck and dodge, trying to avoid them. The exhibition is to teach us that water can't be used to douse incendiary bombs, that the water only makes the fire worse. We believe them.

As we look at the final death of the "bomb" and the last wisps of white smoke, a cloud of what looks like more of the same floats directly at us. I move out of the way, just catching the edge of it. Suddenly my eyes burn as though they had acid or pepper thrown in them. The chemical warfare crew, smiling and laughing, tosses tear gas canisters everywhere. Now, I have to use my gas mask. With my eyes nearly closed I fumble at my case, unsnapping it to pull out the rubbery mask. I clasp it to my face, securing the straps. Behind my mask, tears seep down my cheek. I sweat in the heat and humidity, and, where the gas comes in contact with the dampness on my skin, it burns, especially around my neck. I trot out of the whitish fog, heading for the far edge of the field. Once in the purer air and out of the path of the gas, the sting slowly fades. With my mask off and my eyes exposed to a fresh breeze, I return to normal.

*   *   *

Sometimes it seems as though we live in our gas masks. We often are required to wear them in the barracks for an hour at a time. We wear them when we march or during calisthenics. We look like mutant elephants, our hoses resembling trunks, or microscopic views of mosquitoes with their great eyes and long proboscises. The condensation from our breathing mixed with sweat drips out when we take them off. The rubber smells like the mask the nurses put over my face as a child when I had my tonsillectomy.

During special gas drills we must keep our masks on for thirty minutes regardless of what we're doing. Roaming officers wander through the barracks checking cadets for violations. Any cadet caught without it on will immediately be taken to the base hospital where he must undergo treatment for gas inhalation, said to be a very unpleasant procedure. The threat keeps us in line. In the afternoon we march in the heat for forty minutes with them on again, the discomfort adding to the excruciating irritation of our prickly heat.

*   *   *

We gather in a dimly lit building that houses the pressure chamber. Rounded and silver measuring eight feet in diameter and twenty feet in length, the chamber looks like a miniature submarine. Word had circulated among us that six weeks before, during a freak accident in the pressure chamber, one cadet had died and several others had been hospitalized. We had also heard about other cadets who had suffered from claustrophobia, had beaten their fists on the steel door, begging to be let out. With that one frantic episode they had washed themselves out. I wonder about my own reactions.

Ten of us enter the chamber through the small, round opening, jostling past two thick steel doors. The interior, illuminated by bluish fluorescent lights, resembles the inside of an airplane fuselage. We take seats behind small desks, the oxygen lines and masks near each chair. I try to remember what I learned in the lecture before we entered. The chamber crew shuts the two heavy doors, securing the outer one with a large wheel that exerts pressure enough to make an airtight seal. I see the face of one of the operators at the thick viewing window.

At first they decrease the pressure inside the chamber to simulate an altitude of 5000 feet. They instruct us to work at clearing our ears by swallowing and working our lower jaw back and forth like cows chewing their cud. Four cadets, unable to clear them, are let out of the chamber. With our oxygen masks adjusted and pressed firmly against our faces, the operators take us up to a simulated altitude of 38,000 feet, leaving us there for an hour and a quarter. With the pressure greatly reduced outside our bodies, we forget all modesty, burping often behind our masks and passing gas at will. For our own comfort we're encouraged to do so. Suddenly one cadet leans forward from the waist in obvious pain.

"I've got the bends," he shouts.

"It's only trapped gas," says the operator over a speaker. "The pain will go away. Just hang on."

Easing us down from high altitude, we now "fly" at 18,000 feet. The officer in charge tells us to take off our oxygen masks.

"We're now going to take you up slowly to 30,000 feet", the officer says. "All of you will begin to feel the effects of anoxia, but those symptoms will vary with the individual. You need to know what your particular symptoms are. Do not apply your oxygen masks until you feel you are just on the verge of passing out."

Apprehensive, we sit at our desks as the pressure gradually lowers. Finally several of the cadets, feeling faint, quickly strap on their masks. At 26,000 feet I still don't have my mask on, but my fingernails are becoming blue. Although I don't feel consciousness slipping away as yet, I put on the mask. The oxygen is like fresh air as I inhale deeply. They'd told us that without oxygen at 38,000 feet we would die in five minutes; no sense taking chances.

Once out of the chamber, the tests passed, I'm listed as an airman with an "unlimited ceiling" which means that I'm qualified for any plane that the Army Air Force flies. Again I feel a boyish pride that I can keep up with any of the men no matter how much more they look like men than I do.

I understand that becoming familiar with gas masks and preparing for poisonous gas attacks is important. Any of us could be sent to a base where a sudden chemical attack could send us scurrying for protection. I know too that dealing with high altitude, recognizing my oxygen-deficiency symptoms and my adjustment to cramped spaces is good training. On the other hand, I believe their main objective is discipline and personal testing, a plan of putting us through hoops, presenting us with personal discomforts and trials to see how we react to them. Hours of hot, sweaty, constricting agony behind gas masks is more than is needed to simply get used to them. The officers hope the cadets will follow orders regardless of how uncomfortable they feel or how irritated they become. They look at us constantly, as though asking, "Who will complain? Who will say they have had enough? Who will disobey? Who will quit?"

FROM LUSHNESS TO DUST

Dust swirls in through the open train windows, settling into an irritating haze. Sitting in the last car of the train, we catch most of the powdery soil churned up by the swaying cars. Because of the heat, we can't bear to close the windows. Dust collects on our faces, our sweat fixing the grains to our skin. We wear it like a mask. I grind the tiny grains between my teeth. The grit accumulates in the corners of the floor, around the steel supports of the seats and on the window ledges. I can draw marks along the windowsill and the exposed portions of our seats with my finger. The emptiness of the plains and small dried-up Texas towns pass by our windows.

Aside from the dust and oppressive heat, I'm weary from having had to sit up all night. Two thoughts run through my mind as I try to cope with my fatigue. Even though I've made many friends among the cadets, I keenly miss Carlo Zuniga, who had shipped out to another gunnery school the week before. I feel the absence of his easy kindness and his acceptance of me. We enjoyed our companionship from the time we were assigned seats together on a troop train out of Fort MacArthur. The chances of our ever getting back together are unlikely. As I swelter in the bone-dry heat of southwest Texas, I long for the lush green trees and fields of Houston and the moist air we left behind.

We had boarded the Missouri Pacific troop train at Ellington Field late yesterday afternoon, chugging away from the base in the early evening. During the night the train traveled a roundabout route through Austin, San Marcos and Braunfels in order to reach San Antonio by morning. Once we arrived, the cadet officers marched us down the street to a restaurant where we fell upon a breakfast of ham, eggs and potatoes. Back on the train, we began the long, straight journey to Laredo on the Mexican border where the Army Air Force had established one of its largest aerial gunnery schools.

Sometimes the train stops at isolated towns, their wooden buildings parched and warped by arid heat and, I believe, pathetic loneliness. A few souls wave at us. Several of the thirstier cadets, not knowing how soon the train will leave, decide to dash into town for soda pop, ice-cold beer or even half-pints of whiskey to top off bottles of Coca-Cola. A few chance it, running back, sacks in hand, just in time. When we arrive in Laredo at three-thirty in the afternoon, the mercury hovers near 112 degrees.

*   *   *

Laredo Army Air Field, a collection of low-lying, cream-colored barracks and temporary wooden buildings, nestles among low hills and open slopes dotted with brush. The clay-like reddish soil supports only rugged shrubs, mesquite and a few stunted pepper trees. Flat-bottomed cumulus clouds float high in a blue enamel sky over unbroken miles of open desert. The modern airfield with its long concrete runways lies on a low plateau next to the base. Oven-like heat sucks the moisture out of everything it touches.

The mess hall doesn't approach the high standards that we'd come to expect at Ellington Field. I hadn't been served mashed turnips since I was a child, and I hated them then. One of my friends, John Sacks, who asks for an extra slice of bread, is denied it by sour-looking privates who appear to hate cadets. When he argues with them, one of them hits him in the head with a metal tray, inflicting a small gash on his forehead.

We also discover that we have no footlockers in which to store our belongings, needing instead to stash them in our barracks bags. We are to have no sheets, only two thick, scratchy army blankets. The luxury and comforts of Ellington Field are not to be had here.

*   *   *

Believing that idleness leads to discontent and trouble, the officers fill our time with activities before our classes begin on Monday. We line up to have our pictures taken for our passes, and we spend long hours in darkened rooms watching training films. Officers lecture us, orienting us to the base and its operations, emphasizing regulations and explaining our up-coming gunnery training. In the searing heat they take us to a remote field where we again must endure detonations of chemical warfare gases. The tear gas attacks make us weep, and our skin burns where it reacts with our sweat. Because of our dejection we don't fall out into the field with the proper enthusiasm, so, to teach us a lesson and insure strict discipline, the officer in charge drills us in the sun for over an hour and a half.

At night a few of us at a time walk over to a building where medics test us for night blindness and night vision. We sit twenty feet from a screen upon which is projected a thick circle with a segment out of it. We then turn a dial to complete the circle. With each trial the light grows dimmer so that near the end of the test we can hardly see the circle. I pass. We walk back to the barracks in the night as the wind sweeps up clouds of tawny earth, billows of it whirling past the dim outside lights.

On Sunday morning our tactical officer, a first lieutenant wearing his pilot's wings, orders a sudden inspection. He restricts us all to the barracks, preventing many of us from attending church services, a travesty we consider inexcusable.

He also denies us open post for any part of the weekend. I hate his exaggerated straight posture, small, serious mouth and gleaming silver bars. "What a lousy, unreasonable jerk!" I mutter. "If he were a fit pilot, he wouldn't be down here flying a target plane four and a half hours each month to collect his flight pay." Labeling him makes me feel better.

Our uniform for the base is gray-green fatigues, open at the collar, sleeves rolled up to our elbows, appropriate for Laredo's climate and more comfortable than the suntan uniforms we'd had to wear at Ellington Field. On one arm we wear a large green band that says "Student". For protection from the scorching sun most of us wear olive-drab pith helmets, like explorer's hats, with our shiny brass wings and propeller insignia fixed to the front.

I'm assigned to a class of ten under the leadership of a sergeant who appears to be a good teacher. He explains the schedule with great enthusiasm and interest.

"Your first four weeks will be spent on the ground studying the operation of the 30- caliber and 50-caliber machine guns," the sergeant says. "You'll also shoot skeet, fire 22s and pick off cardboard airplanes with BB guns. You'll fire from turrets and stationary guns on the ground. After the fourth week you'll fly in the AT-6s and fire a 30-caliber machine gun at a tow target, then the final week you'll fire at tow targets from turrets mounted in AT-11s and AT-18s. If you get 10% hits, you'll get your gunner's wings."

I look forward to the training despite the unpleasant weather, the spartan conditions and the desolation of the base, even the unreasonable officers and unnecessary activities. The shock of our arrival wears off, the food improves, and the camaraderie of being with other cadets keeps up my spirits. I feel fit and confident even though I stand at the brink of a new world of flying, action and guns, a world I know nothing about.

COLD STEEL

Cold and heavy, the metal parts slip into place with precise, hollow clicks. The smell of steel and machine oil drifts up from the scattered components and our glistening fingers. A trace of blue, like the night sky just before dawn, tints the steel. A baffling array of machine gun parts lie scattered on the wooden table before me. Like a child who has taken apart the family alarm clock and wonders how he will ever get it back together, I struggle. By the end of the week I must be able to disassemble then reassemble the entire machine gun while blindfolded, a task that now seems impossible. In class I took pages of notes about the elements of the Browning M-2 50-caliber machine gun. I tried to learn the names of each part and how they fit, but there were so many.

This weapon, the bewildering anatomy of which now confounds me, fires 800 shots per minute at a muzzle velocity of 2900 feet per second, and it may, sometime in the future, save my life. Arranging pieces into groups helps me visualize the gun as a whole and learn nomenclature. Gradually the groups become familiar---the back plate group, the bolt group with 26 separate parts, the oil buffer group and the barrel, retracting slide, casing and cover groups. Each time I sit around the table with the disemboweled gun before me, the instructors wandering from one cadet to another, I become more familiar with each element ---its name, its position in the gun and its function. What had seemed impossible really is attainable. Field stripping the gun becomes simple. By the end of the week, with a blindfold tied around my head, I use my sense of touch and the visual pictures in my mind to completely take the gun apart and reassemble it.

The following week, with cotton stuffed in our ears, a group of us gathers behind a mounted 50-caliber machine gun, its muzzle pointing toward a remote bank of sand and dirt. A row of the guns stands poised, all directed at the same barrier.

"Most of these guns have something wrong with them," shouts the sergeant. "Some will fire normally, others will fire then quit and some won't fire at all. If the gun malfunctions, it's up to you to find out what's wrong with it."

I try to remember the many reasons a gun might malfunction, the possibilities that we had studied in class whirling around in my head.

The first cadet steps out of the group and up to the gun, his face taut, lips tight together, not knowing what to expect. He pulls the trigger. Staccato blasts split the morning. Rapid puffs of bluish smoke and the sharp scent of cordite erupt from the muzzle, bullets tearing at the bank of sand. Even with cotton crammed in my ears, I absorb the explosions, the concussions rippling through my chest and intestines as though jackhammers pound away inside me. Once we recover from our wide-eyed silence, we turn to each other, smiling at the wonder of what had happened, laughing nervously to break the tension. The experienced sergeant doesn't flinch, of course, and enjoys our reactions. We have finally touched reality, and the touch is stunning. After days of painstakingly learning the names of each part, assembling and disassembling the guns, looking at diagrams, studying graphs about ballistics, listening to lectures about its operation, we still didn't really know the gun. Only after becoming enveloped in its thunder and smell and pulsing energy do we at least partially understand it. The full reality of the weapon still exists somewhere outside of my imagination. Its sheer violence is alien to the gentleness and serenity I have known all my life.

"So the gun fires perfectly," shouts the amused sergeant. "Let's step up to the next one now and see what we have. Okay, Stevens, it's your turn."

Still recovering, I position myself. I swear the gun is much larger than the ones we had handled in class. I approach its cold savagery with the tenderness of my soft fingers, hoping to God that the mechanism will be faulty, that the gun won't fire. With my muscles as tight as guitar strings and my face already wincing in anticipation of the blasts, I squeeze the trigger. A single click, then silence.

"Okay. Why won't it fire?" asks the sergeant.

After lifting the cover plate and peering in at the mechanism, I discover that the gun has a broken ejector, preventing the bullets from feeding into the feed way. We move on to the other guns. I halfway hope they won't fire yet want to be swept up in all that pounding excitement again.

* * *

Back at Ellington Field just a few weeks before, standing fifteen yards from a large paper bull's eye, my arm extended from my shoulder, I aimed carefully down the sights of my .45 pistol. I'd never held a real gun in my hand except in our classes where we learned to field strip it. I'd never handled a gun loaded with a magazine of live ammunition. Although the weapon felt strange in my hand, I was exhilarated by the idea of learning to shoot it.

"Remember! Hold the pistol as still as possible, line up your sights with the target and squeeze, don't pull the trigger!" shouts the range officer. "The .45 pistol is the most difficult weapon you'll ever fire, and the most dangerous. Okay. Fire when ready!"

With the bull's eye directly in my sights, I squeezed off the first shot. The pistol jerked upward in my hand as though someone had kicked the barrel from beneath, and the loud crack of the report started a low ringing in my ears. The bullet hole appeared at the very top edge of the target, far above where I aimed the gun. The next was no better than the first. The third and fourth struck nearly in the same place. Not understanding what I was doing wrong, I decided to lower my aim, reasoning that if I sighted on the lower part of the target, the bullets would strike the center. At 25 yards one of my bullets actually hit the bull's eye. With my ears ringing and my arm still tense, I learned that my score was a woeful 62 points out of a possible 140. The news depressed me until I learned that three-quarters of the cadets scored lower.

*   *   *

Guns had never been a part of my life, not in the suburbs of Los Angeles.

Neither my grandfather nor my father had owned guns when I was around, although as a teen-aged boy my father owned one while he lived on his Indiana farm. I had seen the sepia photograph of my father proudly holding the eagle he had shot, its magnificent wings spread out in feathery death. He appeared, at that moment, to have passed through the gates into manhood. The bird had been raiding chicken yards in the area, and the local newspapers lauded my father for bringing it down.

The neighbor boys and I often chased each other with our cork-in-barrel pop guns, water pistols and cap guns as we played our eternal games of good versus evil---Indians against cowboys, cops against robbers, the Germans against the Allies. The toy guns wove themselves into our epic fantasies as we galloped across imaginary plains, sped around city streets or shot at each other from trenches. It was a world where no one ever screamed in agony or bled from gaping wounds. It was a magic world where dead men rose like flattened cartoon characters, restored again to perfect health.

Later some of us had air rifles with shiny copper BBs that we trained on tin cans and bottles perched on old boxes or at lead soldiers strategically placed around the yard. Playfully we loaded our weapons with chicken feed then took turns shooting each other in the rear end. As we bent over, our eyes shielded and turned away, the chicken feed barrage stung our bottoms through our cords. We also tried hunting butterflies with air rifles filled with chicken scratch, but we could never bring one down.

*   *   *

With my shotgun aimed where I think the clay pigeon will appear, I yell, "Pull!" The black clay pigeon, sailing like a small, fragile plate flies out of the skeet shack. I quickly take aim, lead it to compensate for its speed and squeeze the trigger. The shell explodes, the recoil of the shotgun ramming the gunstock sharply into my shoulder, but the target flies on unharmed, finally landing softly on the desert floor. I had neither been ready for the loud crack of the gun nor its wallop. The next one flashes by just as safely, the buckshot charge passing well to its rear. I continue to shoot and miss, but with each shot I learn to understand the gun, and my innate apprehension subsides. The following try nicks the pigeon, knocking off bits and altering its course. The next powders it, the dust appearing like a puff of black smoke that drifts away in the wind. All my last five attempts from the most difficult position pulverize the pigeons. A warm oozing of confidence replaces my fear of failure.

As I improve from day to day, skeet shooting becomes fun. It passes from being a strange activity outside of my life to a pleasurable sport. I hold my own among the other cadets and compete for scores with them. We shoot at single pigeons or sometimes two at once, quickly using alternate barrels. We shoot from a standing position, fire from towers and even from moving trucks. Each shot, however, adds another minute bruise to my right shoulder that is now solidly and painfully purple with mottled green and yellowish overtones. I wince as each blast drives the gunstock into the massive bruise. We all suffer from the same condition, and there is nothing we can do about it but continue to shoot and stoically bear the pain.

In a special room, I slip into a fully operational Consolidated turret, the type mounted on a B-24 bomber. I nestle into the seat with a wide-eyed sense of wonder, inhaling the machine smells and marveling at the controls and the complex of hydraulic lines. It is as though I've arrived, that I've entered into that magical realm of bombers and flyers that I'd only thought about for so long. I place my hands on the controls, the mechanism responding delicately to my touch, hissing and humming, turning to the left and right, the twin guns rising and falling. "Splendid," I mutter to myself as I slither out of the turret.

I spend hours in the Consolidated and Crocker-Wheeler turrets chasing a spot of light that waltzes erratically all over a wall. I follow the elusive spot with my optical gun sights, pushing the trigger switch when the two line up. The trigger mechanism sets off realistic machine gun chatter, giving me the feeling that I'm really performing, that I fire volleys of bullets at a phantom enemy. An automatic counter records all the shots that would have struck the target. I'm silently pleased that 419 of my 500 bullets riddle the dreaded enemy.

The all-electric Martin turret softly hums and whines as I manipulate it. After taking pages of notes about its operation, I finally settle into its mechanism. "What a sweet-running turret," I say to myself. But the sweetest of all is the Sperry ball turret, the type mounted on the underbelly of the B-17, the Flying Fortress. I enter the small door of the ball, lowering myself into the tight sphere. In the cramped quarters I curl into a fetal position and peer through the Sperry automatic computing sight, a mass of gears and wheels that compensates for all forces acting on a bullet.

We take tests---turning them 45-degrees in azimuth while we simultaneously raise it 45-degrees in elevation, leaving and entering it properly and knowing all of their operating procedures. We struggle through written examinations on the mechanisms of the guns and turrets. We enter a machine for range estimation with simulated machine guns that rattle, attacking airplane images angling in on us with their engines screaming.

In a sense we still play like children. The guns are real, but the bullets rip into banks of sand, pepper paper targets or powder clay pigeons. No one dies, no airplanes are destroyed and no one shoots back at us. When we operate simulators where imaginary bullets fly and enemy airplanes are only shadows on a screen, we might be in any midway amusement booth. Yet we do edge closer to the grim work. The metallic smell of cold steel and exploding powder has touched our nostrils, and our hands and arms tingle with the murderous throbbing of the guns. I like the excitement of bringing novelty into my life, and being part of it all. I'm proud of what I do. With my blitz cloth, I polish the brass casings of all the types of shells that I have fired, the .45 pistol, the .22 rifle, the 30-caliber machine gun and the 50-caliber machine gun and send them home for my parents and friends to see.

GROUND RANGE

Thick fog obscures our usual sharp view of the desert. The ghostly rectangles of our barracks fade away with distance until they are completely hidden. We mill about, muttering to each other in our muted voices, enjoying the moist breath of the morning. Like a balm, the chill mist kisses our skin and steals into our fatigues, soothing our prickly heat rashes and adding an extra spring to our steps.

By 0700, after the thinning fog shifts away from the field, we scramble into the backs of open trucks. In a coughing of engines and a whining of gears, they assemble into a convoy trailing out along a narrow desert road. We have twenty miles to ride before we reach the ground range where we'll be each day of this week. We slouch down close to each other as the cool wind rips over us. Speeding along the dipping road, we pass brush-studded hills, dry washes and, what looks to me like total emptiness. Some men chat with others, but most of us are quiet, thinking. Before every new experience rumors march like drum majors out in front of a band. One says, "That place out there is lousy with rattlesnakes!" while another says, "It's really rough out there. It's primitive as hell, and they work your tails off!"

Stiffened by the blustery ride, we tumble out of the trucks. A chill still lingers in the air as we walk toward an unusual skeet range where shotguns protrude from aircraft turrets. Each of us must gain the feel of the turret by tracking the sights on clay pigeons and blasting them out of the air. They streak across the desert sky, some of them disintegrating in sooty puffs as our weapons blaze away. The reports of my guns reverberate inside the turret. I soon dispose of the 100 rounds I'm allotted.

The trucks again haul us over to a nearby range where we fire 30-caliber machine guns at targets 200 and 500 yards away. These weapons seem small, almost like toys, compared to the 50-calibers we had fired previously. Confidently and with less trepidation about the gun this time, I squeeze off the first volley of shots, but the bullets churn the dirt into dust far in front of the target. Embarrassed and angry, I spin off expletives into the desert air, but the blasts of the others drown them out. I pride myself on my marksmanship, and my embarrassing display of shooting makes a fool of me in my own mind, even though other cadets on both sides of me also pepper the earth. Harmonizing the sights and aiming higher improves my score.

At lunchtime we file through a large camouflaged tent set up as a field mess hall, where bored servers slap food onto our metal plates. After lunch we must wash and dry our own plates, cups and utensils. I like the novelty of eating in the field. Lining up for food under these rugged conditions, all of us in our fatigues and heavy shoes, makes me feel like a real soldier. It's as though we take time off to eat near a remote battlefront; I become one of the grizzled soldiers that I had seen so often in the newsreels and Bill Mauldin cartoons.

In the pleasant warmth of the afternoon, we hunch behind wooden machine guns with real gun sights on them as an AT-6 training plane skimming over the hills hurtles toward us on a mock strafing run. With earphones clamped to our heads we listen to the pilot's crackling voice calling off his range as he zooms over large distance-numbers placed at intervals along the ground. We train our guns on him, noting how much of our circular sights he fills up at different distances. He streaks over us with a deafening roar, our bodies vibrating to the shuddering sound. After a graceful climb, the plane banks sharply, its silver wings gleaming in the sun, then circles far out over the brown hills for another pass.

After dinner in the field mess tent, the trucks trundle us back to the 30-caliber machine gun range where the sun has just set over the desert, and the air has noticeably cooled. As twilight fades and the star-sprinkled darkness replaces it, we look out at ghostly targets so dimly lit that we can barely make them out. Our guns blast and chatter into the night, shattering the dark tranquility of the desert. I score well, restoring my tarnished self-image.

By ten o'clock, after a demonstration of distress signals, we begin the long ride back to the base. We slump low again to avoid the wind ripping over the truck cab. Exhausted, I think of sleep, but it's too cold. Headlights illuminate the narrow road ahead of us, and the tail lights of the lead trucks appear and disappear over the rolling hills. The silent stars watch us go.

*   *   *

Leaving early from the ground range on the second day, we roll over the undulating desert in the warmth of the afternoon, our thoughts dwelling on a restful evening in the barracks or a good movie at the base theater. The ride out to the range in the early morning had been chilly, but without fog. My bruised shoulder aches and throbs from skeet shooting. Riding in the backs of trucks, we had passed twenty-five trap houses, each one ejecting clay pigeons in different directions. Some flew straight at us while others tailed away or sailed behind us. I shot twenty-five rounds in ten minutes, each shot forcing the gunstock back into my tender bruise. Just the thought of repeating the same run the next day is painful. I feel secretly smug because I'd been top man for the day when we fired machine guns at 6' X 6' moving targets hauled around a track by a speeding jeep.

The officer in charge of us sits quietly near the truck cab, a rifle at his side. He casually scans the sky or looks at us with a blank expression, a hint of a smile on his lips. As we pass a black buzzard turning in tight, wobbly circles over a low hill, he takes up his gun, aims, and then fires two shots, both of which miss. The bird wheels on, hopelessly out of range. The officer had hoped to be lucky. We timidly tease him as he smiles sheepishly. As we rumble over the hills, he continues to look upward, always keeping one hand on his gun. As we speed down a level stretch where the telephone lines run close to the road, he suddenly raises his rifle and fires one shot. The small, dark body of a songbird drops from the wire, tumbling into the brush. Some cadets cheer the officer's accuracy as he beams with satisfaction and places the gunstock on the truck bed, cradling the gun loosely between his legs. The cadet next to me, a fellow from Boston, turns to me and grumbles, "He didn't have to do that! He shouldn't shoot a songbird like that!" The wanton act saddens me.

Seeing the bird's body tumble to the ground reminds me of the hummingbird I had hit with a clod of dirt as a boy. I had thrown the clod on a whim, with out thinking, as the tiny bird perched on a telephone wire over the vacant lot behind our house. I never dreamed I would hit him, but the adobe lump struck him broadside, knocking his thumb-sized body down into the weeds below. Searching the lot until I found him still alive, a trickle of blood running from his needle-like bill, I nestled him in a shoebox softened with cotton, hoping to nurse him back to health. He died during the night.

The officer obviously has no such feelings. His marksmanship is what is important to him, not the bird. I feel him to be callous and unthinking, like the few boys who lived near my neighborhood who shot birds with their air rifles and bragged about it. The officer loved his gun, keeping his hand on it at all times as though fondling a woman. He enjoyed shooting it, whether at targets or anything that moved. I suspected he would relish shooting enemy soldiers, picking them off one by one as they dashed over a shell-pocked field. I liked learning about the guns and how to shoot them. I liked improving my scores and competing with the other cadets, but I didn't love guns.

*   *   *

Standing before the latrine mirror, I cup my hand over my chin then slide my fingers down until they meet underneath. I like the reflection I see there, three days growth of whiskers, a crop of dark stubble shadowing my sun-tanned face. I stroke my cheeks, proudly feeling the stiffness of my beard. I think to myself that the Texas heat must be bringing it out or maybe I'm just maturing. I like looking rugged, tough. I'm glad that daily inspections have been waived while we're on the ground range. While a light rain drips from the roof outside, I write a letter home in the dim light of the barracks. I want them to know that I'm not the same smooth-faced boy they have always known.

You know, I haven't shaved for three days, and my face is just black. Believe it or not, I am proud of my whiskers, but I am going to shave them off. They bother me.

I had always heard thick-bearded men complain that when they didn't shave, their faces itched. I fancy kinship with them.

Light rain showers brush the ground range the following day, the clouds blocking an eager sun that would otherwise turn the insides of our Plexiglas turrets into stifling greenhouses. I nestle in the seat of a truck-mounted Consolidated turret, 50-caliber machine guns on each side, my sights nearly aligned. The target bracketed and tracked, I activate the guns, their pounding filling the turret with bone-jarring sound. To my astonishment, the bullets rip into the desert sands, scattering the dust that lies just beneath the rain-dampened soil while the target speeds by unscathed. The sights haven't been properly harmonized with the guns. I aim the next volley above the jeep-mounted target, but the bullets still fall short. I continue firing, aiming even higher and hoping for the best. Suddenly the right gun jams, the recoil from the left gun jolting and shaking the turret so that the sights trace a crazy path. I blaze away in short spurts with one gun until the last of the chain of shells pass through the chamber. Angry at my bad luck and obvious poor score, I crawl tight-lipped out of the turret. As usual, I sink into a numbing darkness when things go wrong. A strong wind in the afternoon spoils all our shotgun scores.

For the remainder of the week we fire shotguns and machine guns both by themselves and in turrets. On the ground range and at the base the week before I had squeezed off a total of 650 shotgun shells, 425 of them from the shoulder, and had fired 1300 rounds of 30-caliber and 600 rounds of 50-caliber machine gun bullets. I learn to enjoy shooting guns, and, in spite of occasional disasters, I compensate with generally good marks.

My parents ask in a letter, whether I 'm beginning to feel at home with a machine gun.

Yes, I am. At first there is a certain feeling of, maybe we should call it a 'mistrust' of the gun, but that gradually goes away. The first day on the 30-caliber range, I got over that feeling. You must get over that little something about the gun.

THE SKEET SHACK

Stewart and I walk slowly toward the skeet shack, our shoes kicking up little puffs of dust. It's our turn to release the clay pigeons. The other two cadets walk out of the doorway. They give us a few pointers about operating the machine then go on their way. Inside the hot, stuffy shack we sit on a wooden bench built into one side. Aging paint sloughs off the wooden walls, and higher up several spider webs festoon the corners. Before us lies the spring-loaded machine that flings out the clay pigeons. We cock the machine by pulling a large lever that compresses a thick spring. Nearby stand stacks of clay pigeons, all upside-down like a tower of reversed ashtrays. When the cadets are ready on the line, and shout, "Pull!" we release the lever that sends the pigeon on its way.

Stewart and I, having loaded the machine, wait for the signal. I had known Stewart since Preflight, had gone to town with him several times, even traveled with him to his home in Port Arthur, Texas. I always liked him because he was gentle and kind, open and friendly. We had become fast friends.

"Why don't we arrange it, Stevens," says Stewart. "My brother and I will bring our own girls, and we'll bring one for you too. We could all have fun together, and you might really like her."

For a moment I don't answer, but my mind, panicking, asks quick questions. "What does he mean, get a girl for me? What am I to expect? What am I supposed to do with her? Does he expect me to make love to her? Would she expect me to?"

180

Hesitating, flustered, I answer, "Oh, I-- I don't know Stewart. I really don't think so."

Believing he's doing me a favor, he turns to me with a perplexed expression." Why not, Stevens?"

A shout of "Pull!" comes from the firing line. I release the lever. The compressed spring stretches to its full length with a whack, and the clay pigeon leaves. I take another off the stack and reload.

"I really don't want to make love to a girl, Stewart. I want to save all that for marriage."

Still trying to understand my reaction, Stewart shifts forward on his seat, looks at me intently. "Oh, Come on, Stevens. Being with a woman is just natural. What possible harm can come from it?"

"I don't know Stewart. I just can't do it."

"Pull!" Another pigeon flies out of the shack. Some cadet shoots twice, missing it the first time then trying again with the other barrel. Stewart grabs another one and cocks the lever. I remember all my mother has told me---"Men do not like women who have been around, who would do that with just anyone---You should never have sex before you are married"---She talks to me about the loose ones or the girls that are "not exactly all they should be." She neither warns me nor speaks sternly or self-righteously. Her words simply flow sweetly on wings of kindness.

When we were little she told my sister and me about the egg and the sperm and their mysterious joining to bring about the miracle of life. We sat on either side of her aproned lap as she slowly turned the pages of the book and explained how babies come about. A dot on the page represented the egg, and I thought the sperm resembled the pollywogs I'd caught in the rain pools in the vacant lot. As she read, there was no doubt that the man and the woman involved in this union were married. I didn't quite understand the mechanics involved, how the sperms got from the man to the egg in the woman. I knew it had something to do with a penis, but I didn't know what. She told us nothing of the act or the pleasure---the tingling nerves, the ecstasy. I learned everything about sex except what it was. By talking with my friends and from looking at graphic little dog-eared books with groups of boys huddled on the playgrounds, I found out more.

"Look, Stevens. There's nothing wrong with it. It's perfectly natural. It's just what men and women do. There's nothing to feel guilty about."

We send out another pigeon and reload. He looks at me incredulously.

"I just can't Stewart. I just can't do it."

And God would know. My mother had always told me that God sees everything and knows everything. She often quoted a passage from the Bible--- "Not a sparrow falls but that the Lord knows and cares." An all-seeing God would know if I ever did such a thing. It was one of the commandments, I thought--"Thou shalt not commit adultery" I often turned off my erotic thoughts, believing that there was something evil about them and that God would know what I was thinking. I transformed them into a purer form--a future wife and children.

I had seen the films, one after the other, in brilliant color of sickening sores that made me want to turn my head---chancres like red craters festering on penises, putrid pus oozing out of others, men with the bridge of their nose eaten away by syphilis. Men with their minds rotted by the spirochete, their lips blubbering nonsense. The posters were everywhere---the portrait of a beautiful girl, wholesome and lovely, but underneath her fresh, virginal face the shocking words, "She may look clean--But!" It was clear that even "the girl next door" might harbor the spirochete of syphilis or the bacteria of gonorrhea. We often had "peter parades" in the early hours of the morning---the lights glaring into our eyes, the callous medical officers shouting, "Okay. Everybody up and stand by the head of your bunks!" Bleary-eyed, half asleep, we stagger to the proper position. The officers walk down the rows of stupefied men, commanding each cadet to "milk it down" as they pass. With the officers gone, the barracks dark and wonderful again, I think---"What if I had massaged down a gob of infectious pus?" I couldn't have stood the shame.

"Pull!" I trip the trigger, and the target flies away followed by the blast of the shotgun.

Stewart reaches across for another, cocks the spring and says, "These will be nice girls, Stevens. We'll have fun, and if one thing leads to another, that's just the way it is."

Uncomfortable with the proposal and torn between compromising my beliefs and hurting the feelings of a good friend, I mutter without looking at him, "I don't know. I just don't think I'd better."

My track coach, Coach Arnett, stands in my mind, the shade of his hat brim shielding his squinting eyes, clearing his throat as he always did before he spoke. The great God Arnett, whose gospel I believed implicitly, was about to announce another of his moral pearls.

"Nothing can ruin a good man like a loose woman. A man should never touch a woman unless he's married to her. Let me tell you how low a man can sink into moral degradation if he allows himself to. There was a powerful politician in San Francisco who bolstered his wealth by running a string of prostitutes on the side. As the owner, he had the privilege of trying out each new girl brought in to his operation. One fateful night he was called to break in the newest recruit, an exceptional woman, pretty and wholesome-looking. Upon entering the room where she waited, anxious to see her and charged with erotic anticipation, he beholds his own daughter. Stricken with remorse, his hands clasped over his face in utter shame, he tearfully staggers out of the room, renouncing his sordid way of life and vowing to change."

"Pull!" The Texas sun bearing down on the skeet shack slowly turns the wooden enclosure into a sauna. A tear of sweat creeps down Stewart's cheek just below his sideburn as he reaches over to prepare another launch. He's silent now, perplexed by my attitude, not knowing what to say.

I don't want to do it, and yet I do. I feel the sense of Stewart's words, a brand of earthy wisdom from a kind and respected friend, yet I'm clamped in a vise that has been slowly tightened for eighteen years. My supreme wish is to marry a good woman, and raise a family exactly like the wonderful one that nurtured me. I look upon women as possible friends or even as potential wives, not as women for the night, to be forgotten the next day. Most of them around the base or in town appear coarse to me, a contrast to the girls I remember from back home, in my own neighborhood or at school or church. In my mind at least they were sweet, caring, and wholesome. Girls like that must surely live in San Antonio or Houston or even here in Laredo, but they're in neighborhoods far from the base, out of sight. With good reason those girls and their parents didn't trust a guy in uniform, a man who was obviously feeling a new freedom and was out after only one thing.

I dislike the cadets who wander back late to the barracks with lipstick stains on their mouths and cheeks and whiskey on their breath, who boast about their conquests. I think our physical training instructor crude when he ends the calisthenics drill by placing his fist between his legs, extending one finger outwards then pumping his hips in mock intercourse. As he gyrates he shouts out over all of us, "Okay. The last exercise is to get you ready for town. Back and forth, in and out. Let's go into town now, and remember what I told you. In and out. In and out."

"Pull!" The pigeon fractures on the catapult, shattering against the wood around the exit hole. We replace it with another then launch it. Stewart doesn't press me anymore about the girl. As sensitive as he is, he understands and tolerates the way I think. I feel guilty refusing such an offer from a good friend, but I would have felt even worse had I accepted.

I have the same biological feelings as other cadets. I thrill to the sight of a pretty woman with shapely legs and bulging breasts. I feel the same heat in my loins as they do. I notice attractive women on the streets in town. I drink them in with my eyes then walk by them while other cadets simply follow their feelings free of inhibitions. They talk to them, flirt, try to pick them up, even lead them off to a strange bed. They have no guards at their gates while I have a whole array of them standing firm. My mother stands at one gate---"You should never have sex before you are married!" My coach stands at another---"A loose woman can ruin a man!" A doctor dressed in a white coat leans against the next gate---"We've shown you in the films what can happen to a man. It's up to you!" God watches the last---"Thou shalt not commit adultery!"

"Pull!... Hey, pull!" Still thinking, I belatedly send the pigeon on its way.

"God, it's hot in here," complains Stewart.

"Well. We should be about finished. How's your bruised shoulder?"

"It's still tender," Stewart replies. "I hate thinking about more skeet today."

We both become quiet.

Outside we hear the footsteps of the two cadets who will replace us. We open the door, relishing the fresh air. "Welcome to the oven," we say. The cadets joke about their scores and rub their sore shoulders as they enter. Stewart, as friendly as ever, despite my rebuffing, chats with me as we walk back to the firing line. I know he won't insist on his plan. I'm relieved, yet just a bit disappointed in myself---I might have really liked the girl.

FIRST FLIGHTS

For months we had honed our mental skills in classrooms, hardened our bodies on athletic fields and accepted uncompromising discipline on the parade grounds, even in our barracks. We had been tested, taught and toughened, but our feet remained firmly on the ground. That is about to change.

Lively conversations, jokes and nervous laughter wash through the flight line operations room on our first day there, but a deeper undercurrent of apprehension lies beneath. The idea of flying, the reason for our joining the Army Air Corps, is about to mesh with the actual experience. It will be the coming together of idea and experience, the blending of the abstract with the concrete. I wonder whether the two dimensions will match. Will flying be as natural and wonderful as it is in my imagination? Will I freeze with fear?

I sit in a wooden chair, chatting with Stewart while keeping my eyes on a large chart at the end of the room. Filling the neatly gridded blackboard are airplane numbers, names of the pilots, tow plane numbers, the names of the tow plane pilot and the tow operator. Our flight times are shown as well. My flight approaches. Thrills, like fingers, run through my body, play across the whole of my emotional scale---from excitement and joy through anxiety and fear. I've heard the usual stories about how reckless and crazy the pilots are, about cadets who were buffeted into airsickness, who vomited in paper bags. I knew about cadets who suddenly discovered that flying paralyzed them. How would it affect me? I know that failing could wash me out or change the direction of my service career, even my life.

When our flight time arrives, the officer in charge calls our run, shouts our names, "Stevens, Stewart, Spano!" We each check out at a desk in the operations room, a sergeant carefully marking off our names. We walk straight to the armament room, a large shed where rows of dark 30-caliber machine guns rest in ordered racks. A corporal hands me one, jotting my name and the gun's number on a columned sheet of paper. The black bulk of it pulls my hands and arms down at first. I hadn't remembered that they weighed so much. Outside, I harmonize my gun sight with the bore of the gun's barrel then return it to the armament room for a final checkup.

With the weapons nestled in our arms, we walk to the parachute room where orderlies fit us into large backpack parachutes. With the straps firmly cinched about our shoulders and buckled in front, we bend under its cumbersome weight. I slip my head into a leather helmet with earflaps and earphones, and then snap on flying goggles. I push them up to my forehead until I need them. Waddling like turtles, we plod over to our last stop at the ammunition room. Another orderly hands us two heavy metal cans of machine gun bullets all linked together into a long, deadly chain. Like a flat metal snake, they coil in the metal box. Blue paint covers the tips of mine so that when or if they strike the canvas tow target, they will leave a blue mark around the hole. Looking like a string of sinister lipsticks, Stewart's red-tipped ones slither out of the can. Spano's are tipped with green. We run the bullets through a link machine, checking for short rounds that might stop the gun's action. Satisfied that the cartridges are all right, we return them to their metal containers.

Busy with the gathering, testing and lugging of our equipment, we have very little time to think about our flight, our apprehensions dissolving in our activity like sugar in hot coffee. We struggle along the concrete ramp with our loads as the sun burns through a partly cloudy sky. Beneath my fatigues and parachute my back begins to sweat, aggravating my prickly heat rash. After a rare cool week on the ground range, the sun has returned with a vengeance, and so has my rash. Burdened with machine guns, ammunition and parachutes, we decide not to walk to our planes but to wait for the line taxi, a kind of open, low platform on wheels pulled by a small, rubber-tired tractor. It arrives crowded with loaded-down cadets, their machine gun barrels bristling skyward in all directions. We squeeze aboard, hoping not to fall off. All along the flight line, airplane engines burst into life, filling the ramp with their throbbing.

Like a fully loaded pack animal I struggle over to the waiting airplane, a gleaming silver AT-6, an all metal, single winged training plane. The pilot, already sitting in the front seat shows me a half-smile through the open canopy, a smirk of superiority. Inserting the toes of my shoes in small slots, I climb up to the open cockpit to mount the machine gun in its swivel and load one can of ammunition. As I settle into the rear seat, the engine whines, sputters then smoothes itself into a steady, deafening roar, the blur of the whirling propeller with its dancing reflections scattering the lingering puffs of blue exhaust. I fasten my safety belt then snap a special gunner's belt to a U-bolt on the floor. This would prevent my falling out when I stand up to fire my gun. I secure my leather helmet, clip in my radio connection and slip my goggles down over my eyes.

The pilot taxies the plane out to the runway. The wind from the propeller shrieks over the canopy in front of me as the vibrations from the engine ripple through my body. As we hurtle down the runway, immersed in sound, the pressure of acceleration pushing my back against the seat, I'm swept up into an emotional limbo. The pressure softens as we sweep into the air, angling toward the scattered clouds. I peer out at the shrinking runway and the bush-stippled hills and plains, the snaking Rio Grande off to our left. Every twist, turn and bulge of the land below fascinates me. Lost in the grandeur of what I see, I forget my apprehensions.

At 4000 feet we poke up through the clouds, at first losing ourselves in their moist translucence then dashing out into the clear again. At 5000 feet we level off just above them, the sea of white fluffiness below strikingly beautiful to me. Between the clouds, bits of land flash by--- a dry wash, a dirt road, a brush-dotted hill.

We join two other planes in our flight then fly in a tight formation with them. Far off to our right is the target plane, the sun beaming from its polished skin, towing a canvas sock far behind on a long cable. Since I'm to shoot first, I release my safety belt then stand, thrusting my head into the hurricane wind that rips over the canopy. The strength of the air stream surprises me. I hunch behind the machine gun as I line up my sights on the white sleeve, now seeming very far away. Taking the proper lead, I pull the trigger, the shots sounding like staccato pops in the din of the engine and the wild wind. After only twelve shots, my gun jams. The pilot slips our plane beneath the other two then slides into formation on the opposite side while another cadet shoots, and I work on my gun. I push out a round that is too short to extract from the belt, and I'm ready to fire again. Suddenly the target collapses, falls back, then drifts slowly down toward the desert, the cable severed by a bullet from one of the others. We have to return to the field.

*   *   *

Disappointed that I'd shot so few rounds, but buoyant about flying and the sights I'd seen, I walk with the other cadets on the flight line as we head toward lunch. The fierce heat rising from the concrete fails to dampen our excitement. We amble along, laughing and recounting our experiences to each other. One cadet among us walks silently. Tall and slender with perfect military erectness, he is one of our leaders. With his dark hair combed straight back, his handsome features tanned by the Texas sun, he looks the model of a future officer. With perfect composure he says, "I'm not going up again. I just can't do it. Flying is not for me." He speaks almost stoically as though he'd made his decision based entirely on reason. Surely he must suspect that we see this as a serious character flaw or as a confession of cowardice, but his dignity and his deliberate calmness demand that we accept him. He must also feel the sting of disappointment, yet he carries that burden with a kind of nobility that projects courage rather than weakness. None of us taunts him or teases him or urges him to try again because the strength of his character commands so much respect. I feel his silent hurt.

*   *   *

In the afternoon the airplane bounces around in the rough air as though it were a speedboat dashing through a turbulent sea. I have three hundred rounds to fire at the tow target from a wildly bucking platform. I squeeze off the first one hundred rounds, trying desperately to fix my sights somewhere near the bounding sleeve. I can only hope that a few of my bullets have ripped through it.

My first can of ammunition emptied, I remove it from the side of the gun and reach down for a full one. The heavy container feels doubly awkward and unmanageable as the slipstream catches it. For a moment I feel the beginnings of panic, a paralyzing thought that I might never be able to put it in place. I summon all my strength as the wind tears at my head and shoulders and my struggling hands as I reach into the can to pull out one end of the cartridge belt. The serpent chain quivers in my hand, threatening to uncoil itself. Holding firmly to the writhing cartridges with one hand, I lift the gun's cover plate then insert the first round of the chain into the chamber. With a deep sigh, I blast away again at the cavorting target.

Reloading the second time is just as difficult, but having succeeded once, I know I can do it again. As my last cartridge disappears inside the gun, the pilot, watching me in his rear-view mirror, tips the plane into a steep right bank then rolls it over on its back. Still struggling to slump back down in the seat, I look up to see shrub-sprinkled hills and dry washes instead of the sky. As I try to orient myself and reconnect my safety belt, he drops into a dive. He pulls out of it suddenly, the G-force pressing me into the seat, flattening my rear, thrusting me back against the seat rest. When I recover, we're in formation again, now on the other side. Despite the sudden surprise, I think it's fun. I bask in a new smugness. I hadn't been terrified. I have a story to tell the other cadets and a new adventure to write home about.

The following day we fly at only 1200 feet beneath a solid gray overcast. Scattered veils of rain showers sweep over the desert. The pilot avoids them, but I find myself wanting to dart through them even at the risk of getting wet. We shoot first at tow targets then drop down just over the desert floor to strafe dummy airplanes. We fly low enough that I watch some of my bullets rip into the wooden planes as the sand dances around them.

Returning to the field alone on the last day of AT-6 training and after being separated from the others, another AT-6 suddenly settles in close to us, just off our right wing. I recognize Stewart as the gunner in the rear seat, and I know his pilot is named Davis because we had talked about it before we left to fly. Even back at Ellington Field we had heard about the infamous Davis brothers whose reckless and daring antics had grounded them several times. One of the brothers had been disciplined for flying underneath the International Bridge spanning the Rio Grande between Laredo and Nuevo Laredo.

Grinning like a teenager about to pull a prank, he places his wing directly over our tail. Laughing all the while, he then flies with his wing not a foot from our rudder. Knowing his reputation for recklessness, I hope he'll go away. I think about being scattered all over the desert just so this hotshot pilot can enjoy himself. My pilot holds our plane steady and grins back at him, apparently not as concerned as I am. Still with a cocky, boyish smirk on his face, Davis sticks his wing between our wing and tail, his wingtip almost close enough to touch. If I could have, I would have pushed him away. I can see all the rivets on his wing. Finally he edges away, still laughing, then banks steeply to the right. I breathe easier.

Away from the antics of the senseless pilot, we speed toward the landing field. My pilot, deciding to fly at a lower altitude, abruptly noses the plane down into a dive. We plummet straight down for 2000 feet as I swallow hard and move my jaws to clear my ears. The temperature changes rapidly, and the air speed indicator reads 230 mph, very fast for an AT-6 used to cruising at 160. We level out at 1000 feet.

As we touch down for our last landing in AT-6s, my spirits soar. My imaginary visions about flying have met with reality, and I've found the blending rich and satisfying. I've overcome another obstacle. I've enjoyed every moment in the air, and know that I've made the right choice in joining the Army Air Corps.

The author poses with his sister Charline at home in Inglewood
wearing his private's uniform from Fort MacArthur

Charles "Norm" Stevens as a cadet at the San Antonio
Classification Center.

The obstacle course at the bombardier preflight school at Ellington Field, Houston, Texas

AT-9s used for pilot training at Ellington Field. They would often buzz our drill formations, flying just over our heads.

AT-6s used for gunnery training at Laredo, Texas. The gunner sat in the rear cockpit and shot at a sleeve towed by another plane.

Stevens pictured as a cadet in the bombardier training yearbook at Midland, Texas.

Calisthenics kept the cadets in shape at Midland

More Jacob's ladder.

On the obstacle course at Midland

Cadets walking tours as punishment for any violation of the base's strict rules.

A bombardier trainer dubbed the "bug". Learning to manipulate the Norden bombsight on these was required before flying.

When a bombardier was trained sufficiently on the "bugs" he
was ready to drop bombs from an AT-11.

The bombardier aimed at targets in the desert, dropping sand-
filled practice bombs from AT-11s.

Charles Stevens Reports to No. 1 Bombardier School

MIDLAND ARMY AIR FIELD, Midland, Tex.—Picked as one of the men whose job it will be to train America's deadly bombsight on Axis targets, Cadet Charles N. Stevens, son of Mr. and Mrs. Charles K. Stevens, of 535 Brett street, Inglewood, has reported at the "nation's number one bombardier school" here for twelve weeks of intensive training.

In the process of winning his silver bombardier wings and a commission as second lieutenant or appointment as flight officer in the Army Air Forces, he will undergo what army officials have described as "one of the most thorough, all around courses of training ever devised for fighting men." In addition to acquiring an intimate knowledge of the complex workings of the famous bombsight, this tyro axis blaster will study navigation, camouflage detection, automatic flight control devices, enemy ship and aircraft identification. He will study maps and charts of vital enemy targets; he will learn how to load and fuse his bombs, as well as to drop them.

At an outlying "combat camp" he will get the feel of operations from an advanced airbase on the fighting front—living on short rations, ducking into foxholes during simulated air raids and gas attacks, and carrying out missions against "enemy" targets day and night.

A clipping from the hometown newspaper in Inglewood, California announcing Stevens' entry into the bombardier school at Midland.

Graduation from Midland as a second lieutenant and his bombardier's wings.

After training at Alexandria, Louisiana the crew poses in front of a B-17 at Polebrook, England, home of the 351st Bomb Group with Stevens in top row right.

BOYS' TOWN

I don't know why I've allowed myself to get into this situation.

The cab driver knew exactly where we wanted to go, finally letting us out on a dusty incline in a fold of gentle hills. A scattered group of small weathered houses stand on them like monuments to poverty. A half dozen of us walk up the slope in the late afternoon, our shoes stirring up the dust, our long shadows stretched out over the bare dirt. The rustling of our suntan uniforms and the sound of our shoes over the dry Mexican earth are broken only by our nervous wisecracks and mindless chatter. Two of the cadets know where they're going; the rest of us follow. The decrepit houses and shacks cast warped shadows. My feet keep up with the rest, but in my mind I long to be elsewhere. The men with me are my good friends, all of them "S" men--- Stewart, Spano, Southwell, Spence and Senter, who had been with me since Ellington Field. Yet they lead me into a strange and worrisome situation, only my curiosity keeping my legs moving.

As we approach one of the shacks, I notice a woman sitting outside in a wooden chair near the doorway, taking advantage of the afternoon shade. As she tilts back against the sun-parched boards of her house, only the back legs of her chair touch the ground. Her black hair is drawn back flat against her head, then gathered in back and held with a comb. She appears to be nearly middle aged, but she might be younger, the dry sun and the poverty of her life weathering the classic features of her deep brown face. She wears a faded print dress and high-heeled shoes without stockings. The hem of her dress rides high on her thighs. She parts her bare brown legs, a deepening dusk lying between them, the heels of her shoes hooked over the chair rung. She calls to us as we pass, but we only glance at her, and move on.

I feel sorry for the pathetic woman, having to submit to the hungers of the young American military men to support herself. There is resignation in her call, a tone that says," *I know that you probably don't want me, but here I am. Why not?"* I'm not remotely attracted to her, feeling instead a blend of mild disgust and sadness. The sight of the woman convinces me that I don't want to be here. I want to bolt, turn on my heel, wave goodbye to my comrades and jump in the first taxi back to town. But then I would be alone, have to find my way out, picking my way through the dangerous streets of Nuevo Laredo to the bridge and over the border. Surely the others would taunt me, question my bravery, even my manhood.

The vision of the lone prostitute sitting stoically in her chair, even though pathetic, is a new experience, I tell myself. Thoughts tumble around in my mind. I'm curious yet terrified about this "show" we're to see. We move on in the slanting sun; I know not where.

A small Mexican man with a black moustache had been watching us. With a smirk on his face, he approaches us.

"Hey. You boys want to see a show? Come with me."

We obediently follow the little man. Some of the men joke as we tag along behind him, but I feel as though I'm walking slowly to my death. If an angel would appear offering to sweep me immediately back to the base, I would gladly accept. I vow never to let myself ever get into a situation like this again. I thought I had learned that lesson in high school---to never go anywhere or do anything that was not right for me regardless of the pressure from others.

*   *   *

Bob Young leans against the railing at high school. "Why don't we all meet down at the park tonight," he asks the knot of boys around him. "You want to go? You want to go?" he asks each of them.

Hovering around the outside edge of the group, I lean in to hear what he's asking.

"What about you, Stevens? Do you want to go?"

Before I can think, I agree to meet at Centinela Park that night with the rest of the boys. I have no idea what we'll do there, but Bob and I have several classes together, and we're casual friends, so I feel what ever we do will be all right.

"Let's all meet down by the baseball diamond about seven o'clock," he says.

My parents, skeptical about why the boys should meet in the park, ask me what they are going to do.

"I don't know," I tell them, "We're just going to meet down there. I told them I would come."

Reluctantly they allow me to go. At the appointed time I walk a mile to the park, passing under the eerie glow of streetlamps nearly every half block. At the baseball diamond, the boys gather in the feeble glow of the park lights. I can hardly make out their faces. I finally recognize a few of them, especially Bob Young who acts as the leader, but I don't know the rest. Other than a quiet greeting, I don't know what to say to anyone. The rest joke with each other, chatter and launch primitive "eeeh's, aah's and oooh's" and all of the other strange noises that boys make. Bob suddenly says, "Let's all go down by the swings!" Everyone follows him along the cool, dark paths of the park toward the playground. A few light up cigarettes, the matches flaring out against the darkness, briefly revealing their faces with a quivering, orange light. The sweet smell of tobacco smoke merges with the fragrance of the dew, now heavy in the still night air.

When we reach the swings, I notice that Bob is smoking a cigarette. He glides back and forth in the swing, the neon glow of his cigarette tip tracing a pendulum arc through the gloom of the night. I didn't know that he smoked, and seeing him with the cigarette shocks me. I think less of him and some of the other boys too. I wonder why I'm here and begin to grow more uncomfortable. Bob flips his cigarette stub with his fingers so that it snaps end over end into a long, blinking arch. The butt lands in the playground sand with a scattering of sparks.

Tired of the swings, the group edges back toward the ballpark, a giant amoeba of shadowed high school boys in another purposeless movement. We all stand on the dugout roof, the park lights strong enough to cast a pale luminescence on our faces. I listen to the nonsensical banter and jungle sounds of the group, thinking of nothing I can really say to them. I'm with them only physically. I'm an unnoticed tree in the inkiness of the park. Finally one of the boys stands close behind me, and, with much merriment, pushes his knees forward into the backs of mine, momentarily collapsing my legs. Even though the prank annoys me, I laugh, almost glad that someone had at last paid attention to me.

Soon after the knee buckling and seeing no point in staying, I leave the group, and begin the long walk home. I imagine that the boys, still babbling and guffawing, hardly know I've left. I feel lonely and disappointed, the evening having been a total waste. I hadn't belonged there. I think about the warm, loving house still far away where my mother and father always listened to me and believed what I had to say was important. I supposed that the aimless boys gathered anywhere just to be together and be away from their unpleasant homes.

Two years later Bob Young stops in front of my house in his noisy Model A Ford. With him is an equally loud classmate named Morrisson. We talk under the casuarina tree in our parkway, the pale streetlight several houses away filtering through its needle-like leaves. Morrisson combs his kinky hair straight back, his long freckled forehead sloping down into his prominent nose. Both beg me to go out with them, to just drive around town and maybe take in a show. I tell them I have homework, and now that I'm on the track team, I want to get plenty of sleep. They both work on me, gradually wearing down my resistance. They promise to be back early.

With the tires screaming as we take some of the corners and the muffler too loud, we speed across town, Morrisson squealing with delight into the wind gusting through the rolled-down windows. When we reach Market Street, the main street of Inglewood, we finally slow down. It's aglow with light and blinking theater marquees, the steady parade of headlights adding to the brightness. Shoppers and theatergoers, young and old scurry down the sidewalks. Suddenly Morrisson yells an obscenity out of the open window at a cluster of young people on the sidewalk then quickly ducks his head below the window level, his eyes dancing with mischief and his throat convulsing with wheezing spasms of laughter. Startled and embarrassed, I slump down in the seat. I stare at the highlights on the short oily waves of his hair, and wonder why he did it. I slouch in the shadows, hoping no one will see me or think that I had yelled the word. Several more times he raises his head to hurl insulting remarks. I don't want to be with this guy. Finally we park the car on a side street, and walk to the theater. Morrisson buys a bottle of Coca-Cola, and takes it into the show. We file into one of the back rows, disturbing some of those around us with our bungling adolescence. With the audience quiet, Morrisson, now finished guzzling his Coca-Cola, sets the bottle on the floor, then, with a push of his fingers starts it rolling. Down the concrete slope of the theater floor, down through the hushed crowd rolls the bottle, clanging and banging against the seat posts and the startled feet of the moviegoers, a hollow glassy din violating the silence of the darkened room. Morrisson's eyes squint with mirth in the flickering light from the screen, his hands clasped to his mouth to stifle another of his senseless laughs. Embarrassed again, I hope that no one I know recognizes me or thinks that I'm responsible for the prank. I sit quietly in the show staring blankly at the screen and wishing I were home. I'm where I don't want to be. I don't belong here.

*   *   *

The diminutive Mexican man with the moustache and sly smile leads us to the doorway of a small, ramshackle house, ushering us into a plain room with a double bed in the middle. He tells us to stand and wait on one side of the bed then leaves the room. We fidget and mumble nervously in stifled tones to each other. I don't understand fully what is to happen except that there is to be a "sex show" of some kind. My mouth is dry, and I shift restlessly from one foot to the other, but there's no turning back now.

After a ten-minute wait, a young woman enters from a small adjoining room. With a smile on her face and without a trace of embarrassment, the raven-haired woman pads into the room completely nude. She greets us, and jokes with us as though she's fully clothed. I can appreciate the sensual art of her body, but I don't find her erotic. I float now, one part of me wanting to run out the door and the other wanting to stay to see what happens.

Shortly, another naked woman enters the room, this one buck-toothed with frizzy hair. Her flesh sags slightly with age on her thin body. She grins at us then straps on a strange-looking device shaped like a man's genitalia with an organ made of stiff leather backed up by a kind of pubic fluff. With the first woman now lying on the bed, the "man" woman assumes a position then proceeds with phony "intercourse."

The show is a variety of positions, each one assigned to a different country---the English, the French, the Mexicans, the "sons-a-bitchen" Germans and several others. Never have I ever witnessed anything remotely close to what I'm seeing now. My head is a dictionary of emotional nouns---revulsion, fascination, fear, sensuality, disgust, wonder, guilt, curiosity, and loathing.

With the "positions" over, I feel a sense of relief that we'll soon file out into the welcome dust again. Breathing the warm dry air and kicking through the desert soil once more will be like walking in the freshness of springtime. The first woman, however, now squats on the floor on the other side of the room, soon getting up to lie on the bed again. This time she slowly gives birth to an egg, working it out gently with the expert coordination of special, well-trained muscles. The slowly emerging egg looks slimy with a sickly greenish cast.

"Hell, that's nothing," whispers one of the cadets to me. "I hear the girls down at Matamoros can flip a silver dollar with it so that it bangs against the wall."

Repulsed by the woman's "skills" and the other cadet's story, I'm more than ready to leave. The woman walks around the room asking any of the cadets if they would like to have her. As she passes me, she pinches my trousers near my fly, her fingers leaving a small grayish smudge. With no takers and the show mercifully over, we tumble out of the door.

As we shuffle through the shacks of Boys' Town on our way out, Senter says, "Let's go to the Casa Blanca. They have good beer there and plenty of girls." Just when I think we're on our way home, this new crisis presents itself. I don't drink beer, and I'm not interested in the bar girls and prostitutes that frequent the place. I'd just escaped from one awkward situation, and I have no intention of sliding into another one.

"I think I'll pass on this one," I say. "I'd rather go back to the base."

"Oh, come on Stevens. We won't stay long. We'll have a hell of a lot of fun over there," pleads sandy-haired Senter who most wants to go.

I know that Southwell has a girlfriend in Houston, and possibly he doesn't want to go with them. I talk with him about returning to the base with me. The officers had warned us not to walk alone in Nuevo Laredo, so I'm anxious to have at least one other man with me. Although the contrasting thoughts of an exciting adventure at the Casa Blanca and the security of the barracks back at the base tear at Southwell, he mulls it over, and agrees to return to the base with me. We part from the others who still can't understand why anyone would pass up a chance for an evening of revelry at the Casa Blanca.

Back in the town Southwell and I stride along the streets toward the International Bridge over the Rio Grande. Small boys begging for coins accost us, walking along beside us for blocks, pleading with their sad little eyes and runny noses, "Give me penny! Give me penny!" "No" means nothing to them. They cling to us anyway even if we growl at them, sticking to us like pesky flies, hoping we'll tire of them and give them a coin just to get rid of them. Yellow flames curl in charcoal and wood-burning stoves outside of small restaurants where slabs of meat roast and release their fragrance into the streets. Inside a narrow dim cafe where disheveled men perch on worn stools, a man wearing a dirty white apron shreds a roast into fibers of machaca.

Near the bridge even more street boys crowd the walks to ask for coins. Makeshift money exchange booths stand everywhere on both sides of the street---5 pesos for $1.05 American. Far down below the bridge a group of boys, their wet bodies glistening in the late sun, search the muddy waters of the Rio Grande for coins tossed from the railing above. The murky water makes retrieving the coins very difficult. Southwell still doesn't know whether he's made the right choice. He wants to go with me, but the lure of the Casa Blanca still lingers in his mind.

"Maybe I should've stayed with them," he says. "I think it would have been fun."

Back at the barracks, I notice that the smudge is still on my trousers where the woman pinched me. It's not merely a blemish on my clean pressed suntans but on my character as well. As long as I can see it, I'll think about the two women cavorting in the shack. What if she had a venereal disease? Would it be possible for those insidious germs to spread from that stain to my body? What if I should get the clap or syphilis from it?

*   *   *

The small smudge still lingers on my trousers the next day. I have no more clean suntans, and I fear touching the foul smear that I think seethes with unseen contagion, even to wash it off. I can hardly bear looking at it. I wonder if others notice it, but no one seems to pay attention to it. Stewart tells us what a great time they had at the Casa Blanca the night before.

"Boy it was nice," says Stewart. "That beer was so cold. It cut that dryness right out of our throats. And the girls! God were they nice. This little gal sat on my lap with her arm around me the whole time." Then, looking dreamy-eyed, and lowering his voice into almost a whisper, he says, "And her leg was so smooth."

He draws out the last two words as though they are a long caress, and uses his fingers to trace the silky curve of her leg.

Southwell says, "Oh God. I should have gone. Why didn't I go?"

In my mind I see the young Mexican woman on Stewart's lap, his hand following the glossy contours of her leg. I feel it in my own fingers. I didn't belong there in that distressing place, but then I wonder why I respond with such interest to Stewart's hushed, satiny words.

ANNOYANCES

Twisting one way then another, I try to find a comfortable position in my bunk. The trapped heat inside the barracks lingers far into the night, open windows and doors doing little to temper it. I can't sleep. Instead I dream about how nice it would be to lie on a clean cool sheet with only my shorts on, my bare arms and legs spread out. But the quartermaster issued us only two wool army blankets, no sheets. Despite the oven-like atmosphere I wear an undershirt to bed because the rough bedding irritates my skin---just the way my dreaded wool trousers did when I had to wear them to Sunday school as a child.

If I don't pull one of the blankets over me, I expose my skin to the ravages of blister bug squadrons. Each night before we crawl into our bunks several of us check the screen doors for them. Attracted to the light, the pale green, inch-long insects settle on the screen mesh with their long legs or lie in wait outside on the barracks walls near the porch light. We swat them all, sometimes as many as twenty, but new ones always gather during the night. They slip in through cracks around the screen door or flutter in when a late cadet or one back from the latrine opens the door. Crickets as large as grasshoppers jump in too, but we don't worry about them. Just yesterday I saw the trail of watery blisters on a cadet's shoulder. It was too hot for the cadet to sleep, so he pushed his blanket down, exposing his upper body. Puffy white blisters marked the footprints of the bug on his shoulder. Several welts burst, spawning new ones. Gritting his teeth against the smarting, he dashed off to the infirmary.

Tonight we smashed two of the damn things inside the barracks before we turned out the lights, but I don't know how many more still lurk in the shadows. I pull the hair shirt-like blanket up to my neck. As the sweat oozes from my back, aggravating my prickly heat, I'm tempted to push it down again, but even this discomfort is better than a visit from one of those vile creatures. Finally, unable to stand it any longer, I throw off my cover, taking my chances. I think about home and the smooth sheets on my familiar bed there, the soothing sea breeze off the Pacific billowing the curtains at the open window, the room free of insects of any kind.

*   *   *

With the barracks much like the inside of a furnace, I sit outside writing a letter home. No matter how I hold my body, my prickly heat rash jabs needles into my skin. It's the worst outbreak I've had since the scourge began at Ellington Field weeks ago. The red rash covers my body from my neck to my knees. I washed it with cooling rubbing alcohol then floured it with heat powder, but the relief is brief. Soaping under a cold shower is no more effective. The miniscule motions of writing or even the act of sweating sets it off.

Sometimes I think I can hardly stand the pain, but I just have to grit my teeth. I sure hope it goes away. The sooner, the better!

By lunchtime my back feels like a seething nest of red ants feasts on it. After lunch, as I crawl in and out of gun turrets, more tiny knives pierce my back and legs. At the end of the day, in a letter to my parents I complain.

Oh that stuff! I'm practically going nuts with it!

Cooler weather the following morning brings some relief.

Did I enjoy that! I wish it would be zero degrees all day if it would drive that stuff away!

I receive a letter from my friend Ray stationed in the tropical heat of the South Pacific who has a bad case of it too. In a self-indulgent mood I pen a letter home where I know I can tap a well of sympathy.

Just five months ago today I was sitting on my first Army bunk at Fort MacArthur. I remember that I had just met Don Olson, and he was going to sleep in the bunk at the foot of mine. It rained that night, and it was very cool. I curled into bed and pulled up the covers for my first night's sleep in an army camp. It was a night I'll never forget. It was all so new, interesting and thrilling. Now I go to sleep with no covers on a hot night in entirely common surroundings. I sure wish I could be in a place where we had to pull up the covers at night. Ever since I have been in Texas, I have not used a blanket over five times. I'm telling you, this place is hot!

I yearn for the winter that is only a few months away and the cooler temperatures of the bases farther to the north where the bombardier schools are. My fellow Texans tell me about "blue northers" and the sleet or snow flurries that I might expect in winter time in northern Texas. The thought gives me comfort.

* * *

"What's this?" demands the lieutenant as we stand at attention by our beds for inspection.

"It's a small board we nailed to the studs to hold our outgoing mail, sir," replies the cadet in charge.

"Ahh," growls the officer.

With an angry swipe he sends the stick spinning to the just-scrubbed floor. It lies there, its sharp nails sticking up.

"Gig every man in this barracks!" he shouts. "The charge is 'sticks on floor.'"

Our faces remain frozen, our voices silent. *Chicken shit! Chicken shit bastard! What is so wrong about making a little device for our mail?* I mutter under my breath.

Tactical officers, always grim, strut down the streets, into the barracks or across the dusty fields with an exaggerated air of self-importance. Slim and erect, as though they walk with a broomstick rammed up their ass, they stride everywhere with their lieutenants' bars gleaming. They rule by fear like miniature Hitlers rather than by leading with the strength of their characters.

We have a lousy, unreasonable jerk of a tactical officer. He is a First Lieutenant, and he has his pilot wings. He flies a tow-target plane out here about four and one-half hours every month. They have to do that. He is not a fit pilot for anything else---just pulling tow-targets. He really gripes me. What a guy!

The sadistic lieutenant inspects us on Sunday morning, then, finding our quarters unsatisfactory, he restricts all of us to the barracks, not allowing some of the devout to go to church or the others to town.

Southwell particularly hates the lieutenant. He, who has a ravenous appetite and a tendency to gain weight, began to swell around the middle, his belly just beginning to sag over his belt and his polished brass buckle. As we stand at attention outside for inspection, the ramrod lieutenant, scrutinizing each cadet, stops in front of Southwell, and, with his lips screwed up into a snarl, merely groans, "Ugh". The gesture of disgust is far more devastating than any critical words he might use.

We all bear the annoyances, tolerating them as tests of our will and endurance. Unaccustomed to trials, except for the economic hardships of the Depression, I struggle to accept them. I, like the other cadets, complain and moan to my friends and seek sympathy in my letters home to my parents, but putting up with prickly heat, blister bugs and tyrannical officers will be insignificant compared to what we'll all face later. None of the annoyances, as pesky as they are, threaten our lives.

VOICES FROM HOME

Still floating on a euphoric cloud, I write another letter home.

Well, I just called you about two hours ago. Your words and voices keep going over in my mind, and I sure am happy. Oh, it was so good to hear you again. You just can't realize how much that meant to me. I'll hear your voices for weeks now.

I placed the call with the operator shortly after noon, but waited over five hours for it to go through. For the final three and a half hours I sat on a hard chair next to the telephone booth in the PX. I didn't mind the long wait. Being blessed (or sometimes cursed) with a volume of patience and buoyed by the anticipation of hearing from home, I took up residence on the wooden chair, shifting my legs and squirming from time to time, as I watched a steady stream of cadets pass through the door. Images of my mother and father drifted through my mind as I thought about what I would say to them in the short time allotted.

The telephone finally rang. I leaped, snatching the black receiver off its hook. "Your call is ready, sir," said the operator. Through the static of a bad connection I heard the loving tones of my mother's voice for the first time in over 6 months. Her words emanated from my other world, the one I left behind, the one I always thought about. As I listened to her I was in contact with it again---my parents, my home, my block with its rows of pine-like casuarina trees, the wind singing in their needles, the neighborhood kids and my friends, the bark of my dog, Pal, who always wagged his tail whenever he saw me, the sound of the evening freight train from the harbor chugging up the long grade.

I was suspended in the strangeness of the moment as I maintained a dizzy balance between my two worlds. I stood at a telephone in a PX on a dusty army base in the wastes of southern Texas talking to my mother and father in the familiar comfort of their small house on the Pacific coast. For months my life had been one of barracks, discipline, studying, taking courses, seeing new places and having new experiences. Now, for a few moments, I touched my other life.

I was like two people. I embraced adventure, the thrill and excitement of the unfamiliar and untried, new places, sights and people. On the other hand I longed to sit on the comfortable couch in our living room at home and sleep in my old bed. I wanted to see my father come home from work. I yearned to sit at the dining room table enjoying my mother's Italian delight, "porcupines," fried potatoes topped with creamed tomatoes, fresh apple pie.

We had no real news for each other. They told me about my sister's plan for being a nurse cadet and my dog that is still chasing cars, the thriving Victory garden I planted before I left and their work in the garage making flexible metal hoses for military planes. Also the latest about the neighbors and the kids on the block. I complained about the merciless Texas sun and my prickly heat, babbled on about the food, the guns we'd fired and the classes we'd taken. But we had written all that in our daily letters to each other. It was not so much what we had to say, it was the contact, our words interweaving along the wires that stretched a thousand miles across the deserts and mountains. It was the sound of their voices, their subtle pitch and familiar overtones that stirred the images and feelings that touched me.

*   *   *

My thoughts inevitably return home during relaxed moments, especially in the quiet twilight just before drifting off to sleep. I mull over passages from the letters I've received from home. In the silent darkness of the barracks, along the rows of men who may also be dreaming of home, my thoughts float like bright banners in the night.

There are guys that are actually stationed in the Los Angeles area while I'm stuck in a hole like Laredo. My God, I wish I could be stationed there.

Some of the soldiers stationed in Los Angeles are going to a folk dance with the local girls. Well, I hate folk dancing, but I think I would enjoy it if I could just be there.

Gladys and Audrey just had new babies to add to Julia's and Dorothy's. The stork is really running wild out there. It must be a screaming madhouse when all of the babies get together. I wish I could hear them. I haven't heard the cry of a baby in a long time.

I think I'll call home. I can reverse the charges. It should only be a couple of bucks. God, I would love to hear their voices. Mama wrote that she might cry if I called. I'll tell her that that would take up too much time or I'll have a joke ready just in case.

So Manual Souza is home for a 16-day furlough. Every time I get a letter it says that Howard Flagg, Floyd Watkins or somebody else is home on furlough. Every time I read the Inglewood paper you have sent there is some one I know home on furlough---everyone but me. I'll get one someday.

So Ray is coming through Los Angeles on a train, and he thinks he might stop there. If I'm ever on a train going that way, I'd pray and pray for it to stop there.

The 'Brett Street Boys.' Jack Post is about to be a Captain and will go over seas. Chuck, Earl, Roy, Dale and Johnny Berringer are still okay. Maybe the Brett Street luck will hold out.

Letters are like silent voices, their toneless thoughts traced on the page like frozen breath. They are a shade less than hearing a voice over the telephone and still farther away from hearing one in person, yet I yearn for each letter, ripping them open as I sit on my bunk, reading them over and over, thinking about them far into the night.

*   *   *

I think of all the possible ways that I might receive a furlough. I learn that cadets sometimes get a 10-day extension when they ship from Laredo to bombardier school. I pray that it will happen to me, and I file the thought away in my mind as an exciting possibility. Having learned that it's possible to hitchhike home on Army planes, I decide that's what I'll do if I should get a leave. As the days go by, a leave seems even more likely.

I find out that a lieutenant is working very hard to get our furloughs. He has to wait for orders from Randolph Field, the Gulf Coast Headquarters. If they don't arrive, he'll wire for them.

I can taste home on my tongue.

*   *   *

Finally finishing my letter home after my telephone call, I write:

I shall dream about you tonight.

SATURDAY NIGHTS

Distant shouting echoes among the buildings. It's midnight Saturday, and half the cadets from our barracks are not in yet, but the commotion outside heralds the return of the first wave. I wince at their raucous laughter and yelling, my covers pulled up close to my eyes. I'm uneasy around drunken men with their unpredictability. The slurred violence of their voices clashes with my quiet demeanor. They embarrass me. How should a sober person react to inebriates anyway? I lie on my bunk with my eyes open, listening to their approaching babble, wondering what the encounter will be like this time.

Heavy footsteps thud on the wooden porch. The screen door slams back against the wall with a sharp crack. They explode into the quietness of the room like the sudden release of a wild, many-legged beast. I remain motionless in my bunk, hoping they won't notice me. While some of the men walk in, others stagger, their shoes stomping clumsily on the floor, bumping crazily into the bunks and tables. Other cadets carry those who can no longer walk, struggling with their dead weight. The whole drunken sideshow galls me.

The first group finally quiets down, when another blasts through the door, shattering any possibility of sleep. One soused cadet, who pretends he's a football halfback charging down the field in the heat of the game, runs down the center of the barracks ramming his shoulder into the tables as though they are opposing players. He yells at them as the table legs screech and bang on the floor. I don't understand it.

Last weekend a baby-faced cadet from Oklahoma, who looked as though he were still in high school, intoxicated on just two beers, splintered the wooden screen door as he charged through it. With his pug nose and country twang, grinning with pleasure about his wild escapades, he seems a perfect adolescent fool to me. Two-beer drunks are common, only a trace of alcohol needed to free them from what little sense they have.

Senter, who always proudly returned from open posts with lipstick smeared around his mouth, dove through a barracks window, shattering glass and cutting his legs and arms.

*   *   *

After sleeping very little during the night because of the revelers, I slip into a pair of fatigues and walk across the dust to the latrine. Sections of the Sunday paper lie scattered and twisted across the concrete floor where the cadets had discarded them, the comic strips' bright colors contrasting with the dull cement of the floor. It's then that I see him. He lies sprawled next to a partition among the funny papers and tattered toilet tissue, his left cheek flat against the hard, cold floor, in silent sleep. In his rumpled uniform he's like death, motionless and quiet except for his shallow breathing. No one attends to him. He probably returned late at night, had been sick then passed out. I don't know the man, as he's a corporal from another group. He would wake up in his own time, stiff and sore, probably with a pounding headache.

After I leave the latrine, I still think about the man. I'd never seen anyone in his condition before. In my innocence, I can't imagine how anyone could allow himself to be so degraded.

There on the filthy floor, he'd lost all dignity.

I'm sure you never have to worry about me even taking a drink. Every time I see a fellow drunk or throwing up in the gutter or making a fool of himself, it really drives the point home to me. I really feel so sorry for them, and pity them. When they are drunk, they don't know what they are doing, and they do so much that they shouldn't do. I shouldn't let it, but it sure worries me. I wish there would be something I could do to help them, but there isn't much I can do.

*   *   *

Stewart, Southwell and I hop aboard the bus for the ten-minute ride into Laredo. Having never been to town here, we're excited about seeing a new place. Most of the people on the sidewalks are dark-complexioned, either Mexicans in town from the other side of the river or Mexican-Americans living here. An old woman balances a great load of groceries on her shoulder with one hand, her other firmly against her hip. In a hurry, she threads her way through the clots of people. We're surprised to see Kress', Woolworth's and Penney's stores, just as in any other small town in America and even two large hotels that rise out of midtown.

Hungry as always, we drop into the Imperial Cafe, a clean pleasant place where we each devour a steak dinner, a welcome contrast to the mediocre food served at the base. It's a rare pleasure to be served by a real waitress in a civilian cafe with regular people all around us. The music of silverware and the soft clanking of plates in the large room relax us as we cut into our juicy T-bones. Full and satisfied, we stroll into the nearest theater to see "I Escaped from the Gestapo," a typical war movie about the cruelty of the Nazis. We give it only mild reviews. With room enough for dessert after the film, we wander into an ice cream parlor to round out our evening with mounds of vanilla ice cream and tall glasses of 7-Up.

The following week we again explore the town, this time beginning with thick Kansas City steaks and potatoes along with chilled glasses of iced tea. After a movie, we end our open post with chocolate malts so thick that our spoons stand up in them.

As is our routine, the very next Saturday four of us fall upon yet another steak dinner, this time at the air-conditioned Plaza Hotel Grill. We relax in its cool comfort, enjoying the luxury of the restaurant and the hotel, a sharp contrast to our austere surroundings at the base. We follow our dinner with banana splits. After strolling into the elegant lounge, we peek into the USO, one of the finest we had seen anywhere. The evening not being complete, we take in the local movie before we return to the base.

Aside from our usual pattern of having a steak dinner and going to a movie followed by a visit to an ice cream parlor, we enjoy strolling the narrow streets of Laredo, walking beneath extended canopies built out over the sidewalk to shade people from the withering sun, structures none of us had ever seen before. We have a good time just being together, walking about town like real people, free of the constrictions of the base. We learn that Laredo had been one of the main American posts when the army fought Pancho Villa. Some of the fellows from Texas have relatives who fought in that war. Fort MacIntosh, presently an infantry camp near Laredo, had been active during those skirmishes.

*   *   *

I conclude that there are roughly two types of cadets, or rather, two types of men, each seeking their special brand of entertainment. There is the kind who head for the nearest bar to get as drunk as soon as possible, who laugh and scream with each other far into the night then look for women, and there is the type who goes out for a steak dinner followed by a movie and ice cream, who enjoy just looking at the town. Neither group understands the other.

I see the first group as uncontrolled and irresponsible, as men wasting their lives and flirting with the dangers of alcoholism. They are men who make fools of themselves, then laugh with each other about it later, even boast. They are men that lose themselves and their pride, staggering around not even knowing what they're doing, then suffer later with nauseous hangovers and emptiness. They are men who, in lusting for women, risk venereal disease and degrade themselves. They don't care about anything or have any interests.

From some of their off hand remarks, they seem to think of us as prudes, as rigid men who don't know how to have a good time, as timid souls who are afraid to take a risk in return for living moments of supreme joy. We deny sensuality in our lives, keeping that part of us under wraps lest we lose control. We lack the zest for life. We bind ourselves with moral chains. We are men with no guts who don't know how to live life to its fullest. We are men who are not real men at all.

As annoyed and embarrassed as I am when the drinkers force their drunkenness on me, I don't look down on them in everyday cadet life. I'm friendly with all of them, counting some of the Saturday revelers as my good friends. I never chastise them about their Saturday activities, and they never criticize what I do. During the week we work and fly together, but on Saturday night open posts we go our separate ways. We know we are all bound together in the same task, that we reach for the same goal, our bombardier's wings and the specter of combat beyond.

WASHING BACK

Every muscle aches. Despite the cooler weather my skin burns beneath my clothes, as I lie sprawled on my bunk. The coarse blanket smells like dust and irritates my cheek and neck. A dull throbbing pulses in my head. I open my eyes now and then, peering out at the orderly bunks lined up in the empty barracks, the dim light of the afternoon filtering in through the windows. Thank God they had excused me from physical training this afternoon. I close my eyes against the light, hoping to shut out the aching and the heat.

Later in the afternoon several cadets straggle into the barracks, their voices rolling around in the room. I keep my eyes shut against them, not wanting to speak to anyone. What I want is a private bed somewhere, some place where I don't have to appear in this condition in front of the other men. I wish I were home.

"What's the matter with Stevens?" one cadet asks another, his voice sounding as though it originated in some other dimension.

"Oh, he's okay," replies the other man. "He's just upset because his last score in aerial gunnery wasn't so hot."

It's true. As my body struggles with whatever grips me, my mind grapples with the disappointment of that poor score. I enjoyed the gunnery run. I did everything right. I bore-sighted the gun before we ever left the ground. I aimed correctly and led the tow target the proper distance, but hardly any of my blue-tipped bullets found their way to the damned target sleeve. Maybe the guns are getting old, and mine was defective. Maybe they didn't count the holes in the sleeve correctly. Perhaps they confused the color marks left by the bullets. But in my heart I know I've failed, and I strive to cope with it. My defeat mires me in a swamp of dejection. I yearn for sleep to shut it all out. I think about not existing at all. My God, if I can't shoot, they might even wash me out so that I'll never be a bombardier!

Unsure whether I'm truly sick or poisoned by the bitter gall of my disappointment, I manage to get up and swallow a couple of aspirin tablets. The aching and fever continue. At long last a deep sleep releases me from having to think.

A full night's sleep fails to cure me. My skin is on fire, and an anvil chorus pounds in my head. My head is a heavy medicine ball leaking its stuffing at the seams. I struggle into my heaviest clothes and push my feet into my bulky GI shoes, then point myself toward the infirmary for sick call. A cold rain speckles my face as I avoid puddles and the thickest pockets of sticky mud.

"One hundred and two degrees," says the doctor in charge. "We'd better x-ray your chest and take a urine sample, then we're going to put you in a hospital bed for rest."

In a clean hospital bed with cool, clean sheets, I sleep the rest of the day and most of the night. The long slumber has tempered the fever and aching, but my left eye waters profusely, and the glands on the left side of my neck are swollen. After a day of liquids only, they offer me a small bowl of warm cereal in the morning. Very hungry by now, I relish the bland cereal, but an hour later, just before the nurse irrigates my throat, I throw it all up in a fit of dizziness.

As I improve much too slowly, a disturbing thought enters my mind. If I remain in the hospital much longer, the commander will hold me back. If I'm not out by Tuesday in time to fly in the AT-18s for turret gunnery, I'll be too far behind. I wouldn't be able to graduate with my class, the men with whom I had forged such a bond during the past seventeen weeks. The thought of severing those friendships saddens me.

My temperature fluctuates during the day, and x-rays reveal the shadows of severe sinus congestion, a condition that would ground me even if I were to be released from the hospital. I'm pleased to learn that the bad weather has grounded all the gunnery planes for the past two days, keeping the class from gaining on me, but now, with the skies clearing, I can hear the sounds of revving engines from the flight line.

With ample time on my hands I think back to the probable cause of my malady. I had never had sinus trouble in my life. It must have begun the first day I flew. Sweating profusely from lugging a heavy parachute, a machine gun and ammunition in the searing heat of the flight line then finding myself eight minutes later in the cool slipstream at five thousand feet must have been a shock my system couldn't handle.

The off-key tones of a portable organ played by one of the patients, a dreamer who only imagines his talent, disturbs my thoughts, and I quit thinking.

* * *

I knew it might happen, and it does. I think about it far into the night as electric-blue flashes of lightning flicker through the hospital windows, and artillery-like thunder shakes the roof. My class will graduate Saturday morning and ship out to bombardier school the same evening. They'll be wearing their silver gunner's wings while I remain flat on my back in the hospital. Over the past five months I had come to know over a hundred cadets, some of them very well. I envision many of their faces as I suddenly realize I might never see any of them again. Rain drums on the roof and streaks down the windows.

Thick fog clogs the air in the morning, reminding me of my stuffed sinuses. The nurses ply me with liquids and pills, put drops in my nose, irrigate my throat and even erect a steam tent over my bed, but I remain just the same. In the afternoon the sky blackens in the west, matching my disposition. The storm sweeps in with dark churning clouds throwing jagged thunderbolts and fits of torrential rain. Just after the squall drifts away to the east, our Commanding Officer, Captain Bussy, personally brings me my paycheck, a gesture of concern that I never expected from an officer. Receiving the paycheck and the officer's kindness lighten my spirits.

* * *

They came to the hospital to say goodbye; Stewart, Southwell and Spano. They would be moving on to bombardier school without me. Despite the somber parting, I'm overjoyed to see them. I'll especially miss Stewart whom I had immediately liked when I first met him because of his kindness, gentleness and friendliness. The closeness of our last names brought us together for nearly every activity. We studied with each other every night and scored well on our examinations, he with a 95% average and I with 94%. We shipped at the same time and had nearly identical gunnery scores. I always went on open post with him---I'd even visited his home in Port Arthur, Texas. We are the same age, and weigh exactly the same although he is two inches taller. I will miss him terribly.

Short, stocky Southwell with his full round face and friendly eyes comes from Molalla, Oregon. He always supported me when I defended California and the West Coast from the verbal attacks of men from other parts of the country, especially Texas. Always known as a hard worker and studier, he's our champion "eager beaver." He doesn't drink or smoke, and is blessed with an abundant supply of common sense. We often enjoyed our weekend passes together.

Spano, from Long Island, New York, with his accent and occasional wild ways, is an enigma to me, but I always enjoy him.

After a good time chatting we shake hands firmly, and they walk away. Seeing them again will be quite unlikely. I'm left with an emptiness that nearly brings tears to my eyes, reminding me of how deep our friendships had been. It amazes me that being together every day, enduring the same hardships and engaging in the same activities, all of us bound for the same end can bond people so. I realize what a strong and precious force camaraderie is.

*   *   *

Finally out of the hospital and settled in new barracks with the other men who have been held back, I walk up to the flight line to resume flying, to make up what I have missed. I board a twin-engine AT-11 with several other cadets for a turret gunnery flight. Touching the aluminum on the inside of the plane is like touching ice, and the interior is as chilly as an icebox. I squeeze into the cramped turret and fire two hundred rounds at a tow target. As we descend for a landing I have trouble clearing my ears, but I yawn and work my jaw furiously to relieve the pressure. After flying in Lockheed AT-18s in the afternoon, not returning until just after sunset, I can hardly believe what I see on the scoreboard in the waiting room. For the morning run I have the highest score, beating out 402 other cadets. Ecstatic, I feel my confidence return.

But maybe they made a mistake!

Making up for lost time, I continue to fly and score well on my gunnery runs. My health and confidence return, and the world becomes brighter. Despite prickly heat, insects, sadistic officers, cruelly hot days, marginal food, homesickness, isolation and the parting with good friends, I have much to look forward to. I value my fast friendships, the ever-changing adventure of Army life and, above all, the fascination with flying.

I really love every minute that I fly. I like to look out of the window when I fly. It's just so interesting to look down on everything.

I enjoy gazing down on the sinuous curves of rivers, the patterns of dry washes and the grids of cities. I like the slopes of hills and their shadows and even the brushy stippling of the Texas desert. I marvel at the highways and the winding dirt roads, the changing hues of fields and the long line of a railroad, sometimes glistening in a slanting sun. I especially admire the moist softness of clouds, their fragile mounded vapor, their cool, gray breath.

The disappointment of washing back and losing my friends gradually fades as I meet new cadets and resume the adventure of flying. Within two days I should be wearing silver gunner's wings on my chest.

GUNNER'S WINGS

Lying in the swaying comfort of an upper berth on Missouri Pacific's Sunshine special, I listen to the rhythmic clicking of the Pullman car wheels on the tracks. I stretch out and pull the smooth blanket up around my chin, glad that it feels softer than the scratchy wool ones I had endured for six weeks at Laredo. At times, the deep-throated song of the steam locomotive sounds out into the Texas night. I remember how haunting the melodious whistles of the Southern Pacific sounded as I lay in bed at night on the farm near Modesto long ago. I wonder if some other boy, not yet asleep in his farmhouse, hears the train I'm on, and responds to it the same way I did then.

Despite my comfort and the pleasure of riding the train at night, sadness travels with me. The furlough that I'd come to believe was inevitable had vanished in an instant. I'd already tasted home, thought about how I would travel. I'd embraced my family and friends in my fantasies. One of the cadets of the eight held back had gone to the commanding officer to find out about our furloughs only to be told that there would be none, and furthermore that in just one and a half hours we had to be packed and cleared from the base. We had a two p.m. train to catch in Laredo, the first of three that would take us to the bombardier training base at Midland, Texas. Stunned and downhearted, we sadly gathered our belongings. Two and a half hours later we boarded the Missouri Pacific train for San Antonio. We would soon learn that getting our hopes up while in the service was always emotionally risky. After arriving in

San Antonio at six-thirty, we had only a half hour before we had to board the Sunshine Special for Fort Worth.

Having overcome some of my disappointment about the furlough, I basked in the glow of winning my gunner's wings, a personal symbol that I was finally getting somewhere. I wore them proudly on the train, sometimes looking down at my shirt where they perched or catching sight of their gleaming silver in the mirror. I noted how other passengers looked at them, sometimes catching them glancing or staring. I reveled in their attention, puffing up with the heady intoxication of self-importance.

* * *

The last two qualifying gunnery runs before we were awarded the wings had been dramatic. The Lockheed AT-18 we were to fly had been grounded all morning because of a problem with its wing flaps. By afternoon the mechanics, sure they had corrected the problem, cleared the plane for flight. Just before entering the small door in the fuselage the instructor said,

"Do you guys really know how to use your chutes? If those flaps go out on us again, we might have to bail out."

We look at each other, our mouths gaping, our eyes wider than usual.

"Yeah, we know how to pull the cord," we assured him. But what choice did we have anyway?

Once we reached altitude, the air was so turbulent that making good sustained shots at the target sleeve was impossible. Tense from the buffeting and our concern about the flaps, we "sweated out" the landing. If one flap worked and the other didn't, the plane might be thrown into a dangerous roll. We descended into a straight-on approach toward the Laredo runway. When the pilot lowered the flaps, and the plane maintained its steady course, we breathed easier. We glided into the runway, but the pilot, perhaps still agitated, bounced the wheels on the runway three times before we settled in for a steady roll. We didn't care how he landed; we were down safely, and the last of our gunnery runs was completed.

*   *   *

At seven in the morning, after I had enjoyed a satisfying sleep in the Pullman berth, the Sunshine Special arrives in Fort Worth. Since our train to Midland is not scheduled to leave until two in the afternoon, we have most of the day to roam the city. After eating breakfast together, all eight of us decide to go our own ways then meet again in the afternoon at the railroad station. As it's Sunday, I ask the station agent directions for a Methodist church close to downtown. I walk nearly a mile along the deserted streets of Fort Worth searching for it. As I stroll past the closed shops and businesses, I think about how long it's been since I've attended a civilian church. I miss seeing "real" people, church people---men dressed in suits and ties, women attractive in their Sunday finest and children, especially them, decked out in their special Sunday school dresses and suits.

Perhaps because I missed my furlough, I especially think about home. Being among a church congregation much like my own back in Inglewood would be almost like being home. I'm not pious, and I don't seek to satisfy any deep religious need. It's just the idea of being with the people, people like me.

I long to be with young women, the nice ones who would inevitably be there. Although I correspond with several girls at home, the letters are no substitute for hearing the feminine tones of their voices, watching their hair shift and tremble as they move or feeling the soft warmth of their hands. I miss the subtle scent about them, the play of reflections in their eyes, the sinuous way they walk. Proud of my cadet uniform and especially my new gunner's wings, I fantasize that they'll view me with special interest and possibly a touch of awe.

I arrive at the church long before the service begins, but I meet the friendly custodians and others who prepare the church for the congregation. Later, during the service, I sit in the cavernous sanctuary, listening to the minister, a lively man who blends wisdom with humor to make his sermon enjoyable. I like singing the hymns that we had so often sung at church in Inglewood. I attend a Sunday school class for people my age, discovering that twenty young women are in the group, but to my surprise and disappointment, so are five cadets from nearby Hicks Field, a primary pilot training school. Generally having a good time, I enjoy talking to the cadets and listening to the twangy nasal Texas accents of the young women.

After church I walk back through the center of town. I had met nearly fifty people that I would never see again, and all of them were friendly. I still feel the warmth of meeting them as I stride past the stone buildings and locked storefronts. Although very nice to me, none of the young women were drawn to me or fawned over me. None expressed a desire to ever see me again or even write. None of them talked to me any longer than was civil. No dreamy-eyed woman was swept off her feet by my appearance or my irresistible charm. No family offered to take me home with them for lunch or simply show me the town. No one even offered a ride back to the railroad station. I walk the empty streets toward the railroad station, my head down, not looking at anything.

*   *   *

At two-ten p.m. the Texas and Pacific train puffs out of the station. Once clearing industrial Fort Worth, we streak across the interminable, brush-dotted plains. The monotonous scene never changes except when we pass through towns. It's the same expanse of flatness we'll look down on for the next three months. The other cadets and I settle back and trade stories about our "adventures" in Fort Worth. We pass through the major towns of Ranger, Eastland, Abilene and Big Springs before we arrive at Midland near midnight. Too late to be taken to the base, we bed down in the Sharmbaur Hotel for the night, two to a room.

A dusty Army truck rumbles up in front of the hotel promptly at eight in the morning. We throw our bags over the tailgate then climb in the back for our ten-mile trip to the base. What we see of the city of Midland appears clean and neat, the tallest building in town twelve stories high. Bouncing around on the hard seats, we watch the country flash by. To me the landscape looks similar to the Mojave Desert in California, out near the eighty acres my grandparents own.

I look down proudly at my gunner's wings again, the polished gleam of them jiggling on my chest with the vibrations of the truck. My hope is to trade them for a more prestigious one, my bombardier's wings, but that prize lies twelve long, hard weeks away.

BUGS AND BOMBSIGHTS

Looking much like a small oil derrick on wheels, the "bug" creeps silently across the smooth concrete floor of the cavernous hanger. On top of the twelve-foot structure, upon a large square platform with railings, I sit in a bombardier's seat peering through the eyepiece of a Norden bombsight. Snared in its crosshairs is a target across the room, a small metal box on the floor with a paper bull's eye marked on top. Pressing my eye to the soft rubber lips of the eyepiece, I adjust two large knurled knobs as well as my untrained fingers will allow, trying to keep the crosshairs from drifting away from the center of the target. I try to ignore the tension in my neck and the moisture gathering on my palms. The vertical hair remains on the target now. I've corrected the drift. Gradually I move the horizontal crosshair, attempting to find the exact range. Now both rest on the center of the target and remain fixed as we slowly roll toward it. As we approach the moment of release, and the angles become more pronounced, both hairs begin to wander. I make last minute corrections as deftly as I can. Despite my best amateur touch, I watch the hairs stray just off center. Down below a solenoid plunges a marker toward the paper bull's eye, the click meaning that my bomb would have exploded.

"Not bad," says my instructor, Lieutenant Cannady. "You'll be dropping real bombs from airplanes before you know it." His encouraging words ease my self-doubts.

Lieutenant Cannady's calm, relaxed manner blends well with my personality. When I hear other instructors on the bugs around us screaming at their students, I'm glad I have him. Most tough-minded instructors believe that chewing out cadets is the only way to get them to correct their errors, but Lieutenant Cannady quietly tells us about our mistakes.

The lieutenant's disarming manner, the casual way he wears his officer's hat, his soft voice, even his slight slouch breaks down the barriers between us. A minor crook angles the bridge of his nose, and, when he speaks, his voice resonates in his sinuses. Most officers I had seen in the service had worked diligently to establish a chasm between themselves and their inferiors, had scowled and strutted stiffly and seemed to enjoy chewing ass.

In erasing the distance between officer and cadet, he helps me learn, but, at the same time, I become careless about showing him proper respect for his rank. I often slip, forgetting to call him Sir. While ignoring some of my lapses, he occasionally reminds me that I must be careful.

"Stevens, you better not forget to address me as Sir," he warns. "You better get in the habit or some chicken shit officer is liable to really rack you back for it."

He encourages my partner and me by telling us that he's never washed out a cadet during his 8-month duty as an instructor. His words reassure us and give us confidence that we can learn, endure the training and eventually succeed. He even offers to help us pick out our officer's clothing. Despite his motivating words, my partner and roommate, Van Aken, has trouble hitting the target from the bugs. An innate nervousness stiffens his hands, making his "bombs" fall erratically.

* * *

The Norden bombsight overwhelms me with its black, metallic presence, its knobs, scales, dials, indicators, levers and windows. I'm acutely conscious that the intricate mechanism in front of me is top secret, that the enemy keenly wants to know the mystery of it. I'm to be entrusted with understanding its interior workings and using it properly. I feel the honor of knowing and sense the smug thrill that anyone enjoys when he's been let in on a secret---that he is one of the exclusive few who knows. More than ever I begin to feel like a real bombardier.

I think about the "Bombardier's Oath":

"In the presence of Almighty God, I
do solemnly swear and affirm, that
I will accept the precious trust placed
in me by my Commander in Chief,
the President of the United States of
America, by whose direction I have
been chosen for Bombardier Training.

I pledge myself to live and act according
to the Code of Honor of the Bombardiers
of the Army Air Forces. I solemnly swear
that I will keep inviolate the secrecy of
any and all confidential information
revealed to me, and in the full knowledge
that I am a guardian of one of my country's
most priceless military assets, do
further swear to protect the secrecy of
the American Bombsight, if need be,
with my life itself."

This is the secret bombsight I had only heard about. This is the instrument that, according to an impressive Hollywood movie I'd seen, can launch a bomb so accurately that a bombardier can hit a pickle barrel floating on the ocean from 30,000 feet.

*   *   *

Only the dim outside lights of the barracks guide us as we shuffle through the darkness at 5:30 a.m. We all wear our A-2 leather flight jackets zipped up against the morning chill. Our trousers rustle in the quietness. Still too early to be fully awake, we say very little to each other. Now and then the revving of engines and the sharp, flat whirring of the propellers drift over from the flight line .The flight crews work through the night so that all of the AT-11s are ready to fly the next morning

We walk along the road from the mess hall where we had eaten an early breakfast, on our way to the bug hanger for pre-dawn training. The road is straight and flat; the whole base is straight and flat. A huge pumpkin-shaped water tower painted alternately with large white and orange squares looks down upon the base like an all-seeing idol. We see it no matter where we are on the vast treeless base. Like a red eye, its light on top blinks on and off in the darkness.

We had trained on the bugs last night until 9 p.m. then I had to study until 10:30. Sleepy at first, I feel more alive in the chilly air. Despite my lingering fatigue, once up on the trainer, I trace four straight trails across the middle of the "shack", the center of the circular target, even though the target moves this time. A faint smile of confidence steals across my lips. In the far reaches of my mind, I'd always worried about the difficult coordination tests we'd taken in San Antonio. Would I have the ability to adjust the bombsight knobs with precision? This run quiets that nagging question.

After finishing on the bugs at 10, we attend a class called "The Theory of Bombing" which lasts until nearly noon. Drilling on the dusty field for two hours follows chow, then a two-hour class about the Norden bombsight. Once the class ends we change clothes and report for physical training. For the remainder of the evening I study in the library, grappling with the confounding complexities of the bombsight. Tomorrow we must again rise in the dark for physical training.

I knew it would be tough here, but not this tough. So far I have understood everything, and I am confident that if I work hard, I can make it through. If I ever wash out of here, it won't be because I haven't tried.

We practice on the bugs day after day, stalking the paper targets, still or moving, from low or high altitude, using two types of bombsights. I live with the bugs and bombsights until the array of knobs, levers and crosshairs, the touch and feel and sight of them, slip slowly into my consciousness and become part of me.

THE BOMBING OLYMPICS

Hissing as it plunges to earth, a practice bomb impacts with a flash and a puff of white smoke. Within minutes another from a second plane explodes farther from the aiming point, a small structure or "shack" standing in the center of large concentric circles. Another bomb swooshes down, its flash and smoke plume nearly on top of the shack, the closest hit yet. As beginners who hadn't yet dropped a single bomb, we cadets watch the show from far across the field. One bombardier blasts the target dead center.

"Hey, that guy's really good! What field's he from?"

"San Angelo, I think," answers another.

The bombardiers in those AT-11 training planes, the three top men from each of the bombardier schools---San Angelo, Midland, Big Springs, Childress, Albuquerque, Demming and Victorville---compete in the Bombing Olympics for the honor of their base. Not only do I marvel at the drama of the exploding bombs, but also at the unerring accuracy of the bombardiers. I long to emulate them, hoping that when I end my training, I too will be one of the top men. We shuffle around on the concrete ramp, shading our eyes from the bright sun, straining toward the hazy sky to watch for the approach of the next plane. Hits continue to cluster around the shack as each plane roars over.

Soon after the smoke drifts away, a flight of B-24 heavy bombers turns toward our field for a mock attack. Fascinated, we watch their approach. As they fly closer, four P-47 Thunderbolt fighters streak off the Midland runways to intercept them. Within seconds the interceptors dive, twist and turn in and out of the bomber formation, harassing them like angry birds chasing away hawks. The bombers, no match for the fury of the fighters, veer away from the field. No sooner do the B-24s limp away than a half dozen thundering B-17s, flying in a V formation like huge geese, storm toward our field. The fighters then jump on the B-17s, attacking them from every angle in violent rolls and sharp dives, their engines screaming with power and precision. Finally the bombers head away from the field, having had enough of the P-47s.

Just when we think the show is over, the B-17s return, making a run directly toward our field. The P-47s are far away, somewhere out in the haze. Closer now, the B-17s roar over the edge of the field, their camouflage paint making them appear dark and ominous. Then, from out of the sun, the fighters, their engines whining, dive toward the bombers, penetrating their loose ranks with their lightning-fast gleams of silver. We stand transfixed in the roaring glory of it. A thrill runs through my body like an electric charge as I think about being part of that exclusive band of men and machines that perform for us today. In my eyes, the men are all heroes and the planes modern wonders. I wish I could see the men, their resolute heroic faces, the silver wings on their tunics glinting in the sun.

With the B-17s gone, the P-47s make a final pass over the runways. They come in low, flashing by us like bullets, their engines full bore, and then zoom up into the haze where they become only bright specks, and then they are gone. Both formations of bombers now return, heading toward the center of the field. They envelop us in their thunder as the B-24s release salvos of practice bombs on the target, smothering the shack in thudding bright flashes and thick columns of smoke. The bombers rumble away, and the dissipating smoke drifts across the runways, my body still tingling, my resolve to become a bombardier firmer yet. I'll make it through our training. I'll become what I imagine those men to be.

*   *   *

Bundled up against the cold, cloudy day, my partner and I stroll down the flight line. We pass so close to a gull-winged F4U Corsair that we can almost touch it. We'd never been near Navy planes before, but since our base is also a sub-depot for transient planes, many aircraft of all types use the field on their way across the plains. We pause to look over the blue Navy interceptor, admiring its smooth-curved lines and its powerful poise. A Navy F6F Hellcat and an SBD Dauntless dive bomber are also on the line.

Nearby, a P-51 Mustang taxies on to the ramp, brakes then cuts its engine. It is the sleekest, most streamlined symphony in silver that we have ever seen. The pilot pushes back the canopy, raises himself then steps out on to the wing. Instead of wearing an Air Force uniform or even a flying suit, he struts across the flight line wearing a suit and tie with a vest and a Texas ten-gallon hat. We watch with amazement as he disappears into the offices.

Several other Air Force P-51s rest along the flight line with P-47 Thunderbolts, P-38 Lightnings, A-20 attack planes, B-17 Flying Fortresses and B-24 Liberators. Even a few outmoded B-18 bombers spend their last days here. One or two olive-drab C-47 transports are scattered among them. Besides the constant flow of AT-11 bombardier training planes, other planes fly in and out any time of the day or night.

The thrill of it all to me is that I belong here. I'm part of all of these planes and the men who fly in them. I'm not just a person passing a base, watching from a highway or from behind a wire fence, the planes wavering in the rippling distance, the men only moving specks. I proudly walk among the men and machines, listening to the airmen's voices and the throb of engines, smelling the pungent fragrance of fuel and feeling the gusts from prop wash lash against my face. I belong here.

*   *   *

Standing nearly six feet tall and weighing close to 180 pounds, the instructor in our Bombardment Objectives class demonstrates how we can calculate the velocity of the wind on a circular plastic computer if we can determine our magnetic heading, true air speed and drift. There is an aura about the man, a subtle brilliance surrounding his handsome features and his curly blond hair. His mystique has little to do with his appearance or the manner in which he presents his material, but emanates from the fact that he's a combat veteran, having returned only a month before from the South Pacific where he'd been a bombardier on a B-25 medium bomber. Stationed in New Guinea, he had participated in the Battle of the Coral Sea and the Bismark Sea Battle.

I listen patiently to his instruction, my attention riveted on every word of his digressions, his experiences as a combat bombardier.

"I loved the B-25," he says. "But you know the B-25 has no protection from the rear except just part way up from the top turret. There is only a Plexiglas window back in the tail. That's all. Some of us, after being attacked from the rear by Japanese Zeros, stuck two broomsticks back there to make them think we had guns."

The class laughs and urges him on.

"Well, my crew took out the Plexiglas, and mounted a .30 caliber machine gun back there. We placed it so it would have a lot of freedom of motion. We tied a cord to the trigger mechanism then strung the other end to the top turret. We loaded the gun with tracers. When Japanese fighters attacked us from behind, the top turret gunner pulled on the rope.

Tracers scattered all over the sky out of the rear end. That kept the fighters off our tail---at least for a while."

In awe of this man, the class continues to invite his digressions. His stories seem more vital to us than learning about the computer and the nature of bombing objectives. He doesn't need much encouragement.

"I'll never forget October 5, 1942," he continues as he looks up toward the ceiling, trying to gather up the facts in his mind. "While we were on patrol, we spotted a group of ships, a merchant ship, a tanker and two destroyers. We sent them the call letter of the day on the proper radio frequency so that they could identify themselves. Instead of sending us back the correct response, they lobbed anti-aircraft shells at us. This was my first enemy engagement, and it all seemed unreal to me. I couldn't believe it was happening. We reported the location of the ships to the home base then urged our pilot to get the hell out! He refused. He wanted to make two bomb runs on those ships, dropping three bombs at each pass."

"Another B-25 joined us in the attack. On the first try the accurate anti-aircraft fire downed the other plane. We decided to make only one run on the tanker. One of our bombs hit it, then we got out of there. On our way home we fought with 16 Zeros. The top turret gunner knocked down three of them. We made it back to the base with no more attacks."

I put myself in the bombardier's place and wonder how I would've reacted. It's a preview of what I can expect, and I project myself into the account. I admire his courage, and, as he is a combat veteran, a man who has been there, I believe his every word as absolute truth. I read into his personality a heroic quality akin to the supernatural.

He tells us about how useless most of our fighters are against the Japanese Zero. He informs us that the Zero's skin is thin and brittle, making it light and fast but vulnerable to damage. He relates the story of his crash landing after the wing of his airplane had been nearly severed, about his back injury in the crash that has grounded him for good.

At Midland I watch flyer heroes in action and touch the very planes they fly. I walk among combat veterans, men who have known the bitter taste of battle. The men and machines reside on a higher plain far above me, and I, a raw cadet who has never dropped a bomb, look up to them with awe.

MIND AND BODY

I struggle to calm the chaos in my head, but my understanding of how the Norden bombsight functions inside is only a blur. Images of caging knobs, mirror drive clutches, crosshair rheostats, worm and drift gears tumble through my mind, bewildering waves and eddies of them. My prospects of surviving the academics at Midland are in jeopardy. I thought the 50-caliber machine gun and the Martin gun turret were complicated, but I had never seen any machine as baffling as the inner workings of the bombsight. I try to remember that the machine gun was once difficult for me, but I finally mastered it.

I warn my parents that I must constantly study, sometimes far into the night, grabbing a spare moment now and then to dash off a letter. In my bombsight and theory of bombing classes I had taken twenty pages of notes, some of them now undecipherable. I would have to untangle them all later.

I find it difficult to grasp a multitude of facts and functions immediately. I have to slowly process them with much study before they fit together into a comprehensive whole. Not being able to understand often leads to a kind of hopelessness, even fear and panic that I can't do it.

If I were not motivated, I would sink into a morass of confusion and probably wash out. But my passion to be a bombardier goads me into overcoming those obstacles. After hours of concentration and study at my desk the terminology and processes become clearer and crisper, the concepts

251

gradually settling in my mind. I score well on my exams, and my confidence rises. I know it's all possible now.

Classes, examinations and studying never cease. We learn about bombing and navigation computers, most of them plastic discs with plastic arms connected to their centers that move over printed values. I catch on quickly at first but later the problems we solve with them become more convoluted. The class brings out another of my mental flaws, one that had plagued me all through high school. I have the tendency to make silly mistakes, minor but careless lapses that do me in. In working the computer problems, sometimes over ten steps are necessary, each one a potential booby trap. Any step missed along the way, no matter how small, destroys the final solution. I know what to do, and the concepts are clear, but I'm anxious about tripping over details. In a practical sense, just one small mistake could take an airplane far from its correct course or send bombs miles from their targets.

Van Aken and I walk back toward the barracks, our shoes crunching over dust and gravel. Now that the colder weather is here, we change into our ODs, our olive drab uniforms, rather than the thinner and lighter suntans we had worn all summer. The cool days cured my prickly heat. No more needling pain.

Both Van Aken, my partner, and I feel downhearted. We recently endured a difficult exam in our computer class, having to work out long complex problems. Being similar to each other in temperament, we both fear we may have flunked it outright. As we return from an hour's drill on the flat dusty field, a cadet who had secured a list of the test scores dashes from the barracks. He reads the results alphabetically, so Van Aken and I have to wait. I don't know if I want to hear it. The scores he reads are very low, with some cadets failing it. We become more anxious. Finally he yells, "Stevens, one hundred per cent." then "Van Aken, one hundred per cent". We both stand dumbfounded before the excitement hits us.

My academic average remains high, and the horror of failure or washing out begins to ease. But we have yet to fly a single practice mission.

* * *

The last of the blue moonlight and the first flush of dawn cast a pale glow on the physical training field. The barracks appear ghostly, and the red light on top of the checkered water tower winks on and off. The occasional revving of airplane engines drifts over from the flight line, blending with the scuffling shoes and complaining voices of the cadets as they line up in the chill morning for exercises.

"Why in the hell are we out here this early?"

"All they're trying to do is make us miserable, toughen us up."

"My ass is frozen!"

My hands ache, and my nose and cheeks are numb in the near-freezing temperatures.

"Okay you guys. Line up! Stand at ease and listen!" yells the PT instructor. "The sooner you start exercising, the warmer you're gonna be. Okay now! Feet apart, hands over your head! Ready, hut-two-three-four, hut-two-three-four!"

Our spread feet come together then out in rhythm, our hands clapping over our heads then slapping against our sides. The dim field fills with our claps and slaps, the sound of pounding shoes, the steaming of our breaths.

"Okay, faster!" shouts the instructor.

We dance to the complex moves of the Randolph Shuffle, dive to the ground for dusty push-ups, then kick our feet as high as our chins. The instructor's right: we're warm now despite the chill.

After pummeling our minds with academics, they pound our bodies with exercises, a balance designed to keep us alert. After group exercises each day they stretch us even further. The routine is:

> Monday-----Run one and a half miles.
> Tuesday-----Games (Usually football)
> Wednesday----Run one and a half miles.
> Thursday---Run the obstacle course.
> Friday------Games
> Saturday---Run two miles.
> Sunday-----Stay in bed.

When we begin to fly we must exercise even earlier, in morning darkness. At the end the instructors test us for physical fitness---the ability to do 114 sit-ups, 10 chin-ups and run 300 yards in under 49 seconds. After only 4 hours sleep, time on the Sperry trainer and three flying missions, I take the physical tests, somehow passing them.

Staying awake in classes becomes a major effort, not because of the teachers or the material, but my near-exhaustion. Finally, back in the barracks for a precious five minutes before the next activity, I lie down on my bunk. I quickly pass into sleep, only the sudden slamming of a door bringing me back to consciousness. I would have slept the rest of the day. Despite the physical training to keep us "physically fit and mentally alert" the rigors of the daily routine keep us in a perpetual twilight.

* * *

"There are three kinds of thunderstorms," explains our meteorology instructor. "Orographic thunderstorms form when unstable air flows over a mountain range, and frontal types occur particularly along a cold front where denser cold air advances into warmer. The last, the convective, forms when the storm develops from rising currents in warm, humid air.

Whatever the type, they're full of up and down drafts capable of knocking down a plane."

Because of my interest in weather, nurtured by my father, I understand thunderstorms, but discussing the subject in class thrills me. I'm sure that when the war is over meteorology will be my field.

I'm even more excited about the weather after we begin to fly. Now I can look at clouds from the top and sides rather from the bottom. I note their thickness and temperature as we are swallowed in their mist. I try to explain it to my parents.

> *You know, I've learned more about weather by flying in it than I have from the ground. You can just go right up to a cloud and see what it's made of and how it forms. I have flown through cumulus, stratus, stratocumulus, altocumulus and even near some low cirrus clouds. It's also funny to watch the temperature gauge and the screwy things it does as we go up---then see what happens to the weather afterward.*

Not as enthusiastic about my other courses, I try to comprehend them nevertheless, studying diligently for all my exams. Most difficult to master is a course about the C-1 Autopilot, the device the bombardier uses to take control of the airplane during the bombing run. It is more baffling than the bombsight itself. Courses follow about Automatic Bombing Computers, Bomb Types and Fuses. I run my fingers along the cold iron casings of gigantic 2000-pound bombs capable of leveling an entire city block. We lift blue practice bombs filled with sand, attach them to shackles in a mock airplane bomb bay. One course teaches us about the causes of bombing errors, another about the maintenance of the bombsight. Finally we devote a large bloc of time to learning navigation, a subject that fascinates me.

Eventually I complete all the courses, having successfully weathered eighteen withering examinations. What at first seemed like a bewildering blur becomes lucid and understandable. I feel better about myself.

FLEECE

Smiling like a boy that has just received a Christmas gift, I pose for a photograph in the sun next to the barracks wall. My just-issued leather flying jacket, heavy, black and fleece-lined, swells the size of my slim body, its arm-binding padding transforming me into a slow-moving robot. With the zipper drawn up to my chin, my broad fleece-lined collar lies flat around my neck and shoulders. If I should ever be cold, I can pull all that soft, warm fluff around my neck. Downy flaps to protect my ears and a strap padded with "fur" hang down from the close-fitting leather helmet. A thin ruffle shows at the bottom of the jacket and around the ends of the sleeves, like those of a dark Santa Claus costume. Leather trousers held up by wide suspenders grip my legs, the bottoms tucked into soft high-topped boots as large as a fireman's. Thick gloves cover my hands. Airmen's goggles, like frog's eyes, rest just above my forehead in the fashion of all the great aviators I have ever seen.

The four of us waddle like proud but clumsy gingerbread men, still unaccustomed to the heavy, unyielding suits. Neither ready to fly, nor even near the flight line, we hover just outside our barracks taking photographs of each other for home consumption. We want to show our folks and friends at home that we're real airmen now, although we've never been off the ground at Midland. We begin to sweat inside the bulky clothing as we strike different poses. We snap pictures of each other individually, in pairs and in a group of four, sometimes laughing with our arms lying over each other's shoulders. Standing in the afternoon sun, mere fledgling cadets, we appear as though we'd just returned from a high altitude combat mission. In addition to this cumbersome equipment, the supply sergeant also issued us each a large aviators kit bag, oxygen equipment, a summer flying suit, an olive drab sweater and a brown leather flight jacket.

Pleased with ourselves, we feel that the clothes link us even closer to the holy brotherhood of flyers. Now, we not only walk among military aircraft and talk to the men who fly them, but look like airmen.

Unlike the barracks at other airbases, one long room with ranks of beds, ours are partitioned into separate rooms, six cadets being assigned to each. With our close living arrangements we become fast friends, all of us being similar in temperament and ambition.

Raymond Bachuber with his handsome smile comes from Wisconsin. He's the only person I've ever met who only eats to live, confessing that he doesn't enjoy food, only eats because he has to. With my keen appetite, I find his quirk unfathomable. Glenn Ballentyne from Spokane, Washington is closest to me in spirit. Friendly and easy-going, he loves to study and hopes that the war will be over soon so he can go to college. Charles Van Aken from Michigan is my partner on the bugs and will be again when we fly. A devout Catholic, he never misses Mass on Sunday. He chides me if I sometimes skip Protestant services. When I tell him that God would understand that I'm too tired to go, he laughs at me, thinking my permissive attitude ludicrous for anyone who professes faith. I never get to know George Parris as well as the others, perhaps because he's not as serious. Hailing from Michigan, he's pleasant and probably the most fun loving of all of us. Duggan from Massachusetts washes out early and moves out of the barracks.

*   *   *

One by one, we file through the quartermaster warehouse and sign for our bombardier kits. An olive drab canvas valise with a handle at the top, it contains all the paraphernalia we'll need for our bombing flights. Back at the barracks we rummage through our kit bag, removing the items one at a time to see what we have. We find four different metal and plastic computers including an E6-B used for navigation and computing drift, a stop watch, bombing tables, a flashlight, a screwdriver, a pair of pliers, pencils, erasers and a clip board.

The kit belongs to us now. It'll stay with us as long as we're bombardiers. We test all the computers, moving the plastic arms around and twisting the metal, windowed disc of the E6-B. We try out our stopwatches, staring at the ticking, quivering hand as it sweeps by the tenths of seconds. With my flying clothes and special equipment, I feel I'm a bombardier already.

*   *   *

Down on the flight line where the shiny AT-11's all wait in a row, the instructor explains what we must do before a flight. A pilot in one of the planes starts his engines. They whine and cough then catch in puffs of blue-white smoke. The spinning propellers are trembling silvery discs in the sun. The pungent smells of fuel and grease blend with the fragrance of the desert sage.

"Okay," the instructor shouts. "This is where you pick up your tachometers, and over there's where you'll check out your cameras. Be sure you know how to use them. It's very important that we have a photographic record of every bomb hit. When one cadet bombs, the other must take pictures of the results. You miss the picture and you're in big trouble. You'll be walking a tour for every photograph you miss, so be sure you're alert and know what you're doing. In that low building down the line is where you'll draw your parachute. I guess by now you all know how to use them."

We familiarize ourselves with the inside of the airplane--- the bomb bays, the photographic hatch and the bombardier's compartment in the Plexiglas nose. We check the placement of the instruments we'll use on our bomb runs--- the altimeter, the temperature gauge, air speed indicator and drift meter.

Van Aken and I have met our bombardier instructor, Lieutenant Fairbrother, and like him very much. Having found out that he had one of the highest bombardier scores ever recorded at Midland as a cadet, we feel especially lucky to have him as our teacher.

We stand on the threshold of becoming bombardiers. All the academic training and studying, the long hours creeping across the hanger floor on the bugs, being issued flying clothes and bombardier equipment as well as the familiarizations with the instruments and line operations will mean nothing unless we learn to hit our targets accurately under all kinds of conditions. Despite my successes so far, my premature pride and grand visions of what I'll become, I suddenly feel humble and a little frightened.

Within two days we'll fly among the clouds, pull the soft warm fleece of our flying suits around us against the iciness of altitude and hope that we have the skill to land Easter egg-blue practice bombs on the centers of targets scraped out of the flat plains of Texas.

CHECK RIDE

Our plane bounces like a bucking bronco as I try to synchronize the bombsight's crosshairs on the target several miles ahead, a circular bull's eye etched in the desert. At six thousand feet, playing tag with plump cumulus clouds full of jostling updrafts, I try to keep the concentric circles in sight. The cold wind roars around our twin-tailed AT-11, and leaks through its minute cracks. The instructor and I shout to each other over the vibrating drone of the engines, the propellers whirling right outside the bombardier's compartment. For an instant I think about what might happen if a propeller blade should suddenly snap off, knife through the compartment, skewering us. As we close in on the target, I refine the synchronization of the crosshairs, each minute turn of the knobs guiding the airplane toward the target. The hairs now remain on its center as a cloud shred drifts across it. The instructor peeps in the sight to check the alignment. A last touch of refinement and "bombs away!."

We actually have no bombs with us. Instead, we practice dry runs across the targets to refine our procedure and synchronization from an airplane, a far different experience from the stable ride of the trainers on the smooth hanger floors. Three of us take our turns at the bombsight as the instructor evaluates us.

"Okay, Stevens", says Lieutenant Fairbrother. "Your procedure is fine, and you're getting those hairs right on the target."

261

His words sound sweet to my ears, and I purr with contentment.

At 10,000 feet the following day, we again fly dry runs, still perfecting our techniques. At this higher altitude we sail smoothly through the blue, but any error in synchronizing is magnified, requiring an even more refined touch. When I'm not using the bombsight, I peer out of the Plexiglas at the scene below, the unending stretches of the Texas plains dotted with brush, the wild, desolate land that is ideal for target practice. To the south, from this lofty height, I can see the towns of Midland and Odessa at the same time. I gaze in wonder at the scene far below, the wide horizons, more of the earth than I have ever seen at any one time. I find it humbling to be so small in such vastness. I feel the same way I had at Ellington Field during the hurricane when I felt my insignificance compared to the power of the storm as it raged all around me.

The instructor again approves my performance, a glow of confidence, even smugness settling into my soul. I know I can do it, and I look forward to dropping our first bombs. As we slowly descend, I swallow and yawn to clear my ears. Feeling mellow from success, I don't mind the rough air we encounter at 5000 feet where the scattered cumulus clouds lurk, hoping though that I wouldn't be airsick the way many of the cadets were the day before. I relax near the center of the plane, not fighting the motion, but instead, riding out each jolt and shove, each up and down, with a loose body. Suddenly the bottom drops out of the airplane, leaving me suspended in the air, slamming my knees against the navigation table and depositing me on my posterior near the door close to the bomb bays. Not hurt and still feeling warm about my good review by the instructor, I laugh along with everyone else and climb back in the seat.

* * *

"Bombs away!," I shout the next day as my first robin's egg-blue practice bomb drops slowly toward the earth. It floats silently then gradually curves down as its nose begins to drop. It fades from sight as we crane our necks toward the Plexiglas waiting for the impact. After what seems an eternity, the bomb flashes then puffs into white smoke just fifty feet from the center, just fifty feet from the shack! "Good," says the instructor. I can hardly believe that I'd come that close on my first try. From 10,000 feet I'd placed a bomb only the distance of an average suburban front yard away from the center.

Puffed with confidence, I begin the second run. The crosshairs neatly quadrisect the target, but then, almost imperceptibly, they drift away. As we close on the target, I quickly compensate, and, in my zeal, overcompensate. The plane banks then straightens out again. Better, but still not right. The released bomb sails down where the bombsight has told it to go, where I have told the bombsight to put it.

"Christ! What happened to that one, Stevens?" shouts the instructor as the bomb flashes far over the bulls eye.

Not even close. Clearly the Lieutenant doesn't like what I've just done. The confidence and self-satisfaction that I'd built up on the trainers, all the dry runs and the success of my first bomb, whistles out of me like the air out of a child's untied balloon.

My next bomb falls equally as wild.

"Come on, Stevens. Settle down. You can do it," yells the lieutenant over the roar of the engines.

The rest of my ten bombs finally pop within the white circles of that pale white eye that looks up at me from the gravel of the plain below, mocking me. My mind fills with the agony of those two errant bombs and the frown, the tight-lipped disappointment on the instructor's face.

At the photography hatch farther back in the plane, I take pictures of my partner's bomb strikes. He scatters them everywhere with only a few catching the target. He's always had trouble, and I feel he'll wash out soon. Maybe I will too, if I have any more wild bombs like I had today. I want to be a bombardier with so much passion that I can taste it on my tongue, like the electric tang of metal.

At 13,600 feet on my next flight, my oxygen mask pressed to my face, I carefully calculate the information I must feed into the bombsight. Using the mask, smelling its rubbery odor, the very feel of it on my face, reminds me of the mask the hospital used when I had my tonsils removed as a young child. Ready now, I align my bombsight with the target still some miles ahead, appearing quite small from our altitude. I correctly follow every step in the procedure, and I have no problem synchronizing, the crosshairs sticking on the target as though they belong there. As we approach, I fine-tune with the small, now-natural movements of my fingers on the knobs. A perfect hit seems assured. The bomb sinks in its long silent plunge to the target as I lean toward the Plexiglas, looking for the impact below, one that I feel certain will be right on the shack or damn close to it.

When the flash and smoke appear far beyond the target, I sit stunned before the bombsight.

"There you go, Stevens. You've done it again. What's the matter?" growls the Lieutenant.

My lips freeze. I loosen my mask and explain that everything was perfect in the sight, that it should have been a shack.

"It's your calculations then. Check 'em over, and make sure you have everything right."

I pore over my readings and figures, searching for any kind of error that would have given me such a stray bomb. Finally I discover that, in my haste, I'd misread the altimeter. I'd fed faulty data into the bombsight.

I recalculate the data and adjust my settings. My bombs fall within the target now, although the hits are not especially good. My bomb runs mercifully over for this mission, I crouch near the photography hatch to take pictures of my partner's bomb strikes. I'd done it again. Everything had been perfect except for that one lousy lapse, the misreading of the altimeter. It was the same sometimes in class. I'd tediously worked out long problems that I'd actually understood quite well, only to be tripped up by a careless mistake somewhere in the procedure, a decimal point or a transposed number. Am I a person who habitually makes small errors that result in big ones? Bombardiers can't do this. The cold breath of fear whispers to me. *They will not tolerate mistakes. They are about to wash you out.*

At 13,600 feet the temperature gauge reads 13 degrees. The blast of cold air rushing up through the camera hatch numbs my face, and makes picture-taking a miserable business. Even with my head encased in a flying helmet, goggles over my eyes, my oxygen mask on and my fleece-lined flying jacket collar pulled up around my neck and head, I wither in the cryogenic flow of air. My heart, heavy with the gloom of disappointment and the fear of washing out, is just as cold.

Having descended now, we lurch through the afternoon convection currents as we line up with the runway for landing. Still feeling the sting of my poor performance, I find myself, for a moment, wishing that our plane would pile into the runway, killing us all, ridding my mind of the bitter specter of failure. The airplane tires squeal on the runway as we glide in for a perfect landing. Once down, I walk away from the plane, carrying the burden of my backpack parachute and my own downheartedness.

I am just hanging in the balance tonight.

*   *   *

He's not my regular instructor. His silver captain's bars gleam on his collar more impressively than the gold bars of the second lieutenants who usually ride with me. I understand why he's with me today rather than my regular instructor, and I know what's at stake. A pleasant man with a reassuring air about him, he, nevertheless, will check me out, judge my performance and make a decision about my future training as a bombardier. The few wild bombs I dropped have come back to haunt me. I'm about to have a check ride.

Even though I feel that my life as a bombardier is on the line and that this very flight might decide whether I continue in training, I feel a wave of confidence surge through me. I'd been aching to fly again, to purge myself of dejection, to prove to that I'm a capable bombardier.

At 6800 feet and with ragged clouds floating low over the plains, the targets are difficult to sight. The captain has trouble locating them too. He scrutinizes my procedure, checks my calculations and carefully watches my synchronizations on the bomb runs. With my resurgence of confidence and his calm, approving manner, I relax completely. On every run my bombs fall on or near the shack, and finally add up to the best score I'd ever had. He compliments me on my work and tells me that everything is okay, that I have admirably passed the check ride.

When the tires sing on the runway, the airbase somehow looks sharper and clearer, more exciting than it ever had before.

ASCENDING AND DESCENDING

Far across the hazy desert lie the chalked outlines of shipping docks. In my bombsight the vertical crosshair splits their boundaries, cutting them in two. Minor adjustments on the knurled knobs stop the crosshair's movement. The bombing course is correct. The compass heading reads 295 degrees. Having control of the autopilot, I bank the airplane 18 degrees to the right then, slowly, 18 degrees to the left, zigzagging back and forth during the bomb run, avoiding hypothetical enemy antiaircraft fire. Now, only 30 seconds from the target, I stop the evasive action, pulling the plane back to center, refining the direction until the compass again reads 295 degrees. In the final seconds, my fingers lightly touch the bombsight knobs, turning them only millimeters, fine-tuning. The crosshairs remain fixed on the make-believe docks. With a click, the bomb leaves the rack, drifting downward until it slips out of sight, eventually bursting near the edge of the center dock.

Combat runs seem easier, and my bombs usually fall within the lines. The initial success with the combat bombing eases some of the ever-present strain of training although I still worry. Even when I bomb well, I suffer a nagging anxiety that I can't possibly keep it up.

Back in the barracks I try to relieve some of my tension by expressing my feelings to my parents.

You have no idea of the strain all of us go through. Honest, we don't know whether we will be here the next week or not. Originally we had 220 men in our class. We have lost 70 men so far, and now have only 150 left. Most of the cadets were eliminated for ground schoolwork and on the trainers. That's why we have to keep on our toes, and why we are so uncertain all of the time. It really keeps us worrying.

Several days later, flying at 13,600 feet, we again sight on the docks, bridges and power- houses chalked on the desert. We sweat out each bomb, as they all count on our record. Each miss whittles down our score. Our 60 combat bombs must fall on or close to the chalk drawings. My first bomb, which I think will be perfect, misses the aiming point. The second bomb also goes astray when it shouldn't have. This time it's the fault of a defective mechanism in the bombsight, but everything had been "right", and I'd wasted several potentially good hits. Even though they won't count against me, I feel robbed, and, this time, more angry than dejected.

Well, I am not worrying about it anyway. Since I have been in the Army, I sure have realized how senseless worrying really is. It's just no good whatsoever. In the air, when something goes wrong, I don't get riled or nervous. I have learned to just relax and take it easy. If it's a stupid thing I have done, I either smile or laugh; it's much easier than getting 'tied up' or nervous about it.

What I have written is not exactly true. It is a philosophy of self-control I think I have or want to have, but I often lose sight of it.

From high altitude, my slippery oxygen mask on, I drop my 15th bomb on a circular target. Used to the vibrating din of the airplane engines in the bombardier's compartment by now, as well as the cold, I concentrate on building up my score. I feel the soft rubber eyepiece of the bombsight pressing against my eye. I can waste no more bombs. Each one carries immense importance. Along with the 60 combat bombs, we must drop 40 on the bull's eye targets, having an average error of no more that 230 feet. So far, so good.

* * *

Speeding down the runway, the small lights at its edge flickering by, we sweep up into the vast blackness of the night. The pale lights of small towns appear like phosphorescence floating in a strange dusky sea. From the dark bombardier's compartment, the night sky opens to a whole universe of scattered stars that twinkle crisply in the clear air. The spectacle reminds me of trips to the desert or the mountains in California when I was younger, that clear, deep sparkling of stars that made me feel as though I peered into the beginning of time. The wonder of what I see, for several precious moments, relaxes me, taking my mind off the task of my first night bombing mission.

The engines oscillate, throbbing separately before the pilot deftly adjusts the throttles, blending the quavering beats until they hum together like two synchronous singers. Except for the small purple eye of an ultra-violet lamp, the compartment is dark, the fluorescing instruments and the tips of switches glowing like a frozen swarm of fireflies. I can read the instruments clearly as I search the plains for the targets, the isolated bull's eyes of light. The numbers on my circular plastic computer fluoresce clearly as I move its small arms to the correct readings. Straight ahead, the first target appears almost secretly out of the black void. Catching it in the web of my bombsight hairs, I synchronize on the rings. Bombing is a much more difficult task at night. That brittle voice in my head crackles again, "This is different. This is difficult. You're probably not going to be able to do it." My muscles tighten and my fingers stiffen. The bomb is away. It bursts on the ground like a bright orange flower then quickly fades. Grazing only the outside rim of the circle, it explodes my spirits as well. The second bomb is no better, but the rest bloom around the shack, instantly freshening my outlook and restoring my confidence. Another voice, " I, Norm Stevens, can fly out into the darkness, find a target and hit it dead center."

When we fly at night we eat breakfast between 2230 hours and midnight then sleep until 0900 hours the next morning, a schedule that turns both our physiological and psychological worlds upside down. Just as we soar and land in the AT-11s, my morale rises and falls with the successes or failures of my bomb strikes. It's as though my whole soul has been swept up into this adventure. The all-consuming nature of it even blots out thoughts of home. With becoming a bombardier being more of a personal quest than a goal, I suffer when I don't perform well.

I haven't written for a couple of days because I hardly had the heart to. I had one of those lousy missions you get once in a while. That tears down my morale so that I hardly feel like doing anything. I want to get through here so bad that the slightest messing up really worries me. I am now only four weeks from graduation, and I would hate to have anything happen to me now. We haven't flown for two days now because of weather conditions, and I wish we could fly because I want a chance to try and lift my morale some. I had a swell mission that afternoon, and then, that night, I screwed everything up. My first bomb that night hit only 50 feet away from the center of the target, and the rest went haywire. I am going to try like mad to make that up.

A cold, gray sky presses down on the air base, an icy wind driving a drizzly rain on the verge of crystallizing into snow. Banners of wind-swept darker clouds streak the smooth underside of the overcast, a type of sky I'd never seen before. No one flies today. "Even the birds are walking today," says another cadet. I long to fly again so that I can restore my faith in my ability.

Several weeks ago the cadets two classes ahead of us graduated. They looked snappy in their new officer's uniforms with their silver bombardier's wings gleaming on their chests. So many new officers passed me near the barracks that I nearly wore my arm out saluting them. With obvious relish, they returned them. I admired those dapper young men in their freshly creased pinks and dark green tunics. I want to be like them.

A full, bountiful Thanksgiving dinner presented to all the cadets in the mess hall temporarily turns my mind away from my bouts of anxiety. The staff prepares roast turkey, gravy, oyster dressing, and snowflake potatoes along with traditional candied yams and cranberry sauce. We also had garden-fresh peas and buttered asparagus tips and salad. We have our choice of spice cake, apple pie, ice cream or mixed candies. The base gives each of us a carton of cigarettes. I give mine to the other cadets in my room to fight over.

President Roosevelt's Thanksgiving message appears on our special menu:

"God's help to us has been great in this year of marching toward world-wide liberty. In brotherhood with warriors of other United Nations our gallant men have won victories, have freed our home from fear, have made tyranny tremble, and have laid the foundation for freedom of life in a world which will be free...For all these things we are devoutly thankful, knowing also that so great mercies exact from us the greatest measure of sacrifice and service..."

His abstract words mean little to me as I concentrate on my particular tasks of becoming a bombardier. But the Thanksgiving dinner warms me inside, and turns my thoughts to the Thanksgivings at home where, with good luck, hard work and a hoped-for graduation, I'll be in a few weeks.

* * *

Skimming over the desert at 1000 feet, I struggle to stay in the bombardier's seat, so violent are the updrafts that buffet our plane. We dash in and out of low clouds, searching for the special target set aside for low altitude bombing. Sudden currents slam into the underbelly of the AT-11, catapulting it upward, only to leave it suspended for a moment to fall in what feels like a vacuum. The wild winds thump us into crazy angles as tatters of clouds and the brush-dotted plain pass quickly beneath us. The pilot, having graduated only a short time ago, fights with the controls, trying to maintain level flight and our 1000 feet altitude for bombing.

In between clouds I spot the target ahead, but with the uncontrollable tossing of the airplane, the bombsight crosshairs travel all over the desert. When I try to correct our drift, the inexperienced pilot can't follow the pilot direction indicator. Giving us his best, but not up to the struggle, he tries to hold our altitude. As capricious as the turbulent atmosphere, my confused, senseless bomb explodes far off the target. My partner has no better luck as he scorches the interior of the bombardier's compartment with his earthy cursing. "God damn it! Son of a bitch!" curls out of the compartment with his other expletives. Once on the ground again, I'm relieved to find that all the cadets have had the same problem, yet I still worry.

Not yet finished with low altitude bombing, we again fly at 1000 feet, this time practicing fixed angle bombing. Even though thrown about again in the rough air, I make a triple drift run that I'm proud of, hitting the wind speed and direction right on the nose. I approach the target with the utmost confidence, feeling that it's mine. When the bomb detonates far over the target, my spirits sink once more. After all that perfection and confidence, I blundered. Instead of using the tangent of the dropping angle, I'd set in the dropping angle itself. A small error had again magnified itself into a disastrous result.

After landing, I discover that every cadet in our squadron had trouble. The whole mission was a fiasco. Only two cadets managed to even hit the target. Six cadets accidentally released their bombs off the bombing range. My regular partner who flew in another airplane today started a grass fire with his first bomb and lobbed his second one into a group of grazing cattle. Another cadet scattered a whole army of jackrabbits.

Flying night and day to take advantage of good or sometimes marginal weather, I feel as though I live in airplanes, that I have lost contact with the earth. Each time we take off for a mission we must spend a minimum of two hours in the air. The icy breath of winter adds its chill to every flight as well as every walk to the barracks, the mess hall or the flight line. We take off at night when the temperatures on the ground are below freezing then climb to altitudes where it is much colder. We snuggle into our fleece-lined flying suits, but still shiver when we open the bomb bays and the camera hatch, the airplane becoming an aluminum deep freeze.

Despite the cold and the long hours of flying, I still enjoy the spectacle of night, the all-enveloping blackness with its scattering of stars and the dim lights of far off towns. One night on the way back from the range, we fly between two layers of clouds, both tinted blue by the light of the full moon. It's as though we're suspended in a vast, vaporous cave of incredible wonder.

I've now dropped all the bombs that will be on my record, both on the combat targets and the desert bull's eyes. Even though I suffered the agony of some poor hits and endured a gut-wrenching fear of washing out, most of my bombs had been good. Like competing athletes, most of us had our good days and our bad, but our thrust had been forward. Ten more cadets, including my flying partner and roommate, Van Aken, wash out in the final weeks of flying.

I think back about my worries. Instead of reveling in my strengths, I'd had a tendency to think little of myself, counting each success as a fluke or a lucky break.

All through training I'd been told by others that the tasks ahead were nearly impossible, and I believed them. But I'd chipped away at the frightful obstacles until they seemed smaller and smaller and finally faded away altogether. I consider thinking more about just who I am.

THE GHOST PLANE

Exhausted after flying missions during the day and another long one at night, I stumble into the barracks with only one thought in mind, to slither into bed after a hot shower and sleep away my fatigue. In our room the five of us chat about our bomb strikes, and complain about how tired we are as we sit on our bunks slipping off our shoes and unbuttoning our shirts. Some cadets already pad down the hallway, shouting to each other on their way to the gang showers. Parris lights a cigarette, one more before his shower. The bluish smoke curls then drifts into wispy layers like thin clouds.

Suddenly cadet officers appear at our door and in the hallway ordering everyone to dress and report in formation outside the barracks.

"On the double now!" they shout. "We want all of you, and I mean every one of you out there in five minutes."

As usual, they give us no explanation, no hint of why we have to report there. Ours is only to do and not to question.

"Christ! What did we do now?" gripes one cadet as he pushes his legs into his trousers. "What the hell. Why are they calling us out at this time of night?" grumbles another.

Resigned now, the complaints cease, and we reluctantly dress as fast as possible. It seems cruel to me to have an inspection at this late hour, but we never know what the officers are thinking.

Out in front of our barracks in the dusky light, we shuffle into our regular positions. Cadets from adjoining barracks also line up. A blanket of low clouds hangs over the air base, a penetrating chill riding on the moist air. The red light blinks on top of the checkered water tower. The low clouds and damp air muffle the occasional sound of an aircraft engine from the flight line.

"All right men," shouts the tactical officer, "I want it absolutely quiet. When your name is called, I want you to shout out your response loud and clear. It's very important that we do this right."

The officer begins calling the names, the cadets answering with a loud, "Hyo!" I can't understand why the officers think it necessary to bring us out here just for roll call. Perhaps someone has gone A.W.O.L., but the whole procedure seems ridiculous to me.

As the cadets continue answering to their names, the group becomes more somber. Whispers circulate through the ranks like a cold wind.

"They lost a plane out there tonight. One of the planes went down."

I swallow it all in stunned silence, realizing that a person might die even in training long before he ever reached the dangers of combat. I think about some of my friends and wonder if they might have been on the flight. I feel my jaws tighten and my intestines roil. The sobering chill of the tragedy tempers the silliness, innocence and naiveté of my boyhood, and I feel instantly older.

As we stand together in our military-straight lines, I hear airplane engines somewhere in the hovering clouds. The droning of them, although muted by clouds and distance, is clear. Struck by the enormity of the accident and the probable deaths of cadets, I fantasize that it's their plane searching for the airport. For a few moments I see the straight, but fog-shrouded beams of landing lights probing for a place to settle in. I imagine it as a ghost plane, the spirit of the crashed plane and its young men hunting for a way back. Gooseflesh travels down the length of my arms.

As my "ghost plane" becomes a normal transient plane coming in for an instrument landing, the officer addresses us in a subdued but clear voice.

"Will the following cadets answer to their names if they are here." After hesitating, he reads the first name.

"Earl Barney."

Only silence. Absolute silence.

"Gerard Cuddy." Again, everyone is quiet.

"Gordon Eskelsen." No voice.

"Gentlemen," says the officer, "It grieves me to have to tell you that we have lost a plane out there tonight and with it, three of your fellow cadets and a young pilot. I'm sorry we had to bring you out here, but it's the only way we can positively identify who was actually on the plane. I'm deeply distressed by what happened. Dismissed."

In loose clumps of somber men we make our way into the barracks. Scraps of information and rumors float from one group to another.

"Some of the cadets saw a fireball on the desert."

"They couldn't possibly be alive."

"When the clouds socked in, the pilot probably had vertigo. You know, with no references he believes what his body tells him and not his instruments then he spun in."

I had known Earl Barney well. With several other cadets I had been chatting with him earlier in the evening. I liked him because he was funny and friendly. No matter how tense our lives became at times, we could count on Barney to make us laugh. I never knew him not to smile. He found life to be a relaxed humorous adventure, discovering mirth in every situation. Unlike me, he excelled without being too serious or tense or depressed. Always talking and cracking jokes, he seemed to stand taller than he actually was, even when he bent slightly forward as was his habit, possibly his antidote for military stiffness. I see him with his cap peaked over his wavy hair, his narrow laughing eyes and an eternal smile on his lips.

The gruesome thought of his torn body among the twisted aluminum of the airplane somewhere out on the dark plains disturbs me all through the night. I think about what he might have been but never would be. I try to cope with the suddenness of it all and the shock of his death.

*　*　*

We hear that one of the Davis brothers, both pilots at the gunnery school at Laredo, had been killed. His AT-6 hit another, killing himself, the other pilot and two student gunners. I remember the day that Davis harassed our plane on the way back to the base. He tucked his wing into us just inches from the fuselage then placed the tip over ours so that they nearly touched. He placed his wing directly over our rudder then lowered it as closely as he could. Like a mischievous schoolboy, he grinned and laughed at us as he played. I didn't like his teasing, and my pilot didn't either. Although Davis was a skilled pilot with lightning reflexes, he pushed his talents to the limit, risking his own safety and that of others.

The accidents did not make me fearful or skittish because I trust the aircraft and the pilots, if they are cautious and mature. Accidents happened in all areas of life, and not being a victim was sometimes a matter of skill or foresight, but usually of blind luck, being in the wrong place at the wrong time, a roll of the dice, a blip in the law of averages.

*　*　*

I don't write to my parents about the accident at Midland because I fear I might worry them. Earlier I expressed my faith in flying in an effort to reassure them, blaming most accidents on pilots, not airplanes.

You were talking about so many aircraft accidents and this investigation. If you want my frank opinion, they don't need to investigate the planes, just the pilots. As long as I have been in the Air Corps, I have only known of one accident. Two student pilots were killed while I was at Ellington. They crashed about twenty miles from the field, and I didn't see it. At Laredo there had been only one crash since the field began. There is nothing dangerous about a plane. It is built to fly and is extremely hard to crack up unless the pilot is fooling around. Most accidents are caused by so-called hot pilots.

I think much more about the lost men than the dangers of flying. I silently mourn for Barney, but I have no hesitation about climbing into the small door of the AT-11 for another flight. As much as his death touches me, I think it inconceivable that it's a prelude to mine. The AT-11s and their pilots that sweep us up into the sky are reliable and trustworthy. My own death seems as remotely imaginary to me as the ghost plane that flew through my mind for those few moments that tragic night.

NEGLIGENCE OF DUTY, INSUBORDINATION AND OTHER SINS

Glaring at me as though I'd personally insulted him, the sergeant repeats his question.

"Where's the scale, Stevens? If you don't have it on you, you're gonna have to walk back to the plane and get it."

Other cadets in their flying suits crowd into the small office to return their equipment, jostling each other as they hand over their scales, tachometers and tables. The sergeant flips the pages on his clipboard as he checks off their names. I back away, sitting down on a wooden bench to search for the silly little scale, a strip of metal about six inches long and a quarter inch wide that fits on one arm of the bombsight. I fumble through my kit and probe my pockets, but I can't find it. Finally I have to confess to the disgusted sergeant that I just don't have it.

"Okay," he grumbles, "Back to the plane then---and I'm not going to stay around here all day."

Weary from an uninterrupted procession of flying missions, I push out of the screen door, letting it bang behind me. I trudge along the concrete flight line, heading straight for the plane that had just brought us back after a two-hour mission. Without a line taxi in sight, I plod along the ramp, passing along the straight lines of silver AT-11s. Nearby, a mechanic tests the engines on one of them, the propellers racing in diaphanous discs. The changing pitch of the propellers spins out a flat rapping violence that carries far out into the plains. My airplane still appears to be a quarter mile ahead. I can feel the difficulty of the last mission and my lack of sleep in the heaviness of my legs as I struggle along the grease-stained concrete. An AT-11 turning toward the taxiway bathes me in its dusty, exhaust-tainted prop wash. I glance down at the concrete, thinking I might have dropped the tiny scale on the way in.

Once in the plane, I scurry into the Plexiglas fishbowl of a nose to check the bombsight. When my first glance tells me that the scale isn't on the bombsight arm, I feel a vacuum in the pit of my stomach, like I've felt in an elevator when it descended too fast. I search the rest of the bombardier's compartment, the crawlways, the navigation room and the catwalk between the bomb bays, all without luck. Empty-handed, I begin the long trek back to the equipment office.

"You're in trouble, Stevens," scowls the sergeant. "I'm gonna have to report this you know."

I bump my way out of the screen door, and amble back to the barracks alone. I don't know how they'll discipline me for the loss of the equipment, but I know from the facts of cadet life that, at least, I'll be walking many white-gloved tours.

*   *   *

Punchy after a long, high altitude bombing mission, I wander off the flight line into the ready room to check the board for my next mission. Possibly my oxygen mask had leaked or the oxygen system in the plane had been inadequate, or maybe I'm simply suffering from fatigue, but I walk around in the room as though I'm in a trance. The shuffling cadets, some wearing parachute straps over their flying suits, the Coca-Cola machine and even the square-paned windows seem distant and out of focus. Edging over to the schedule board with all its lines and squares and chalked-in names, I look for information about my next flight. Wanting to plan my time, especially to find an hour or so to rest, but not finding any details, I search for someone in authority who might know.

Finally I spot a tall officer in a dark green uniform at the edge of a clot of cadets. In my unthinking stupor, I amble over to him.

"Say, can you tell me when they're going to put up the schedule for the next flights?"

At first he stares at me with a blank, unbelieving look, his mouth open, his dark eyes boring into me. He screws up his face in an expression of bottled rage.

"Haven't you ever learned to address an officer as Sir, Mister?"

Suddenly I realize the enormity of what I've done. Much taller than I, he now seems twice as tall, his uniformed eminence towering over me, his polished silver first lieutenant's bar gleaming with blinding light. Fire leaps out of his narrowed eyes, his face flushed with anger.

"How long have you been here anyway? This is about the worst incident I've ever seen! We're not going to stand for any insubordination around here! What's your name, Mister?"

Nearly speechless and feeling helpless, I reply in a weak voice, "I'm sorry sir. My name is Aviation Cadet Charles N. Stevens."

"What flight are you in?"

"43-18, Sir."

"This'll not be the last of this, Mister. You've shown the most blatant disrespect for an officer that I've ever seen."

"Yes, Sir."

The lieutenant storms away carrying a white card in his hand with my name and flight number and I know not what else.

I had no intention of being disrespectful. I simply hadn't thought. I couldn't explain my actions or offer excuses. I had to swallow it all. I can still hear Lieutenant Cannady, my instructor on the trainers, warning me after I'd failed to address him as "Sir."

"You better watch out, Stevens. You better get in the habit of calling me, Sir. If you don't, you're liable not to say it to some chicken shit officer, and then you'll be in real trouble."

What he had so kindly warned me about that day, I had done anyway.

* * *

After forgetting about the incidents for several days, I receive a notice in the barracks that I'm to report to Major Smith promptly at 1300 hours. I know why he wants to see me. Later, with my tie straight and my uniform clean and pressed, I walk down the asphalt street towards the major's office. Butterflies flutter and grasshoppers jump in my belly.

Once inside the office, I stop at the aide's desk. Looking up from his typewriter and neat stacks of orders, he tells me the major is waiting for me, that I should go right in. I march straight from the doorway to his desk, snap to attention, salute smartly.

"Aviation Cadet Charles N. Stevens reporting, Sir."

The stone-faced major looks directly at me.

"At ease, Mister."

I spread my legs comfortably, and join my hands behind my back, but remain standing in front of his massive desk.

"Two serious charges have been made against you, Mister, charges we don't take lightly in cadet training. On separate occasions within the past few days you have been charged with negligence of duty and insubordination. You failed to return a sensitive piece of equipment that had been charged out to you and signed for, but the most flagrant of all was your glaring disrespect for a superior officer. What do you have to say about all this, Mister?"

With firmness and with as much honesty as I can muster, I utter the only reply possible.

"No excuse, Sir."

"You know, Mister," he continues, "we don't just train bombardiers here, we train future officers. Those officers will always carry out their duties and show the utmost respect for any rank above their own. We can't function without this discipline. We have to decide whether you are officer material or not, or whether you even belong in cadet training. If any more serious charges are leveled against you, you'll find yourself a flight officer rather than a second lieutenant when you graduate, or you may not graduate at all. I've ordered you to walk tours this entire coming weekend. Perhaps you'll have time to think about your actions while you walk. Dismissed!'

I give him a crisp salute, execute an about face and march out of his office.

* * *

With a tie binding my neck, white gloves stretched over my hands and a phony rifle slung over my shoulder, I pace the gravel lot in a straight line. Reaching the end of the yard, I perform an about face then walk the other way, hour after endless hour. The major's words are still with me. Thoughts spin in my mind like scraps of paper, dust and bits of brittle brush in a whirlwind. Others would not guess, seeing my stoic expression and my straight-ahead, far away look that so much action stirs behind my forehead.

Many other cadets also walk tours. We appear like a child's game, marching back and forth in our single line, like animated tin soldiers to be shot at by little boys with cork guns. I had walked tours at Midland before for neglecting a haircut, missing pictures of another cadet's bombs, being seated improperly at the mess hall and not passing inspections. Most of us had walked tours at one time or another because the perfection demanded of us had been simply greater than the capabilities of normal human beings.

I had wanted a pass into the town of Midland, but every weekend some unknown situation would arise to prevent it. Tours could only be walked on weekends, and I had a number to walk. Once, a violation of correct procedure in the mess hall had restricted all of us to our barracks. Several weekends I had had to study in order to pass my examinations, and the onset of winter weather had so delayed our required flying time that we had to fly on weekends. Perhaps there is not much to see in town, but I'm curious nevertheless.

The major's words; negligence of duty and insubordination! The terms sounded as though I had placed the whole Air Corps, possibly even the entire country, in jeopardy, that I had profaned my uniform, violated my sacred trust and stained the good name of the armed services. Actually, I had only lost a little piece of metal, and had, in a moment of fatigue, neglected to call an officer, Sir, acts that don't seem very serious to me. They are certainly incidents that my parents would have understood and immediately forgiven, but the Army Air Corps is another world.

The major had threatened me with the rank of Flight Officer when or if I graduated, a rank just below second lieutenant. Flight officers wear a small blue bar, rounded at the ends, rather than the full gleaming gold bar of the second lieutenant. A certain percentage of all graduating cadets were always commissioned flight officers, but none of us understood how the cadets were selected to fit each category. I feared that it was determined by the age of the cadet, and since I had just reached my nineteenth birthday at Midland while the rest were all in their lower or mid twenties, that I was sure to become a flight officer. Now with the warning from the major that I had screwed up so miserably in his eyes, I'm sure that, should I happen to graduate, I'll be a blue-barred flight officer.

I walk on, the sound of my shoes and those of the other cadets crunching on the dusty gravel. Our toy-soldier shadows lengthen in the afternoon sun, stretching out across the bare drill field. Our tours are nearly over. I like flying, and I like being a cadet, but I'll never fully understand or tolerate the rigid, unflinching, discipline of the Army Air Corps.

THE WAY WITH SOME TEXANS

"The moon is prettier in Texas than it is in any other state," boasts the curly-headed cadet in his nasal Texan accent. "You just look at it," he continues. "The full moon coming up over Texas is better than it is anywhere else. Damn it, all you have to do is look at it."

As we chuckle and roll our eyes at him, we remind him that the moon looks good to us in our states too, but he remains adamant. Most amazing is that while he makes such an outlandish statement, his facial expression is deadly serious. Funny at first, I soon understand that the cadet actually believes what he's saying. Those piercing brown eyes set in that tanned face clearly challenge anyone to differ with him.

"Texas brags" is a slogan I learn early. Not only is it the largest state, but also the Texans claim to have the biggest and best of everything---the greatest cities, the prettiest girls, the sweetest oranges, the bravest men, the finest cattle and now the most beautiful moon.

* * *

"Oh, a prune picker," taunts another Texan when I tell him I'm from California. "Ah California," he goes on. "The land of the fruits and nuts."

These Texans also bolster their chauvinism by running down or poking fun at people from other places. They take a special delight in kidding people from my state as they've heard, and firmly believe, that California, with its permissive climate, produces strange people with weird and zany ideas and oddballs who champion crackpot causes.

"I was out there in California once," chides another Texan. "We were going through some hills covered with scrubby brush when we came to a sign that says, 'Leaving Angeles National Forest.' We like to died laughing. They call that a forest? There was nothing but shrubs there."

"That was just land owned by the Forest Service," I say back at him. "The largest and oldest trees anywhere in the world grow in California in Sequoia National Park."

Paying little attention to me he adds, "If you want to see some real forests, come to Texas."

Generally I fend off what they say good-naturedly, but some of their other ideas grate on my sensibility.

* * *

"You've never screwed a heifer?" taunts one cadet, his pale blue eyes full of mischief. "You really haven't?" he asks again as he runs his hand through his short blond hair.

Confused and hardly knowing what a heifer is, I clip off a quick "No."

"Hell," he goes on, "You're not a man in Texas unless you've had a heifer."

He clearly enjoys the shock value of his words. Thinking it's only a joke, I hardly know what to say.

"Well, I guess I'll just remain a boy then," I respond.

"We've all done it, but you've really got to watch those heifers. This 'ole boy I knew, he lined himself up in back of the heifer, dropped his coveralls and was about ready when it dumped a load right in his pants. God damn he was mad at that fool cow."

I chuckle at his story since I think it serves the guy right for being such an idiot.

"Some guys really get it bad," he rambles on. "I heard about a soldier that got drunk and crawled into a cattle truck looking for some action. They found the guy the next morning sound asleep on the cattle truck floor covered with dung."

The stories sound to me as though they originate from outer space, strange signals emanating from some dark corner of the universe. They are so alien to my way of life, and my experiences, that I can hardly comprehend them.

I find many young Texan males to be obsessed with "being a man" and the necessary steps to become one. Being a man or becoming manly is important to me too, but to the Texans it's a passion. Perhaps it's the final gasp of the frontier spirit when a "man had to be a man" to survive or perhaps they still live out the legend of the cowboy. I'm proud when my beard grows faster or that I can compete athletically with other men, but I have no list of what I must do to become a man. To me, their concern for manhood seems exaggerated and ridiculous.

* * *

Derogatory nicknames for other races or religions had never been used in my home or by anyone that I knew well. My parents always had respect for other groups and so had I. Hearing these names used as loosely and naturally as any other term disturbs me. Expressing contradictory thoughts about races, especially about Negroes, always brought the same response.

"Yeah, well out in California you don't live among 'em. You don't know 'em the way we do. Down here they know their place."

No middle ground exists. A person either hates black people or he is called a "nigger lover," a term often applied to me.

"We've got a sign in our town," says another cadet from Texas. "It reads, 'Nigger, Don't let the sun set on you in this town.' Believe me, they don't hang around after dark."

With other southerners, the Texans talk about whether they would ever salute Negro officers.

"Not me," says one. "I'm never going to salute one no matter what rank he is. If I see one comin', I'm gonna pretend I don't even see him. I'm gonna walk right on by."

"You're not saluting the man, you're saluting the rank," argues another, but he's hooted down.

I'd seen separate toilets and drinking fountains for coloreds and whites, the most outward symbol of segregation. There are no Negro cadets at Midland nor do Negroes associate with us in any way except to serve us in the mess hall. They wear dark trousers with white coats, politely bringing steaming bowls of food to our tables and clearing our dirty dishes afterwards. They perform all the drudgery of K.P. work, as the cadets have no time for it. An all-Negro group competes in our marches, sometimes winning over the WAAC's who are also segregated.

Giving races names dehumanizes them the way names like "Jap" and "Jerry" dehumanize the enemy, making it easier to hate them or stereotype them. It's easier to kill a person who " is not quite human."

* * *

I felt sorry for my Japanese school acquaintances---Yukiko Katsumata, Michiko Matsunaga, George Sato and even "Fuji" who used to pester me in junior high school. After Pearl Harbor, they'd simply disappeared from school. Newspaper photographs showed large groups of Japanese-American families with their meager possessions stepping off of Pacific Electric red cars at a collection center at Santa Anita Race Track, and others being dispersed by train or buses to relocation centers inland. Because several Japanese-American vegetable men in Inglewood markets had been beaten up, I felt that the relocation camps would protect them.

I'd winced on the local Inglewood bus when the driver turned to some of the passengers in front, his bus grinding up the Hyde Park hill, and said, "You know what I'd do with those Japs. I'd put 'em all on a raft, tow it out to sea, then sink it." I knew I didn't feel that way about the Japanese people as a whole, just the men of the Japanese army and navy who were killing American men.

Some of the Texans I knew, with their primitive hatred for anyone different, saved a very special part of their ire for homosexuals.

"The pasty-faced bastards," snarls one cadet. "You can always tell queers by the way their faces look and the way they mince around. We had one of the bastards in our town. A bunch of the guys cornered him one day and beat the shit out of him. Served him right."

I knew very little about homosexuality or even whether I had ever seen a homosexual or not, but pummeling someone just because he was different seems cruel to me. We had always laughed and joked about homosexuality among ourselves with standard kidding remarks like "wearing our shorts backward" or "playing 'drop the soap' in the shower" or even "two-handed grab ass", but they remained jokes, nothing more.

Some Texans and other Southerners seem to still fight the Civil War, talking about it often, shouting their defiance and calling anyone from the north a "damn Yankee." I gather that the defeated remember defeats much more than victors remember victories. The Texans' fighting to the last man at the Alamo, a battle they still sing about in their "national anthem," is thought of more as a war fought by a country than a state. They are also fond of declaring that "Texas can secede from the Union anytime it wants to," and that's what some want to do, have a country of their own.

In my effort to make sense out of what I see and hear, I conclude that a real Texas man is Texas-born, white, Protestant and heterosexual. He's leery of anyone different from himself---any other race, any other religion, and any persons who deviate from the sexual norm or anyone from outside his state. He's the most self-centered primitive I've yet met.

All Texas men, of course, are not like this. My closest companion in the service is from Beaumont, Texas, and has none of these tendencies. He is fair, honest and gentle, doesn't worry about whether he's a man or not and doesn't run down other races. But enough of the cadets from Texas do. My mind naturally groups them together. My harshness in judging them is even sharper because I've been in the state too long, away from home. I'm tired of the endless nothingness of the Texas plains, the nasal twang of Texas voices, their homespun metaphors, their blind intolerance and bragging. I'm sick of their puny sour oranges and long for a good sweet California one. I'm even weary of how big the state is; we travel for hundreds of miles in any direction, and never get out of it. I write to my parents that if we should ever take a trip across the United States after the war, we are to avoid touching Texas. I'm homesick. It's time to go home.

THE SQUEAK OF SNOW

Walking gingerly over a thin carpet of fresh-fallen snow, the crystals squeaking and crunching beneath my shoes, I pull the collar of my officer's trench coat around my neck against the icy wind. Having never heard snow squeak beneath my soles before, I, like a child, delight in its strange sound. Behind me I leave dark, shallow footprints. With sunrise still an hour away, only the outside lights guide my way past the barracks and supply buildings. Streaming past the lights like swarms of wind-driven moths, the snowflakes slant downward in cold muffled silence. The flakes drifting by the lights remind me of the only other snow I had ever seen---that wonderful morning nearly ten years before when a rare snow storm whitened my hometown in California, the town where I hope to be again in a matter of hours. Back then the snow swept past our porch light in the same way, our frightened cat with a white layer on her back bounding up to the porch and dashing into the warmth of the house.

I hunch my shoulders against the frigid morning and take care with each unsure step, but I feel a warm glow inside. I try to comprehend the great change in my life and what the coming hours and days will hold. I had won my bombardier's wings, graduating as a second lieutenant rather than the flight officer I expected to be. Not only am I an officer wearing my fresh uniform and silver wings beneath my trench coat, but I'm also about to go home for the first time in eight months. I can hardly imagine how I'll feel walking into my own home again, eating once more at the dinner table, basking in the warmth of family and friends. I think about presenting myself to them in my new, razor-pressed pinks, my fresh tunic with its gleaming gold shoulder bars and silver wings. If all goes according to plan, I should reach home on Christmas Day in time for gifts, dinner with the whole family and the crisp scent of the Christmas tree. Will Pal know me? Will he bounce up to me with his tail wagging and punch me in the stomach with his paws or will he bark at me as though I'm a stranger?

Nearly a week before the graduation ceremony, as we filled out forms, I knew I would be a second lieutenant, but the sensation didn't seem real. I feared they might have made a mistake, and then would have to correct it later. I saw it on the page, looking back at me, "Charles N. Stevens, 2nd Lt., serial number 0704242." Tailors from Midland came out to the base for last-minute alterations of our uniforms, and pictures were taken for our officer's passes.

Yesterday we signed about a thousand forms. One of them is my Honorable Discharge from the United States Army. Now I'm in the Army of the United States. Silly, isn't it. These legalities in the Army are really queer sometimes.

*   *   *

With a scattering of parents in attendance, the graduation ceremony was short and simple. I rejoiced in the pinning on of my wings, as I had worked so hard and suffered so much apprehension to get them. They made me feel that all the sweating had been worth it. I'd tossed in a turbulent sea of worry, sunk into the abyss of depression when I failed, and studied until I thought my head could hold no more. I flew what seemed a hundred hours, prepared for examinations and endured physical training to the point of exhaustion. I felt the uncompromising sting of army discipline, but now, looking down at the wings on my chest, I'm content.

With all the trials now passed, I think back more fondly about my twelve weeks at Midland. I loved hurtling down the runway in the AT-11s enveloped in the vibrating din of their engines, the pressure on our backs, the swift rising over the brush-dotted desert, our ears popping as we rose. I thrilled at the unparalleled views of the earth from high altitude and the magical sensation of flying at night with its intricate patterns of blackness and lights. I had the sheer joy of touching clouds, being in them and among them, the clouds that I had only seen from the earth for so long, the same parade of clouds that fascinated me since boyhood. I learned to ride the violence of air currents and let my body flow with them. I felt the satisfaction of scoring a good bomb hit, the thrill of "getting a shack."

I had formed fast friendships with Van Aken, Bachuber, Ballentyne and Parris. We talked, complained, studied and flew together. We all wanted our wings and our officer's bars, and our attitudes meshed amazingly well. I felt the warmth of their friendliness as we walked to the base theater, our feet scuffling through the night with our bubbling laughter, to see the latest Hollywood films, "Henry Aldrich Haunts a House," "Gildersleeve on Broadway" or "Thousands Cheer" with June Allison, which we managed to see three times. We sucked up thick vanilla malts together in the PX then shopped for toilet articles and special Air Corps stationery. I cherish our camaraderie, especially now that we are about to be dispersed in many different directions.

I hadn't realized how much I could learn with diligent study and without tempting diversions. I never understood the value of a burning goal, a channeled direction. I didn't know what my capacity was until I felt the glow of top grades on examinations. I learned what I never dreamed of in high school, that I was as capable as nearly anyone else. I acquired a self-discipline that made my efforts in high school seem childish and anemic. In my newfound confidence I discovered the seed of a thought---that I might attend college after the war.

I relished the well prepared and pleasantly served meals at the mess hall. Always hungry, I was curious and excited about the steaming bowls of food being carried to the tables. I ate ravenously especially at breakfast when I nearly always heaped my favorite food on my plate, fried potatoes.

I even enjoyed the novelty of our three-day bivouac out on the plains where we pitched tents among the brush and dug shallow foxholes in the gravely soil. We slept out under the stars in our tents then retrieved our shoes the next morning, stiff and whiskered with frost. We dashed into our foxholes when low flying AT-11s bombed us with small bags of flour, ate out of mess kits at field kitchens and filled our canteens from Lister bags hanging down like great udders from tripods of poles.

*   *   *

I'm giddy with thoughts of home and the realization that I'm actually going. Nearly oblivious to the drift of snowflakes, I think about what I've requested at home, what I've been promised and what I want to do there. Strohmeyers pledged a chicken dinner in their home, a promise I hope they don't forget. I'm anxious to taste the sweetness of California oranges again after a steady diet of the Texas variety. I want to see my mother's aunt, "Auntie" to me and my sister, who has been ill, and my grandmother who suffered from a stroke.

To my parents I've made special requests for dishes I've missed. First is "Italian Delight", a wonderful mixture of noodles, ground beef, tomatoes, onions and corn. Second are tamales, large, luscious XLNT tamales tied together with string at each end, and, beneath the paper wrapper, real cornhusks that surround thick masa and the fiery insides. My father taught me to adore them laced generously with tomato catsup. Never had any Mexican food been prepared for us in the Army mess halls, and I'd sorely missed its spiciness. I want canned Boston brown bread, steamed, sliced and lathered with butter that melts down into it. Lastly I want to taste my mother's baked beans, her famous recipe that she always created lovingly from "scratch." Every relative admired them, and I wanted that special taste again, with all its associations.

Most of all I want to stand in my own house, feel the power of my father's grip, the warm embrace of my mother and hugs from my sister. I look forward to the music of their voices, the light in their eyes, their tender looks. I want to see Pal curled on the floor shaking and whimpering in his dreams, my mother rustling in the kitchen and the sigh of wind in the casuarina trees. In my mind I see my old room in the garage again with the large map of the United States on the wall, the picture chart of cloud types on the ceiling and the provocative photographs of Veronica Lake and Alexis Smith on the wall above my bed. I think about strolling through my backyard past my wooden weather tower, the chicken yard and even the old rubbish heap. I hope to hear roosters crowing again in the morning, the Santa Fe freight train chugging up the grade in the evening and the hollow rolling of the number five cars on the rails by the cemetery.

I'm about to melt into the source of the daily letters I'd received and close the gap between my loneliness and the warm, gentle-voiced people who love me. My parents and friends sent me letters and even newspapers from home, and, now and then, I received cookies and walnuts, handkerchiefs and socks. A cadet next door ate most of the walnuts, and the cookies vanished quickly in the larcenous fingers of cadets who heard about my cache. I welcomed a package of California oranges and a watch with a luminous dial from my parents. I received a leather writing kit from my girlfriend, a box of cookies from my relatives, Louise and Justice, and a container of fudge from my Aunt Mary. The other cadets and I agreed that they were the creamiest and tastiest we had ever popped into our mouths. Now I would see them all again.

With the snow still squeaking wonderfully beneath my shoes, I plod on. Within hours we'll leave, a half dozen of us in two cars with drivers from Midland who had agreed to drive us to points in California, Oregon and Washington for a price. With trains and airplanes solidly booked for the holidays, this is our only alternative. The snow falls softly like a hushed sinking of the darkness, but in my mind, I speed westward over the Texas plains, each moment drawing nearer to the people and places I love.

A TRIP NORTH

      Gazing out of the Pullman window at a wintry world, I immerse myself in the warm memories of my just-ended furlough at home. I also think about resuming army life again at yet another new place, Salt Lake City, Utah. Snow had blanketed the ground even below Caliente, Nevada. As the Union Pacific train rolls northward, the snow only becomes deeper, whitening the desert floor and fluffing every shrub with cotton. The sheltered sides of rocks, isolated trees, weather-beaten cabins and gas stations appear black in contrast. Whey-colored clouds hide the sun. The landscape lies colorless---a frozen wasteland of white, gray and scatterings of black. Clouds of steam from the locomotive drift by my window, linger in the freezing air.

      The Pullman wheels click over the rails as the porter finishes putting up the beds and reassembling the green seat cushions. Many of the passengers wear service uniforms, all of them on the move to bases scattered over the country. A few fresh lieutenants like me are on their way to Salt Lake City. I recognize or know some of them, especially Walter Kelson whom I have known since San Antonio. Shorter than I, he compensates for his lack of height by assuming a military bearing and a serious expression. I always liked him, and we often went places together, sharing our common interests and the intensity of our goals.

      I had a long time to think before the rocking and swaying of the upper berth lulled me to sleep. I thought about my ten-day furlough at home, the leave I dreamed about for eight long months. Before the furlough, I constantly thought about being home, polishing the idea in my imagination so much, that my mind transformed it into a gleaming magical place, an Eden or Utopia. I thoroughly enjoyed my stay---seeing my parents and friends, my girlfriend again, immersing myself in the familiar---the house, my room, the yard, my dog. I strolled the streets of my hometown again and sat in the same theaters where I once watched Saturday afternoon matinees. I tasted home cooking, enjoying the delectable dishes I wished for. But the reality of being home could not possibly match the vision of it that I nourished in my imagination.

Nestling my head on the Pullman pillow and listening to the faint whistle of the locomotive echoing out over the desert, I continued mulling the furlough over in my mind. I was ecstatic when I first met my family, hugging them warmly once again, hearing their voices. They admired my new uniform and my wings, and I stood back puffed with pride to let them gaze at me. I liked being taken care of again, and being surrounded by people who were interested in me because they loved me. I slipped into the familiar much as an exhausted traveler might slide into a bed lined with smooth, silky sheets.

As the furlough days flickered by, however, I began to feel that I'd never been away. I was a boy again in my own house. I felt that I'd only dreamed of the adventures I'd been living for so long. All my military experiences began to become ethereal, as though I only imagined them, but there it was, hanging on the closet door, my officer's uniform with its gold bars and burnished wings. I always wore it at home, never wanting to dress in civilian clothes because I liked who I had become. As much as I loved being home, I began to feel like a child again, not the man I wanted to be.

I enjoyed talking to my parents and friends about my experiences, but I sensed that they, especially my mother, couldn't really understand them. They listened politely, paid attention and responded when they could, but they couldn't feel how it was for me. To them my adventures were all abstract, merely words thinly dressed with what few associations and emotions their minds could supply. Possibly I tried to tell them too much. I began to realize what I should have known, that only those who have lived an experience, have had it traced on their nerve paths and pumped through their blood can fully comprehend it.

I also began to realize the power of longing. While I was stationed far away from home for so many months, I yearned to be home, but after I arrived, there was nothing to long for anymore. That whole dimension, that passionate wanting to be home had been lost, leaving me with an unexplainable feeling of emptiness.

*   *   *

Nearing Salt Lake City, I see little change in the bleak picture outside of my Pullman window. The weathered fence posts and telegraph poles flicker by, all plastered on one side with snow. Already I've begun to think fondly of home again, and I'm apprehensive about resuming barracks life, yet I look forward to new places and new experiences. A double helix of thought wraps itself around my mind. On the one hand I want the warmth, love and security of my home and family, to be a boy again, and on the other, I desire the excitement of new adventures, striking out in new directions, being an independent person with my own life to live, being a man.

My parents saw me off at Union Station in Los Angeles, my father struggling mightily with my barracks bag crammed with all my belongings. We finally gave it to the Railway Express Agency to take care of. I bid them goodbye with the same enthusiasm with which I had greeted them when I arrived. I would miss them. As I'm thinking about them, Kelson stops by, sitting in the seat opposite me. He was

on furlough at his parents' house in El Monte. We plan to go
out to the air base together.

When the train stops at the Union Pacific station in
Salt Lake City, Kelson and I walk carefully across the snow and
ice on the platform, wincing at the sharpness of the cold air that
nearly takes my breath away. Steam puffs out of our mouths,
out of everyone's, and more steam escapes from the hose lines
beneath the couplers of the passenger cars as we make our way
toward the warmth of the station. The voices of passengers and
the scuffling of their feet echo in the cavernous but attractive
waiting room. We sit down on one of the polished wooden
benches to get our bearings and plan our next move.

Two other men from our group who arrived earlier
from the east greet us then sit down with us.

"We met these two nurses on the train", says Mueller,
his eyes like pale blue beads and his small teeth gleaming
beneath his prominent nose. "We had no trouble getting them
into bed. They were really eager. Do you know what mine
said? She said, 'Most women just do this because the men like
it, but I do it because I like it'."

They both laugh then Jackson says in his slow southern
accent, "Yeah. I'd never had a piece before. Now I don't know
if I can ever stop."

I feel that I'm really back in the Army now, listening
again to the endless stories of men's proud triumphs. They
laugh heartily again then move off to another part of the
station. Neither says anything about his furlough.

*   *   *

Outside in the cold again, huddling in line with the
rest of the people, we wait for a taxi to take us to the air base.
A steady procession of them drive up, steam curling out of
their exhaust pipes, tires crunching and popping on frozen
chunks of mud-stained snow. They drive off on the compact

ice as though it's not there, the cabs' back ends sliding around the curves. The cabbies drive with a blend of recklessness and expert control. While we wait, I look up toward the city, impressed with its broad, open streets. A pall of coal smoke dims the buildings and nearly hides the wintry crags of the Wasatch Mountains behind it.

After a hair-raising ride over the slippery roads to the air base three miles west of town, we sign all our papers and are assigned to our barracks. A foot of powdery snow blankets the air base, making walking difficult except in the places where it has been tramped down by a parade of shoes or smoothed out by trucks and cars. Great icicles hang like stalactites from the eaves of the barracks buildings, a number of them from two to four feet long and several five feet with three or four inch diameters. I had never seen anything like them before. Long and tapered and as solid as rocks in the freezing air, their severe beauty fascinates me.

The pungent smell of coal smoke fills the barracks area as sinking brown wisps of it ooze out of their stacks. The plain, single-storied barracks with sterile wooden floors, much like the ones in Laredo, depress me. All the windows are closed tightly, and two pot-bellied coal stoves, one near each end, blaze and rumble constantly to ward off the bitter cold. With home now far away, I begin to think of it longingly again.

I am already homesick, and would take the first way home if I could. My ten days didn't last half long enough for me. Those ten days sure meant a lot to me. In a while they will all seem like a dream, but a very pleasant one.

A TASTE OF WINTER

For the life of me I can't understand why it's necessary to be out here. What could the commanding officer possibly have to say that would warrant our assembling in front of his office in weather like this? I wear fleece-lined flying boots, a pair of rabbit fur-lined leather gloves that I purchased in town the first day and every item of clothing I possess, including my trench coat, its collar pulled up around my ears. Despite my layers of clothing, the biting chill of the winter morning seeps in at every opening, through every minute pore. At least the near-zero air is calm, the heavy frigid mass of clear air settling over Salt Lake City like a quiet, invisible glacier.

The commanding officer, bundled up, as warmly as military decorum will allow, speaks to us from the railed porch of his office bungalow, his words forming puffs of steam like slowly dissolving smoke signals. He has nothing vital to say to us, only a welcome to the air base and an overview of what plans they have for us. We learn that the temperature stands at only eight degrees, but that earlier it had been five degrees below zero. When we shift our stance the crusty snow cracks and pops beneath our shoes. The icicles hanging from the eaves of the barracks hadn't melted a single drop in the two days we'd been at the base. Yellowish-brown coal smoke tumbles out of the barracks' flues then sinks along the roofs, releasing its sharp creosote scent into the otherwise pure air. It reminds us of the warmth back in the barracks and how comfortable we'll be when we're once again inside. I can hardly feel my feet any more and my ears, nose, cheeks and chin are numbing.

The commanding officer could have given us his information in a bulletin that we might have read in the coziness of our barracks, but tradition demands he speak directly to us.

The lowest temperature ever recorded in my hometown in California was twenty-four degrees, a cold snap that froze the citrus crop in the valleys despite the smoke from the smudge pots that turned our skies black at every horizon. At home the water set out for the chickens and in the crock for the dog and passing birds froze solid, even the water pump on our Model-T Ford. So far, the temperature in Salt Lake City had not been that <u>warm</u>. Perhaps the men from Minnesota, Michigan or Maine think nothing of this weather, but for a California native like me, with orange juice and sunshine in my veins, the iciness is overwhelming.

*   *   *

Sitting on my bunk in the barracks, I write the last letter that I owe. An orderly throws another load of coal into the stove, the flames glowing a fierce yellow-orange through the air slots. I move away from the violence of the combustion and the searing heat until the fire settles down. The barracks still smells faintly from the stench of a melting plastic Utah tax token that someone purposely placed on top of the stove.

With nothing to do but wait until our classes begin, probably several more days, we each attack boredom in our own ways. I read magazines, talk to others and write letters. The only airplanes near this air base are the DC-3 airliners that fly into the Salt Lake City airport about one mile away. We'll not fly here. Our only task is to complete two weeks of classes then wait for shipping orders assigning us to crews at fields anywhere in the United States. Some of the men spend their time gambling, sleeping or braving the weather to go to town. Being too busy is easier to handle than not having enough to do. We are used to our cadet life that was structured at such a fast pace.

I look forward to meals at the officer's mess where we pay twenty-five cents for each one. The food is so tasty and ample that I don't mind paying the price. Even walking to the latrine a block away over a snowy road is a welcome break in the stagnation. At night we go to the movies on the base despite the theater's chilly interior. Tired of a steady diet of war films, we see *So Proudly We Hail* and *Cry Havoc* one night and *Hostages* and *Harvest Melody* the next.

Finally the base supplies some activities, the first being a lecture and film about malaria and mosquitoes, a subject quite remote from the winter of Salt Lake City, but welcome nevertheless. We also watch films about how to survive in the wilderness after a crash landing and listen to lectures on field sanitation, first aid kits and the pressure chamber. Some subjects are dull, but we're ready to listen to anything. They inform us that within the next few days we'll enter the pressure chamber for tests, take a yellow fever shot, and, after a brush-up on the .45 caliber pistol and range procedures, go out to the frozen firing line for practice, a trial that I don't relish.

Despite the cold that left my feet like blocks of ice, I had gone into the city three times during the first week. I especially enjoyed going in with Thomas, one of the fellows who rode in the car with us from Midland to California. We ate our dinner in a nice cafe, saw a double feature at a theater in town then finished off the evening at a hamburger joint where I consumed a hamburger, a glass of root beer, a glass of milk and two donuts. The chilly weather stimulates my appetite.

Several days later I go into town with a B-17 pilot. After seeing a movie, we walk into one of the three "Hamburger Barns" located along the main street. Long and narrow like real barns, they have no seats or tables, only long counters along each side where people stand to eat. An artificial cow peers in a barn window at one end. The hamburgers are delicious and so are the fresh donuts, deep-fried right on the premises. Eating is a good way to fill time.

*   *   *

True to their promise, the range officers take us out to the firing line in the bitterly cold weather. I thought they might not follow through, but they did.

Yesterday morning we went out on the range, and fired the .45 pistol. It was very cold out there, and it was extremely hard to fire a gun. When you would take your glove off for half a minute, you couldn't even feel the ends of your fingers anymore. My hands even hurt through my fur-lined gloves. Here is what I had on out there: undershirt, shorts, shirt, pants, tie, wool socks, knit sweater, leather jacket, winter flying shoes, winter flying helmet, my officer's cap, my trench coat and, of course, my fur-lined gloves. I was still cold, so you can tell from that just about what the temperature was out there. I always took my right glove off when I fired the pistol, and every time I did, my hand just started aching something awful. Gee, that cold hurts! We all went out in big tractor and trailer buses , 'cattle wagons' we call them.

Near the end of our ten days at the barracks, the temperature moderates, melting a small amount of ice and snow. The icicles facing the afternoon sun melt very slowly, the water dripping off each point one tardy drop at a time. As soon as the sun sets, the icicles stop dripping, and the slushy snow freezes into crispy hardness again. The weatherman predicts more snow. The combination of breathing coal smoke and walking around in freezing temperatures finally stuffs my sinuses, spreads a dull aching through my muscles and irritates my throat.

THE FAIRGROUNDS

Happy to be in different facilities and delighted with the prospect of a vigorous daily routine, I explore our new quarters. My double bunk is one of nearly one hundred and fifty lined up in orderly rows on the second-story floor of the Manufacturing and Industry Exhibition Hall on the Utah State Fairgrounds. The largest building in the complex, the hall measuring nearly one hundred feet by four hundred feet gives us a sense of openness and freedom even though it limits our privacy. Steel rafters and the beams supporting the great roof are nearly a hundred feet above me. Large paned windows let in daylight at both ends. After the oppressiveness of the other barracks, the vast space and the light streaming in raise my spirits. The wooden floors, worn and grooved by the shoes of thousands of fair-goers over the years, could use repairs, but they're adequate. Four large furnaces burn constantly to keep out the winter chill.

Here on the fairgrounds, officially called Sub-Base Number 1, we have all the conveniences: a theater, a PX, tailor shop, barber shop, post office, chapel and what is rumored to be the best mess hall in the 2nd Air Force. All our classrooms are here. The instructors will fill most of our daytime hours, seven days a week, for the next two weeks. After completion of our classes we must wait patiently for shipping orders assigning us to our crew and heavy bomber training bases.

Just outside our quarters stands another hall that serves as our movie theater, the films changing almost nightly. Out near the boulevard that leads to town, flanked by winter-bare poplar trees resembling inverted whiskbrooms, are the guardhouse and the entrance guard station, manned at all hours. Blue-white snow softens all the roofs and covers the ground so completely that no dark earth is visible anywhere.

A half-mile away the freight yards of the Union Pacific, Western Pacific and the Denver and Rio Grande railroads serenade us during the night with their variety of whistles, the puffing rhythm of their switch engines and the percussion of coupling freight cars. I love the sounds, and I listen to them far into the night. They remind me of home.

Standing alone not far from our quarters, its rounded roof capped with a soft hat of fresh snow, is the State Fair bandstand, a large gazebo-like building now open to the icy winds. The blasts of brightly uniformed bands with their burnished instruments, the crowds around them in shirtsleeves and summer dresses are only a memory. The racetrack and stands too lie idle and frozen, the roar of the crowds and the thunder of flying hooves now mute, victims of war and winter.

*   *   *

Wrapped as warmly as possible in my trench coat and wearing my fur-lined gloves and winter flying boots, I trudge through the foot-deep snow to class. The snow had drifted down all night and into the morning, leaving a thick, powdery layer that reminds me of sifted flour lying smoothly in the bottom of a mixing bowl. It's so fresh and even that I feel guilty disfiguring it, but I must reach my classroom. With each step I lift my foot high then plant it in the fresh snow just ahead. With the others I laugh at our struggle. Each time I lift my shoe out, a dollop rests on its tip, some of it tumbling back into the hole I've just made. Not used to the procedure, I soon discover how much labor it is and begin to feel warm beneath my trench coat.

Each day, walking to class is a different experience. Sometimes the snow lies deep everywhere, but after a few days it begins to melt, and the constant tramping of heavy shoes compacts it along the most traveled paths. A few warmer days turn it into wet slush that sometimes oozes into the tops of our shoes where it melts and runs down into our socks. When the slush freezes, the paths become treacherous, and we must be very careful about how we step. My legs become sore from bracing myself on the ice, trying to avoid a fall. Once, after most of the snow had melted, leaving a quagmire of dirty slush, mud and deep brown puddles, a new snow covered it, hiding the thin-crusted puddles with fresh white fluff. Not sure where the puddles are beneath the snow, we found out only when we suddenly broke through, bathing our shoes in ice water, sending us to class wearing damp, dirty socks and shoes.

Walking through falling snow always thrills me. I'm taken by the hushed silence of it in contrast to the drip and clatter of rain. I like the way the drifting flakes dim the brick buildings and the naked poplars, softening them and enclosing them in a cold, misty quietness. I marvel at the translucent pearl-gray sky, sometimes with the weak sun silvering through, the driving snowflakes black against its light. I'm amazed by the variety of flakes, falling as a smothering of downy goose feathers one day and a flurry of frozen grains on another. I enjoy the flakes as they bounce softly against my face, sometimes curling into my ears. I look with wonder at the pristine snow when it drifts in the wind, forming what I think to be the earth's most perfect smoothness.

*   *   *

Thick gray fog shrouds the fair grounds as I make my way with several other men to our eight o'clock armament class. The damp chill penetrates my trench coat, sending a shudder through my body. The mist still hides the classroom building, but we know our way by now. Frost clings to every branch and naked twig of the few trees we pass, transforming them into webs of fragile white filigree. Even the telephone wires stretch like pale crystalline lines that disappear into the mist.

As I've not worked with armaments since gunnery school, the class renews my interest in them. We study and manipulate large Consolidated and Emerson gun turrets, the type that fit into the nose of the B-24 bomber and take up so much of the bombardier's space. I hoped that I'd never be assigned to a B-24 bomber with its squat, dumpy look and its scant bombardier's compartment. I yearn for a B-17, an airplane that looks the way I think a heavy bomber should look, sleek and lethal, with plenty of room for the bombardier to move around. We also operate the Bendix chin turret, the type installed in a B-17. I hoped we'd fire them on the range despite the cold weather, but we never do.

We reacquaint ourselves with the Browning .50 caliber machine gun, reviewing once more how to take it apart and put it back together. I'm surprised when my fingers seem to know what to do. I'd disassembled and reassembled the gun so many times at Laredo, sometimes blindfolded, that its mechanisms are firmly imprinted on my nerve paths.

Each day we practice Morse code, a monotonous task that we all dislike. Our main class is a two-week concentrated course about navigation. I'd enjoyed navigation at Midland, both in the classroom and in the air. I had the satisfaction of giving a pilot a heading to an airport nearly one hundred miles away, checking for drift and ground speed then giving the pilot a corrected heading and an estimated time of arrival. We "split" the airport and arrived on the exact minute. My elation was greater than that of hitting a "shack" on a bomb run.

I slip easily into the complexities of navigation instruction. We plot courses, learn about Mercator charts and keep a navigator's logbook. We hone our dead reckoning skills and learn about radio navigation---learning to fly on a beam and shooting a radio fix to find our exact position at any time.

I walk back toward the old, coal-stained brick building now serving as our home, a little furnace of excitement about navigation burning in my belly. Except for the usual haze of stratified coal smoke, the fog has cleared to a sunny day. The delicate white frost that laced the trees and wires has now melted. I hoped I would learn celestial navigation from the navigator on our crew when we finally meet, but he'd have to teach me to find the stars and give them names. At this point in my life they are only bluish points that speckle the night.

Upstairs in the great hall I stretch out on the bunk to rest.

SALT LAKE CITY

Turning east out of the fair grounds gate, I point myself toward town. Most of the snow has melted from the walks, but I keep an eye out for globs of mud and dirty piles of slush. Walking in the crisp air, inhaling it deep into my lungs, invigorates me after being cooped up at the fair grounds all day with nothing to do. Now that classes have ended, we wait day after day for shipping orders. Only eating, sleeping and discussing the latest rumors occupy our time. Alone, believing that no one else would want to walk to town, I feel free and alive. With all of us bunked in the single large room, I sometimes yearn to have time to myself, to do what I want. Even though it's five o'clock, I'll have just enough daylight left to walk the mile and a half to town then possibly another mile to the State Capitol Building. Having studied all the state capitals in school and especially at home as a young boy, I'm excited about seeing it.

Once past the smoky railroad yards with still over a mile to go, I turn north on the street leading up the hill where the capitol building dominates the crest. I'm fascinated with this unusual city with its grayish, coal-stained buildings and its wide, nearly empty avenues. As I plod up the steep, sloping street, my legs tighten, and I struggle for breath. Having had very little physical training since Midland over a month ago, I 'm out of shape, but I'm determined to reach my goal.

Finally at the base of the capitol stairs, looking up towards its massive columns and great dome, I pause to catch my breath and appreciate its magnificence. I'd never seen the capitol building of any other state. Up until now the capitals had been only names on a cardboard circular game that I had as a boy. If I turned the pointer of a cardboard wheel to the state, I could read the name of its capital in a small window. Impressed by just standing in front of a structure with such mystique, I begin to trudge up the granite stairs leading to the entrance. I glance at my watch. The hike from the air base had taken exactly 41 minutes.

Standing beside a column beneath its Greek portico, I look down toward the city. I gaze out over a panorama of buildings and streets, dimmed at its edges by coal smoke haze and the fading light of day. From this vantage point I begin to understand the layout of the city. Salt Lake City nestles within the curved but jagged arm of the snowy Wasatch Mountains, much of the city with its geometric grid of streets built on a gradual slope that levels out near the river bottom. I peer out over the city until it's nearly dark and the lights begin to appear in the windows of the fading gray buildings. I'd never seen any scene quite so stirring.

*   *   *

Two days later, again tired of being penned up with everyone else all day without any duties, I decide to take another solitary walk. Without knowing for certain where I'm going, I begin at the center of town, walking east until I can go no farther. Once more I appreciate the simple pleasure of being unconfined and alone. I feel my legs unraveling, and I sense that my blood flows again, pumping and pulsing through my limbs rather than festering in stagnant pools during my day of inactivity. I draw deep drafts of cold fresh air. The temperature hovers near freezing, but the briskness puts an extra spring in my step.

After nearly two and a half miles I reach my limit, the eastern edge of the University of Utah campus. Beyond this point a long snow-covered field rises toward the foothills of the Wasatch Mountains. The attractive halls and administration buildings of the university, the winter-bare trees and snowy lawns lie shadowed in the dimming light of late afternoon. As I stroll along the cleared paths on campus, I come upon many A.S.T.P. men who train at the university to become future officers. I nearly wear my arm out returning their salutes. Having been in the army only a short time, the men salute with an awkward eagerness, even smiling when they bring their hands smartly up to their caps.

With darkness approaching, I begin the long trek back into town. I still like being alone, but paradoxically I miss talking to someone. Most of my many trips to the city had been with other men. I had often visited Ballantyne at his hotel court where he chose to live instead of at the base. Ballantyne and I ate dinner together several times and bowled many games at the local alley. We even attended a vaudeville show together, sitting right up front so that we could get a good look at the girls. With others I ate at a variety of restaurants, bowled far into the evening, sat in nearly every movie theater in town, puttered around in the penny arcades and yelled from the bleachers at a local high school basketball game.

What I had done with others is what men enjoy doing together, cutting into juicy tenderloin steaks as large as our plates, laughing together at a movie or competing with one another on the bowling lanes. Walking to the capitol building from the air base or striking out to the east from the center of town is not what most men would enjoy. I do that alone.

The night before, after spending the early evening with Ballantyne, I was returning to the base alone when I noticed the unusual brightness of the full moon. From one spot I had seen the city with all its sparkling lights, the mountains outlined in black behind it and another range facing the moon, brilliantly blue-white with its deep covering of snow. The moon filled billowy clouds with its bluish light. A mild breeze had blown all the usual haze away, leaving the city to twinkle in its moonlit surroundings. I stood there a long time, admiring a kind of beauty that I had never experienced before.

Had I been with others, I might not have noticed the striking quality of the scene, or, if I had I would have been compelled to pay attention to the other men. If I stopped to admire it, I think they would not have understood. Some moments are better experienced alone or with someone of like spirit, someone whose heart is on the same beat.

*   *   *

Perhaps the wide streets of Salt Lake City make it seem empty, but I'm struck by how few people use the sidewalks. Downtown Los Angeles had always been crowded with shoppers and businessmen. The people that I pass on the streets seem distant and aloof. Rarely do they smile or even look at me, treating me much as if I were a lamppost or fire hydrant or, even worse, non-existent. As our small base is the only one around the city, the streets are not flooded with service men. We can't be so common that they don't notice us.

Back at the base one of the men offers a good explanation for their attitude. In the early days, around the 1860's, the Mormons practiced polygamy. The United States government, frowning on the idea of a man having more than one wife, passed laws to stop it. To enforce the anti-polygamy statutes, the army sent soldiers to nearby Fort Douglas. The Mormons objected vigorously to the soldiers or anyone who tried to tell them how to live. The antagonism developed into a feud between the people of Salt Lake City and the Army.

Several years later a completed statue of Brigham Young was to be unveiled in Temple Square. Mormons from all over Utah flocked to Salt Lake City to witness the ceremony. During the night before the unveiling, several soldiers from

Fort Douglas sneaked into the square, ducked underneath the shroud, and placed a banana and two apples in the crotch of the statue. The Mormons were outraged when the veil was lifted the following morning. The Mormons, determining what had happened, complained loudly to the authorities at Fort Douglas, reviving the feud that apparently persists in a modified form between the citizens and the military. Perhaps the story explains why the people of Salt Lake City hardly ever give us a ride, "take us in" or even look our way.

I stand on a breezy street corner in town, waiting with other pedestrians for the signal light to change, my hands down at my side. I feel someone or something take hold of my hand, something warm and small. I look down to see a little girl about three years old, her hand clasped to mine, looking up at me, her deep brown eyes dancing under the dark wisps of hair spilling out beneath her knit cap. With her other hand she holds firmly to her mother's. Not quite knowing what to do, I say, "Hello, there." She says nothing but smiles broadly and holds my hand tighter. As we cross the street she releases my hand, hanging on to her mother who seems to be in a hurry. All the way across the street, walking awkwardly as she looks back at me, she smiles, almost breaks into a laugh. At least one person in Salt Lake City had been friendly. The smile and the touch of the little girl's soft hand combine for a perfect finish to my final day in Salt Lake City.

MORAL JUDGMENT

The dice thump against the side of a footlocker draped with an army blanket then tumble back across the rest of it laid out on the floor. Brand new lieutenants and flight officers, who had just been paid their travel money, sit or squat around it, hoping to fatten their wallets. Cheers and curses erupt from their twisting, shifting bodies as the winners reach for the pile of crumpled bills on the blanket. Their eyes burn with excitement, turn glassy with greed. Cigarette smoke curls out of the circle of their pressed bodies, rising among them like incense from a noisy shrine. They reach for more wrinkled bills wadded in their pockets, snapping them at each end to straighten them out before tossing them into the pot.

I observe the men with detached amusement. I neither understand the game nor care to learn it. I watch them gather their winnings, jamming the cash into their pockets. For every winner there is a loser, or several, and those who walk away from the game with empty pockets seem foolish to me. How can they stay in so long and lose all that money? My stash, the little that I don't send home, remains safely in my wallet.

At a small table in the next barracks I watch a poker game. Here the mood is quieter, more somber. The stony faces around the table remind me of the gambling scenes in bar rooms and river boats that I'd seen in Western movies. Four hundred-dollar bills, neatly spaced, peek out from the shirt pocket of the current winner. He wears them like a medal of his prowess.

From my viewpoint, risking good money by gambling is wasteful. We never had much money at home. Perhaps that's why I value it so much.

This rest we are taking here so far is pretty hard on some guys' billfolds. There have been a lot of crap and poker games going on around here today. I have never seen so much money flying around in my life. A fellow in one crap game won $458. The other fellows lost all their money, and now they are broke. Tough, isn't it? I don't feel sorry for them.

I can't help but look down on the men who don't use their heads and appear to have no self-control. At the same time I feel my difference from them. My attitude separates me from the gamblers, making me feel like an outsider. I shake my head at their antics, but feel the chill of loneliness. They probably think I'm afraid to take a risk, have no zest for the excitement of the contest, or don't know how to have fun. But I think I'm being prudent and right. Fortunately a few others feel the same way I do and become my best friends.

I send most of my money home---with instructions.

Today we were paid our travel pay...I wrote out a money order for $150 which I will enclose in this letter. Here is what I want done with it. Put $100 in the bank, use $37.50 for a $50 bond, then each of you take $5 for your Christmas presents from me. The extra 50-cents, you can fight over. Buy about ten Milk Nickels when the Good Humor man comes along.

After receiving our regular pay, I write home again.

We got paid today. I got $217.50 that I was very glad to get. I had plenty of money to last me this time, so I can send home quite a bit I think...I can send almost $180...I kept $68 last time. I had many good times, paid for all my food, bought magazines, newspapers, candy bars etc., loaned $22 and still had $8 left over today. I don't like the idea of loaning money, but this time it was understandable. Some of the men diddled their money away until about a week ago when they found out they were broke. They had to have money for food, so I had to loan them some. I loaned *money to Ballantyne to pay his hotel bill. Maybe next month they will plan their money more carefully. They all paid me back, so I know that I can trust them.*

*   *   *

Many fresh lieutenants were either engaged or married during their furloughs. It's as though becoming officers and winning their wings as well as our nearness to combat is the appropriate time for sweethearts to pledge their love to each other. The number of them that hint, announce or boast about their new status amazes me. I congratulate them, but wonder whether engagement or marriage is smart at this point.

Being committed to a woman seems to make little difference in the way they act toward other women in town. They chase after them with the same vigor they always did. Still needing to prove their manliness to each other and themselves, they continue to pick up women and brag about their conquests.

Their unfaithfulness and what I consider weakness of character astounds me. I think about how surprised their women back home would be if they ever found out how their men behave when they're away from them. As one man explains it to me, "I just need that stuff"---as simple as that.

As always, I vent my feelings to my parents in a letter.

It seems to me that about half the guys that came back from their leaves are now married or engaged, mostly married. In most of the cases it's a shame because their wives don't seem to mean much to them. They brag about their engagements and marriages then go on as they usually did. I hope for their sake that they married girls just like themselves, because if they didn't, the girls would be very hurt to see them now. I know if I had a wife at home, I sure wouldn't want her to run around with every guy in town. Even I have thought of getting married sometime, but I sure don't think I would dream of it until after the war. That is one reason that I am trying to save as much money as I can. I may have enough by that time to get a start after this thing is over.

Several men in the barracks claimed that, "Maybe these Mormon girls don't drink or smoke, but they'll do everything else." Both the married and the unmarried men fan out into the city to test the saying.

Flight Officer Seagrave, as yet unmarried, lives for women. They are the only real interest he has in life. His conversations bubble and boil with his experiences with this woman or that. He's short with just enough fat under his skin to mask a good physique. Light blue penetrating eyes look out from below the dark luxuriance of his wavy hair, but the deep natural contours of his face etch an expression that some people interpret as a sneer. I can never understand what the women see in him, but in every city he has eventually found what he wanted. Within days of our arrival in Salt Lake City Seagrave finds a "good situation," a virgin who has told her friends that she's ready for experience. He's only too happy to oblige. Night after night he goes into the city to see his woman, until near the end of our stay, he tells me he's not going to see her anymore. As he crudely puts it, "we're all fucked out." The passion spent, it's time to find a new woman.

I don't understand Seagrave. He has no feeling for any of the women he "loves." To him they're merely vessels for his pleasure, and when he finishes with them, he discards them like empty toothpaste tubes. The women parade through his life anonymously, his relationships with them good only for stories he can tell his friends.

* * *

My moral position, ingrained in me by my parents, especially my mother, the Methodist Church and my influential track coach is quite clear. Money should never be piddled away on needless luxuries or frivolous activities. It should only be spent on necessities and wholesome recreation. As much money as possible should be saved for after the war when it will be needed for marriage, education or emergencies. Gambling is a total waste. A man should not have sex with a woman until he marries. He should always be faithful to her thereafter.

Few men hold the same moral ideas I do, or if they do, they don't practice them. Even though I pass moral judgment on the men, I keep my thoughts to myself. I have no compelling need to convert them or change their ways. I go about my life while they go about theirs. I remain friendly with them because I like them and value many of their other traits.

As my barracks mates sometimes say, "It's these quiet guys like Stevens who get it all. They have women all the time, but they just don't talk about it." All I can do is smile, and let them believe what they wish.

TRAIN WHISTLES

I am homesick again. We can hear the train whistles from the base here, and ever since I have been in the Army, a train whistle in the distance has made me homesick. It seems like all of them are going home, and I can't be on them.

Somewhere out on the snowy plains a steam locomotive vents its deep-throated harmony into the cold, still air. The plaintive far-off notes sing through the red bricks of the exhibition building, and sweep across my bunk. That train could be on its way to Los Angeles, and I imagine myself on it, going home. I think about what I have just written in my nightly letter to my parents. Train whistles and home are one, the fusion of a sound with an idea.

Even though I miss home, it doesn't seem as far away as it did when I trained in Texas. Airliners arriving from Los Angeles, only a two-hour flight away, often bank into their landing patterns over the fair grounds. We readily pick up two powerful radio stations from Los Angeles, KFI and KHJ, both bringing us local news and many programs I often listened to at home.

The news continues to pour in from home through frequent letters from my parents. It's everyday stuff, events that might happen at any home anywhere, but these happenings are from my world and assume cosmic proportions. My dog Pal has been chasing chickens again, this time Mr. Shaw's chickens next door. He had let them get out---so what is a bird dog supposed to do? Mr. Shaw is angry and wants us to tie up the dog---My parents are thrilled at an Army-Navy show in the

323

Los Angeles Coliseum. The buzzing of the stadium by a P-61 Black Widow night fighter electrifies the crowd---Pal has a difficult time standing up on the newly waxed floor---First the temperature is 81 degrees in Los Angeles and then 82 degrees the next day. My father drives his 1933 Ford V-8 with the windows rolled down and his sleeves rolled up. (I think about our frigid weather and the snow lying deep all around us)---My sister Charline has a sty, and wrestles with writing themes and studying for her physics tests in high school. We're proud of her good grades.

I've asked Charline to buy two records for me, "On the Sunny Side of the Street" arranged by Lionel Hampton and "Take it Easy" by Guy Lombardo and his orchestra, a group I don't usually like. I want her to save them until I come home. My parents send me professional photographs taken on my furlough. My father sends me Brylcreem for my hair, and my Aunt Mary mails a silver identification bracelet. Each item represents just a little bit of home.

* * *

Rumors circulate around the barracks and classrooms about where we might be sent for our crew training. Most are about when and what type of heavy bomber we'll fly, B-24s or B-17s. My fervent wish is to begin training immediately after our classes at a B-17 base as near California as possible. Each rumor affects my mood according to how well it fits into my ideal plan. I'd like to ship out with bombardiers I know well, but the likelihood is remote. Most of the shipping orders affect only small groups who are headed for bases scattered throughout the United States.

The word is out that bombardiers trained at Midland will be sent to B-24 bases because they are familiar with the Sperry bombsight, the one used in that bomber. I'm disappointed, and begin to picture myself in that squat airplane, stuffed in the cramped bombardier's compartment with a bombsight I don't like. One group of men is sent to Casper, Wyoming, a forsaken place with more severe winters than those of Salt Lake City. Some are shipped to Wendover, still in Utah. I have three bases in mind for myself, Blythe and Muroc, both in California, or Tucson, Arizona, all of them within reach of home on a weekend pass.

Rumors begin to fly thicker and faster, working us all into a state of nervous apprehension. We hear that some officers have been given delays in reaching their destinations, allowing some of them free time to go home for a few days, provided they live close to the base. The talk gives me hope, but I know from experience that rumors are like soap bubbles--- their colorful iridescence floats lazily through the air, only to burst into a few paltry drops.

With our classes finished, shipping orders are announced each morning. I hang on each word for my name or the names of my friends. In the disinterested baritone of a sergeant's voice lie the words that can send my life in one direction or another, perhaps changing its course forever. I don't hear my name, but the list of my departing friends grows long. Nearly every man with whom I could laugh or accompany into town, or talk to easily, packs his belongings and goes away, leaving empty bunks soon to be filled by strangers. I begin to feel lonely. I try to imagine that matters will work out for the best. Parris ships out to Casper, Wyoming, and my close friends Ballantyne and Bachuber leave for Sioux City, Iowa.

At last I hear my name. A thrill charges through my body. I don't know where I'm to be sent, but I know that my new destination is 1587 miles away, definitely not one of the three bases I'd hoped for. I learn from hearsay that it's Alexandria, Louisiana, but if that's the destination, at least I'll be a bombardier on a B-17 crew. With more snow pelting down outside, I think about the sub-tropical South---warmth and lush green grass and trees, bayous and thunderstorms.

I still hear the locomotive whistles across the snowfields. One of the trains is surely bound for L.A. Within a few days a new arrival, perhaps bedding down in my old bunk at the fair grounds, will hear the whistles, some of them from trains speeding toward his hometown. He might even hear the melody from my own train on its way to Louisiana.

BACK TO THE BAYOUS

Lacy frost patterns etch my Pullman window, blurring the scene outside. Clearing a small patch with the back of my glove, I look out on an arctic landscape beneath a low, gray overcast. Snow whitens the roofs of railroad sheds in the Union Pacific yards, and lies in soft blankets on top of each boxcar. It crowns the peaks of every weathered fence post, feathers the crevices in piles of coal and drifts around switches. While we were traveling across the frozen plains of Wyoming during the night ice formed all around the frame of our window, as well as the metal lift, even the screws.

Our military train left the Salt Lake City station near midnight, speeding north to Ogden then eastward across Wyoming through Rawlins and Laramie. By morning we reached the yards just west of Cheyenne. Shaking the fuzziness out of our heads after a short night's sleep, we slip into our uniforms, trying to look like officers again. A few heavy-eyed men carry their satchels of toilet articles down the aisle, making their way to the small bathroom at the end of the car. I dress faster than usual, the steam heat inside the Pullman car barely holding its own against the polar air outside.

Thomas, Seegrave and Norbut, all bombardiers who trained with me at Midland, are in the same car. Having seen many friends ship out to other bases, I'm relieved to have at least a few along with me. They'll be training at the same base in Louisiana.

Near breakfast time the train leaves the snowy railroad yards, turning toward the south and Colorado. The farther south we travel, the less snow we see until finally only patches remain in the shady spots. Occasionally a misty rain dampens the low, just-greening hills. We pass through Greeley then head toward Denver, the cloud-shrouded splendor of the Rockies on our right.

Despite the season, parts of Colorado with its fields and farms remind me of Central California where my sister and I spent a wonderful summer only two years ago. I think about those warm days near Modesto in that grand old farmhouse next to the cavernous warehouse where sacks of beans were piled nearly to the ceiling. I think about the taste of those hearty farm-fresh meals---pouring thick cream cooled in the tank house on apple pie, biting into plump night-chilled peaches picked off the tree in the morning. The days were carefree and casual then, far different from my situation now as I travel southward to a base for my final training before being sent overseas.

At the Denver station the train stops for a check of its brake shoes, wheels and hose connections. They need to change the locomotive too, so we have plenty of time to stretch our legs outside on the platform. We walk far enough to catch glimpses of downtown Denver. I'm entranced with its large buildings, and vow that I'll return some day to explore it. I again experience the thrill of connecting what had been an abstract name with the reality of actually beholding the city. It's like looking into a dream and touching it. A switch engine hauling a string of passenger coaches chugs by in a swirl of coal smoke, its driving rods clanking.

Near Pueblo, Colorado we turn eastward toward Kansas, finally passing through Dodge City and Newton. At Emporia the train again stops long enough that we can get out and fill our lungs with fresh air, but at Kansas City, Missouri we have a full hour. Keeping the location of the station in mind, several of us start off through the crowded streets of the city, peering into the windows of department stores and shops and into the lobbies of grand hotels. I sense the same dream-like feeling that I felt when looking at Denver. I'm beginning to see more of the United States. Excited and interested, I regret that we have so little time to explore.

After cutting through a tiny corner of Missouri, we enter Kansas again, rolling through Osawatomie, Garnett and Coffeyville, all small towns of little distinction. By the time we race through Oklahoma, through Claremore and Muskogee, night envelops the plains. We see only the lights of small towns as they flicker by. Tired, especially from the short sleep of the night before, I turn in early.

Morning finds us in Little Rock, Arkansas. The brown, muddy river that slithers through it appalls me. I think it's the most repulsive river I've ever seen, and Little Rock, tainted by the river's sliminess, is just as bad. Even as we leave the city and thunder out across the Arkansas countryside, I'm unimpressed. Some of the men tell me that Arkansas is pretty up around Hot Springs, but I think it's the least desirable state I've seen, and hope that I'm never stationed in it.

* * *

Now in Louisiana, looking at green again soothes me like a pleasant massage especially after weeks of snow in Salt Lake City. The verdant southern countryside reminds me of east Texas with its lush thickets of trees and shrubs and the sweet smell of grass. We pass mile after mile of piney woods, the trees smaller than the ones in California. Swamps sometimes invade the forests, abruptly changing the scene to one of thick cypress trees hung with Spanish moss, their knobby knees reflected in the dark mirror-like water. Here and there we pass bayous, a few choked with bulbous water hyacinth covered with pale purple blossoms.

Thoughts float in and out of my mind as I drink in the tropic-like green outside the window. At Alexandria

I'll meet my pilot and co-pilot and, in time, the rest of my bomber crew. I'm apprehensive about what I'll think of them and what they'll think of me. Will we meld into a smooth unit or will we grate on each other's nerves? Will the pilot be a man with whom I can trust my life, or will he be a hotshot risk taker who craves excitement? How will all our personal philosophies, morals and outlooks blend? How will we endure combat together?

As we pause at Monroe, Louisiana, the sun sets. We'll not reach Alexandria until late at night. I think again about my innocent vision of combat and how it will match the eventual reality of it. All I know about it I've learned from movies, newsreels and what I've heard from the very few who have been there. I already know that movies and newsreels lie.

I think too about how fortunate I am. From the first day I entered the army, I wanted to be a bombardier on a B-17 crew, and now that's about to happen. I sometimes look down at my silver wings just to make sure they're there, that I really am a bombardier. Despite my concerns about meeting the crew, the rigorous training ahead and the specter of combat in the near future, I ride a soft wave of confidence.

* * *

Arriving at Alexandria Army Air Field at 2200 hours is like arriving at any new base at night, strange and dream-like. I see only pale slices of buildings in weak shafts of outside lighting and the yellow squares of windows in dark, low-lying quarters. Fatigue, combined with the eeriness of the place, gives me the feeling that I'm imagining it all. The occasional growl of powerful engines cuts into the night and drifts up from the flight line. The warm, humid evening, much like those at Ellington Field, adds to my weary disorientation, especially because the balmy air is so completely different from the arctic conditions we had left only two days ago.

In a stark, poorly lit room we fill out papers and listen to instructions. Meals will cost us 50 cents each, an unexpected expense that will tax my budget. Too exhausted to be interested in what they have to say, I only want the nonsense to cease so I can go to bed. Eventually, cross-looking orderlies check out our bedding and assign us to barracks. The outside of the low, single-story quarters are covered with black tar paper battened down with widely-spaced strips of lath, a look that makes me feel as though we're already in combat at some hastily-built air base. Unhappy about my first impressions of the air base, I slowly store my belongings, and make up my bunk. By the time I turn out the lights and stretch out into my new bed, my watch reads 0100 hours. The bed rocks slightly like the swaying Pullman car I'd been riding for two days, but I soon drop off to sleep.

ALEXANDRIA

Walking on the sidewalks of downtown Alexandria on a Saturday night is like being swept along in a turbulent stream of uniformed bodies while being jostled by a similar stream moving in the opposite direction. A long sea of bobbing heads wearing military caps fills the sidewalks, thousands, it seems, slogging through the mist drifting out of a warm, sticky sky. Stopping to look in a shop window or hesitating in front of a restaurant to check a menu is nearly impossible. Since most of the men we pass are not officers, we edge through the crowds returning a perpetual series of salutes.

Alexandria, a city of 30,000, reminds me of Laredo, the same type of town with a similar mixture of buildings. Its business section clusters along three long blocks, not enough room to fit the deluge of service men that are in town. Within the three blocks are all the commercial businesses as well as two large hotels and three movie theaters. The muddy Red River flows along the edge of town, separating it from its smaller sister city, Pineville, just across from it.

Six sprawling army camps containing 300,000 men, enough to launch an invasion, surround the beleaguered town. For all these bases Alexandria is the nearest town of any size, and it appears that tonight all the men have been released at once. I don't like the town. I vow this visit will be my last, at least on a Saturday. Disappointed with our evening off, we don't even try to duck into one of the packed theaters, but attempt to salvage some of the evening by slipping into a drug store soda fountain for some thick malts.

Even the colored section of Alexandria, a collection of bars, clubs and shops about six blocks long, teems with life. We had come through it on the bus on our way to town. I was amazed at what I saw out of the window. Never had I seen so many black people in one place ---thousands of them it seemed---soldiers and civilians alike, crowding the walks, spilling out into the street, everyone having a great time--- white teeth and black faces in the night.

Not a single black man walks the streets of downtown Alexandria, and no white man mixes with them in their part of town. Segregation is complete. I don't think separation of the races is right, but I know that's the way of the South. All I can do is observe it as another way of life.

* * *

Strategically located along the Red River in the exact center of Louisiana and a natural junction for major roads and railways, Alexandria had been too important to the South for the Union Army to let it stand. They burned Alexandria and Pineville across the river, leveling both towns and destroying most of its antebellum homes, cotton gins, courthouse records, churches and libraries. All the buildings we see today had risen out of the ashes of the destroyed city.

Today the Missouri Pacific, Texas and Pacific and the Louisiana and Alabama railroads converge on Alexandria. So do major highways. It seems now, however, that the main business of the city is the military.

* * *

Having nothing to do on Sunday, my fellow bombardier, Thomas, and I decide to go into town to look around, to see what Alexandria looks like during the day. After riding eight miles on the bus, we get off on the outskirts rather than going all the way to the center. The weather is perfect for walking. A soft breeze rustles the trees, the air is fresh, and puffy clouds float in a deep blue sky. We stride toward town, occasionally walking through cloud shadows. Seeing new territory, breathing in the magnificence of the day and feeling our muscles untangle with the rhythm of our walking is just what we needed.

On this Sunday afternoon only a few soldiers walk the streets in the town center, a marked contrast to the wildebeest-like herds of Saturday night. Once near the business district, we make our way to the bridge that spans the Red River and leads to Pineville on the other side. We stop part way across to watch the muddy river flow under it, the red soil washing into it obviously giving it its name. The sluggish water roils and forms flat patterns on the surface. Sometimes a small tree branch or a stray stick floats by. Thick green trees crowd the riverbanks.

Walking through the small town of Pineville doesn't take us long. With energy left we move on until we come to the campus of Louisiana College, a school neither one of us knew about. The serenity of the campus and the beauty of the Colonial-style, red brick buildings with their dazzling white trim, nestling among the pines and green lawns, captivate us. We stroll along the paths through the campus, taking in its Southern charm.

Thirsty after our long trek, we open one of the unlocked doors of the nearest building, hoping to find a drinking fountain inside. We find two young men in the building who tell us that it's the girl's dormitory, but as it's Sunday most of them had gone home. They also inform us that the entire student body numbers only 300. We think about how tantalizing it might have been had we entered the same door on a weekday and barged in on a dormitory teeming with young women.

Back in Alexandria and still in the mood for exploration, we board a local bus on its way to the city park, but once we arrive, beginning to feel some fatigue, we decide to remain on the bus and ride it back to town.

I'm fond of exploring. Even if what I find in my wandering is not exciting or important, at least I know what's there. It all interests me. I enjoyed exploring San Antonio, Houston, Laredo, Salt Lake City and now Alexandria---little bits of America to poke around in.

A BINDING OF LIVES

All the way from Salt Lake City to Alexandria, I spent idle moments thinking about the bomber crew I was about to join. Lost in the mesmerizing rhythm of the Pullman car on the rails, I thought about the now nameless and faceless men who would become, for a while, so important in my life. I wondered about how I'd blend with them. Would I be accepted? Would I accept them? It would be my most intensely personal military experience. I didn't have long to wait.

On the first morning at Alexandria I meet both the pilot and co-pilot of my crew, Second Lieutenant Johnston and Second Lieutenant Podoske. We chat briefly before going our separate ways for the day, but I already begin to relax, feeling that both are sensible men. Neither is rash, daring or overly adventurous. They both appear to be proficient, levelheaded and serious, the very type I hoped for. Johnston and I even agree that we'll never flirt with towering thunderheads, and we'll always fly a safe distance above mountain peaks.

From this instant on our separate lives will be woven together. Men who would never have met each other will come together at a discordant time in history, be with each other briefly to perform a single task, then return to the places from which they came.

Lieutenant Johnston, the pilot, 23 years old, is from my own state, having attended high school in Alhambra, California and now living in Pasadena. He's already logged 180 hours in B-17s, and understands the plane thoroughly. As far as I'm concerned, he's "on the ball." Slender and nearly six feet tall, he carries his body erectly, more like a fit athlete than the artificial stiffness of a military man. Serious, smiling only sparingly, he carries the look of authority in his deep brown eyes. He readily assumes his role as captain of the ship, and makes sure that we all know it. His voice is rather soft and slightly strained, but is clear and authoritative.

Johnston had been a pitcher in the Coast League with Portland where he was known as "Lefty" Johnston. Having once been acclaimed, he carries that eminence in his bearing as though he still feels special about himself. Always cool, he rarely raises his voice to correct any one, allowing his character alone to carry the weight. I believe that the same gift of coordination that made him a first-rate pitcher will make him a first-rate pilot. The link between his senses, nerves and muscles, along with his coolness allows him to keep a sharp eye on the instruments and the other planes in tight formations while maintaining a strong hand on the control column and throttles. These are skills that I can trust, that might save my life some day.

Always immaculate, his clothes are pressed; his hair cut and neatly combed, his shoes and belt buckle burnished to a shine, and his face clean-shaven. His forehead and reddish cheeks always appear so clean that they actually glow, as though he had polished them.

"My father always told me", says Johnston, "that there is no excuse for not looking sharp. No matter how much money you have or how poor you are, you can always wash, wear clean clothes, shave, comb your hair and keep your shoes polished."

Johnston makes it clear that he's making the best of a bad situation. If he has to be in a war, being an Army Air Corps pilot is his most satisfactory niche. He wants it all to be over so that he can get on with his life---his baseball games, his fiancé and a career with his father in the Carnation Company.

337

"I want to get it all over with as soon as possible," says Johnston. "I want us all to get back as quickly as we can. I don't want anything to delay us either here or overseas. If we have a first class crew we'll never be held back. Once we're in combat I want our primary goal to be finishing our missions as soon as we can, so that we can get back quickly."

We all agree with the goals.

Johnston appreciates my skill as a navigator and bombardier, and he enjoys my sense of humor, often laughing at my jokes and witticisms, but challenging his decisions brings out his stricter side, one that he usually keeps under control. He clearly feels that the pilot is a special person, that his position, skill and training far exceed those of anyone else on the crew. He never expresses this, but we all know he believes it. We smooth over any differences between us, and, almost without exception, work well together.

Lieutenant Podoske, shorter and stockier than Johnston, is not happy with his role as a co-pilot. He would much rather be a fighter pilot on a P-38 or, like many of his former class mates or be training on P-47 Thunderbolt fighters, rather than flying as a second pilot on a "box car" like the B-17. More open and less sophisticated than Johnston, he's more like me. I bind with him immediately. He's accepting of me, and I of him. I enjoy his sense of humor, his wit and the quick little laughs that light up his face. Unlike me Podoske likes his cigarettes and a touch of bourbon once in a while.

At first, we room together and get to know each other well. He has an easy way about him, a personality that invites anyone to know him. He listens well and seems genuinely interested in my life. We are often together at the PX, the base theater or sometimes in town.

Older and more experienced than I, he sometimes laughs at my innocence. He likes women, but he's no woman chaser. They're attracted to his good looks and thick wavy hair.

*   *   *

Several days after I meet Johnston and Podoske, all three of us meet the rest of our crew. In turn, we shake hands with Corporal Stanowick, Private First Class Hannigan, Corporal Diaz, Staff Sergeant Frawley, Corporal Pengra and Corporal Lucas. There are nine of us now, eventually to be ten when our navigator arrives, and, despite our varying backgrounds, hope to fuse ourselves into a top bomber crew. The better we work together, the better chance we have to survive.

Corporal Stanowick from Providence, Rhode Island, our assistant radioman, becomes our tail gunner. He has to sit at the narrow back end of the fuselage with his legs straight out, peering back through a small Plexiglas window while manning two .50 caliber machine guns. A gentle man with a deceivingly bull dog-like face and a soft, rather high pitched voice shaped by a New England accent, he readily assumes his position in the tail. Like Podoske, he's of Polish descent. It's surprising that there are so many men in the army of Polish heritage. A rather quiet person, at least around me, I learn little about him. Respectful and cooperative, he silently goes about his job.

Private First Class Hannigan is with us only three weeks before he's grounded with eye trouble. Because he's such a good man and all around nice guy, we hate to lose him. Corporal Caruso from Pennsylvania replaces him then becomes our ball turret gunner. Small and compact, he nestles into the claustrophobic confines of the ball turret, curling up inside of it like an embryo in the womb. Laughter and jokes bubble out of Caruso as naturally as his breath, keeping himself loose and the rest of us as well. Having been an armament man on a ground crew, he knows guns and turrets, and becomes an instant asset to our crew.

Corporal Diaz from St. Louis, Missouri, the only married man on the crew, lights up the space around him with his friendliness and his lively smile. His dark eyes sparkle below his curly black hair, and when he laughs, he flashes his even white teeth. As we begin to fly, he gradually changes. Rough weather sometimes makes him airsick, and at other times he seems frightened, his face becoming pale, his dark eyes darting this way and that like the eyes of a nervous animal. He stays with us as the weeks of training go by, but obviously he doesn't relish flying or, I suspect, the thought of combat. Near the end of our training he develops eye problems. Instead of the news disappointing him, he appears genuinely happy about his bad eyes. In the final weeks of training the doctors ground him permanently, and he slips away from us, very much relieved. Corporal Kellog, a small, sandy-haired young man with a quiet smile, replaces him.

We're happy to have Staff Sergeant Frawley on our crew. An expert radioman that already had experience in the Pacific, he'll be especially valuable to us. After only a few weeks, however, the commanders in charge of crews decide that he's too advanced to go through unnecessary training with us. They remove him from our crew, and place him on another about to leave for combat.

We grumble about losing Sergeant Frawley, but we welcome his replacement, Corporal Witherspoon, as our new radio operator. Quiet and soft-spoken, slender in build, he becomes, at 27, the oldest member of our crew. I, at 19, less than two years out of high school, am overwhelmed by his education and experience. A graduate of the University of Alabama where he had majored in Spanish, English and Mathematics, he taught mathematics to high school sophomores in Ohio. Despite his superior education, there's a quiet humility about him. In awe of him, I treat him with the greatest respect. Even when a friendly smile plays about his lips, a trace of worry steals across his brow, wrinkling his forehead above his bushy eyebrows. I'm sure he would rather be in a classroom with blackboards and students than in the aluminum body of a heavy bomber with a crew soon to go into combat.

*   *   *

Corporal Lucas, the engineer, in his mid-twenties, despite his lack of height, is probably the most handsome man on the crew with his stylish hair and classic face. I feel that at times he barely tolerates me, a younger officer who outranks him. Although outwardly respectful and friendly, I sense he finds it difficult to accept me. I read it in the unconscious wrinkling of his brow, an occasional near-insolent smile and a subtle rolling of his eyes. I never pressure him, but I feel his distaste for me as a person. When I become the venereal disease officer of our crew, our differences reveal themselves.

The base commander decides that all bombardiers will be venereal disease officers of their crews. Our first duty is to watch several nauseating films showing glistening red, crater-like chancres on penises, all in full color, pus oozing from the ends of them, and syphilitic men with the bridges of their noses eaten away. Fighting off nausea and light-headedness, I endure the films, sometimes having to close my eyes against the horrors on the screen.

As V.D. officer I have to see that the crew all have these prophylactic kits. It's a shame, I know, but most of them will get into trouble like that once in a while. Most soldiers do, even the officers. That's one thing that surprised me when I first joined the army. Most of it is just because they are away from home, awful down in the dumps about something, or under the influence of alcohol---some weren't brought up right in the beginning. It's kind of a serious problem. A lot of it is due to the girls too. In fact I think quite a bit of it is due to them. They stand all over the streets sort of flirting with you. Most soldiers will fall for that easy.

Lucas, very experienced with women, is not about to take any warnings, help or advice from me, an innocent inexperienced kid just out of high school. He works on the upper turret mechanism, his eyes squinting against the sun filtering through the Plexiglas, as he listens to me. I have no desire to lecture him, only to tell him what I had seen in the film and see if he had a prophylactic kit. But I inadvertently express my own opinion.

"Of course the best way to prevent is just not to have sex."

Without even looking back at me or showing any emotion, he says, "But Lieutenant, that would be totally impossible. Men need to have women. Don't you feel the need for a woman once in a while, Lieutenant?"

I sense that his expression, his half-smile, and the look around his eyes means he's laughing at me.

"Sex is part of life," he says. "A man can't go through life without women, at least I can't."

"What about venereal disease?" I ask.

"Most of that is exaggerated," he replies. "They only show you the worst. If you choose your women, and take reasonable precautions, it's okay. A man has to have women."

It's obvious that I have nothing to offer him--that he only plays with me. I stop the conversation and tell him where he can pick up the kits.

Despite the tension between us, we get along well, each of us good-naturedly tolerating the other in the interest of crew harmony.

We had all come together at last, men from all parts of the country, bringing with us our own experiences, attitudes, philosophies and outlooks on life. We'll have to bury any differences we might have and learn to work together if we want to be a first rate crew. We want to survive our training and eventually combat, and we know that a smooth-functioning group increases our chances.

THE FLYING FORTRESS

Buoyant with anticipation, I walk across the oil-spotted concrete ramp with my pilot and co-pilot for my first look inside a B-17. Towering clouds dim the sunlight as we make our way toward the plane. I like the way the B-17, the Flying Fortress, looks poised on the ramp, its clean lines cutting across the backdrop of billowy clouds. I admire the plane's sleekness, the way it angles toward the sky and the sweep of the long fin tapering upward toward the tail. I respect its reputation, its tradition and its mystique.

I buzz with pride and excitement as we approach it, its plain white star insignia blazing in its olive-drab camouflage. The sheer size of the behemoth overwhelms me as we pass under the engine nacelles. Its shadowed wings seem to stretch out forever. Its four engines and three-bladed propellers exude power even when they're silent.

Johnston twists a small handle on the escape hatch door, under the belly, just behind the bombardier and navigator's compartments. The small door drops down then hangs by its hinges as we hoist ourselves, one by one into the opening and the heady smell of aluminum, rubber, wiring and plastic. Curious about my own position on the plane, I duck through to the nose. Passing the small navigator's table, I find that the bombardier's compartment is large enough that I can stand up in it. I look out through a great rounded window of Plexiglas, giving me an unsurpassed view of everything in front of me and a psychological feeling of roominess. The bombardier's knobs, switches and lights seem not as complex as

343

I thought they might be. The brand new bombsight mounted in front excites me as I hadn't seen one since leaving Midland two months before. I sit in the small bombardier's seat just behind the bombsight to get the feel of my new "home." I think briefly of my own home when I discover that the plane had been assembled at the Douglas plant in Long Beach, California, only 20 miles from Inglewood.

I gaze at the bewildering maze of instruments, dials and switches in the pilot's compartment. I have an instant respect for Johnston and all the other pilots who understand them. I decide that I'll gradually try to learn all about the instruments.

We walk back on a narrow catwalk through the bomb bays with only a flimsy rope railing to hang on to. Once past the bomb bays, we step into the roomy radioman's compartment, then the waist. We poke into the top turret, the ball turret and the tail gunner's position, exploring every inch of the craft.

Being a part of a crew on a magnificent airplane like the B-17 feels almost like a dream.

It's the culmination of all that I'd wished for and all that I'd worked so hard to achieve.

*   *   *

Several days later, I, along with several other new bombardiers, follow the instructor, a captain, across the ramp toward a B-17. A light sprinkle dampens the concrete, the bomber appearing especially dark beneath the cloudy skies. The captain's job is to familiarize us with the instruments in the nose compartment. With a few grunts and wheezes we pull ourselves up into the belly through the escape hatch. The captain points out that if we ever have to evacuate the plane quickly, this hatch is the one to use. We should roll out head first with our parachutes.

As we stand in the nose, he points out the air temperature gauge, air speed indicator, altimeter, compass and drift meter, all instruments we'd used at Midland in training, each one necessary for precision bombing and navigation. He explains the bombardier's control panel with its banks of indicator lights and toggle switches and the intervalometer that controls the release and spacing of the bombs on the ground. None of the equipment seems very complex, and I feel I'll have no trouble using them. I'm anxious to fly, and try them all out for myself. After a tour through the bomb bays and a look at the bomb racks and shackles, we've seen it all.

The roominess of the bombardier's compartment with its panoramic view impresses me the most. Room and vision. I yearn to be as unrestricted as possible, and to be able to see as much as possible. Being in the nose of the B-17 is like having a new window on the world, a place where I can clearly observe the clouds and storms and the hundreds of miles of land spread out before me with its cities, railroad junctions, rivers, forests and roads.

Later, soon after we begin flying, I write home.

I sure wish I could take you folks up in the nose with me sometime when we are flying. I bet you would really like it up there. Our whole family, including Pal and the chickens, could easily fit in it. That's the part I like about it. After you bomb, you can get up and stretch and even walk around a bit. I have a regular maze of switches and levers up there to fiddle around with--which I kind of like.

* * *

With the engines at full throttle and the brakes set, the bomber fluttering like a trembling bird, we face the long concrete runway. Johnston suddenly releases the brakes. We begin to roll, the black tire marks and concrete seams passing slowly beneath us. Gradually gathering speed, we seem to hurtle down the runway forever before we finally lift and sail out over the forests and fields around the air base. Used to the relatively quick take-offs of the AT-11s in training, this one seems excruciatingly long. I watch it from the nose where I'm not supposed to be during take-off for safety reasons, but the drama here is too exciting to miss.

For my first flight in a B-17, we have to stay in the air for five hours, and I must drop fifteen practice bombs, one at a time, at a bombing range in Texas. No instructor is along to help me in case I have a problem, and, for some mysterious reason, the bombardier's seat is missing. As the only navigator on board, I plot the course to the bombing range hundreds of miles to the west. Although I'd had a few hours on the bomb trainer at the base, I hadn't touched a Norden bombsight in the air for over three months. The flight seems more like a baptism.

Without a seat, I kneel in front of the bombsight as though praying for a good hit. Despite the uncomfortable position, I manipulate the bombsight as well as I can. I pick up the target, refine my settings and lay the first bomb close to the center. Having a stable platform like the smooth-flying B-17 is so much better than the bucking AT-11s we flew in training.

On the next run I begin to feel the strain in my legs. The tension of my first B-17 bombing mission and my awkward position tighten my muscles. Just as I get the target caught in my crosshairs and the refining nearly completed, a knot begins to harden in my thigh. Leaving the bombsight, I quickly grab my cramping leg, straighten it out and massage the lump of muscle with my fingers. The unmanned bombsight, doing the best it can without me, releases the bomb that sails far off the mark.

With thirteen more bombs to go, I try to relax my leg and concentrate on the bombing. Between each run I stand and work my thigh as though kneading a lump of bread dough, trying to relax the brick-hard muscle. On all but one more run I bomb successfully, but on that one, suffering an excruciating cramp at the last moment, yet another bomb goes astray.

With our bombing mercifully over we are to fly to Jasper, Texas, to rendezvous with several other planes then fly back to the base in formation. As the green pilots are not yet practiced at rendezvousing, we find only one other plane. We tuck ourselves in close to the other plane, flying back to the base only about 100 feet from each other. By the time we land, a landing as smooth as spreading soft butter on bread, I'm exhausted.

Once on the ground, I find out, to my great surprise, that I had the second best bombing score of the day, only 9 feet behind the leader. Considering my cramp-thrown bombs, I'm satisfied.

I'd been properly introduced to the Flying Fortress, and, despite my problems, I'm glad to have met it.

THE UNEXPECTED

Our plane sweeps up into an eerie darkness, softened by the pale blue light of a full moon. I zip my thick winter flying jacket, check my maps and the course then switch off the small map-reading light. I'd never flown with the moon so full and the air so clear at night. I'd heard about a "bomber's moon," and I think that a night like this is what they must have had in mind. In the darkness of the nose compartment, I look out through my panoramic window at the jeweled and phosphorescent villages and cities scattered over the flat blackness of Louisiana. Some of the city light patterns will be landmarks to help me check my course to the bombing range in east Texas.

As our laboring engines gradually pull us up to an altitude of 10,000 feet, I check the temperature gauge. It reads 28 degrees. I strap on my oxygen mask to keep my head and thoughts clear. So far, my jacket has kept me warm in my unheated compartment. The grand view out of my great round window makes me forget about the cold. The brilliant moon suffuses the earth below with pale blue light, bringing out the features of fields and forests, rivers and even roads, all touched with lunar softness. As we fly over wide rivers, swamps and bayous, the mirrored image of the moon looks back up at us.

My God it's exciting to be here! I love hurtling through the night sky in the moonlight amid the thunderous surge of power from our four engines, the roar of the air around our nose, the magical scene below, even the rubbery smell of the oxygen mask. At times like this I embrace experience, the whole exhilarating freshness of it, and I forget for a while how I yearn to be home.

I had set up and calibrated the bombsight and prepared all the bomb settings ahead of time. When we arrive at the east Texas bombing range, I'll be ready. Ten blue practice bombs hang in order on the racks back in the darkness of the bomb bays, all to be dropped one at a time on separate bomb runs. I look forward to the bombing because I'm especially confident: I'd dropped ten bombs in the afternoon for the best score I'd had yet. An instructor was along who praised my accuracy and said that he had no suggestions for improvement.

"Stevens," says Johnston in a strained voice over the intercom, "Can you see the target up ahead anywhere? It's supposed to be near that city down there, isn't it?"

Knowing that we're not near the target yet, I answer, "No. That's not the right city. We still have a ways to go."

We stay on course for about five more minutes when Johnston says in the same tight voice, "We're going home!"

Why does he want to go back? We're not due at the base for another two hours.

Is he angry with me because I disagreed with him about the identity of the town? But I know exactly where we are. Has our plane developed mechanical problems? The engines seem to be running smoothly. For a moment I think we might have been called back because of threatening weather, but the forecasts had predicted continued clear skies.

We bank sharply then turn on a heading back to the field, the bombs I was to drop still hanging on the racks.

"Co-pilot to crew," says Podoske over the intercom. "Johnston's sick. I'm going to take us back to the field. We'll drop down in altitude to make him more comfortable."

A wave of panic ripples through my bowels. Podoske has flown the plane several hours, and he's had training in lighter multi-engine aircraft, but he's never landed a B-17. As far as I know he's never even been shown how! Landing an airplane is the trickiest maneuver of all, and is sometimes the nemesis of even the best pilots.

"Johnston's really sick at his stomach," says Podoske. "He has a stabbing pain in his side, and he's just slumping in his seat. I hope to hell he doesn't pass out. Johnston told me he'd try to land the plane when we get back."

We take off our oxygen masks as we lower our altitude. Podoske holds the plane steady as we head back on course to Alexandria. Johnston doesn't improve. The ethereal beauty of the moonlit night fades away as well as my plans for a good bombing mission.

All the way to Alexandria, I think about the landing. Will Johnston be capable of landing the plane once we arrive? Will Podoske, as green as he is, be able to bring the plane in without killing us all? Will experienced pilots at the base be able to talk Podoske down over the radio? Will Johnston recover enough to land it? Could we try a normal landing or will we have to come in our belly? None of the alternatives sound good to me.

Finally back over the field, it's time for a decision. Johnston, still very ill but conscious, says he will take over the landing, a great relief to me. He turns into the landing pattern, but with his thoughts addled by nausea and pain, he circles into a right-hand pattern when he's supposed to approach from the left. Podoske warns him, and we try it again, this time lowering into the correct left-hand pattern. We glide down towards the runway, its edges dotted with lights. All seems normal, and I begin to relax. The tires squeal on the runway as our bomber lands without the slightest jolt, a landing that any pilot would be proud of.

Once stopped at the flight line, Johnston scurries out of the plane, leaving all his equipment behind. He disappears into the flight room, and that's the last we see of him for the night.

* * *

Safely nestled in my bunk in the tar paper-covered barracks, my thoughts are full of the evening we've just lived through. My admiration for Johnston slides up a notch. Coming in for a perfect landing despite his distress had been a genuine act of courage. He'd brought us through what had been a tense situation. The tenacity he'd shown had raised my confidence in him. In threatening situations, especially those that lie ahead of us in combat, I think he'll always pull us through.

I think about how quickly life can change. Coasting along in a near-euphoric state of comfort and wonder, I'd seen my world shift in a single moment to one dominated by apprehension and fear.

I should have learned by now that the unexpected is part of flying.

A bombardier and co-pilot from our barracks, good friends of mine, had to bail out with the rest of their crew when one of their engines caught fire and began to disintegrate over Oklahoma. They all escaped by descending safely in their parachutes. Another crew, hopelessly lost, had to set down on an emergency airstrip. All of us, sooner or later, would have to deal with the unexpected.

BEFORE DAWN

Rising out of a cozy bed before dawn reminds me of surf-fishing trips with my father. He would shake us out of our sleep at 4 a.m. so that we could reach the beach just at sunrise when the wide stretch of sand would be entirely ours, and the incoming tide would bring the fish close to shore. I remember how much I wanted to go on sleeping, yet I looked forward to the adventure at the beach---my father standing in the foaming surf with his pants legs rolled up, casting the line out into the churning waves, my first sip of steaming hot cocoa from the thermos.

When the orderly rousts us out of the barracks at 0400 for the day's mission, I feel much the same way. I want to pull the sheet over my head and return to my dreams, yet I think about the excitement of the mission ahead, never knowing for sure what it will be. It could be a bombing mission at the practice range in Texas or camera bombing over nearby large cities. It might also be a navigation flight or a gunnery exercise over the Gulf of Mexico. We might fly alone or practice formation flying. Then there was the ever-changing weather that always staged a special drama of its own.

Still trying to gather my wits, I sit on the edge of the bed, my hair rumpled, my eyes squinting at the light. Podoske has already inhaled his first cigarette of the day, the pungent smoke floating lazily about the room. I mechanically make my bed, drawing the blanket tight, turning back a few inches of sheet and folding the spare blanket neatly at the foot. My trench coat and gas mask hang on hooks on one wall, my dirty clothes bag on the other. I walk slowly to my locker just outside our room and slip into my flying clothes. The coal stove next to our door stands cold and useless this morning, as air from the Gulf of Mexico bathes us in its sticky warmth. But the weather changes quickly in Louisiana.

I brush my teeth in the latrine with all the others, most of them rather silent and not fully awake. I quicken my pace, as we must be dressed, fully alert and fed before briefing at 0500. Podoske and I walk out into the sultry darkness, our feet crunching on the crushed shells that compose the pathway. We pass our "lawn" which is mostly mud and the large coal bin against the barracks where each crew gets its coal when the weather turns cold.

The mess hall lights shine out brightly into the darkness. I generally enjoy army food, and don't understand others when they constantly complain about it, but the fare at this base is usually plain and poorly prepared. Not bad this morning though---scrambled powdered eggs, potatoes and limp bacon. The coffee tastes good.

Briefing is never brief, often lasting well over an hour. Today we have a variety of assignments, each crew performing its own special tasks. Our crew is to fly on instruments for three hours then rendezvous with two other crews for two hours of formation flying. I'll navigate, practice tracking with my guns and receiving Morse code.

The weather officer is the highlight of the briefing. With a rare combination of a love for meteorology and a sense of the dramatic, he holds us spellbound with his forecast.

"Oh, there'll be huge build-ups along this front," he begins, his voice penetrating and his eyes almost wild. Reaching with his hands to emphasize height, he goes on. "There'll be cloud tops building to over 40,000 feet! They'll be full of strong up and down drafts capable of ripping your plane apart! There'll be frequent lightning, blinding rain and blasts of hail bigger than marbles! Stay out of them!"

We all smile and chuckle at his performance, but he's made his point---no one will fly anywhere near them.

A comedian pilot who had just announced to the group that he'd been "busier than a cat trying to cover up shit on a marble floor," says he has a solution for some of the crews who have had trouble finding their way home after night missions. "Just do this," he says with a playful grin on his face. "Every crew takes a homing pigeon along that has been fed Feenamint and phosphorus. When they're lost, they release the pigeon then follow his trail through the dark." Everyone collapses with laughter, taking the edge off the grimness of having to get up so early and the prospect of the long mission ahead.

Trucks take us out to our plane. By now, I'm an expert at hoisting myself up through the small escape hatch door into the plane's belly. Once in my compartment, I calculate headings for today's mission. I remain in the nose for take off, watching the runway flash by as we charge down it.

Without much to do today, I plot a temperature-altitude graph for my own information and amusement. The temperature decreases normally with altitude until we reach 1200 feet where it becomes warmer. This lasts until we reach 4000 feet, the temperature again dropping with altitude. We'd passed through an inversion layer, a thick blanket of warm air trapped between two cooler ones. I noticed temperature inversions before whenever we passed through cloud layers, so I predict to myself that clouds will form in this layer.

I continue to navigate as the pilot and copilot practice flying on instruments. Part of their training involves tight turns and rudimentary acrobatics while on instruments. Some of the turns and dives press me flat against my seat, blood rushing to and from my head. My brain feels as though it's being compressed into one corner of my skull and then another. At times my vision dims as though I'm close to blacking out. I'm surprised that a B-17 can make these moves. I'd felt these forces while training in AT-11s at bombardier school and was used to them, but our gunners had very little flying experience.

Two gunners, dizzy and queasy from all of the sharp maneuvers, retch at their stations. I walk through the bomb bay to the radio room just in time to see Witherspoon, his hand desperately clasped to his mouth, send a stream of vomit through his fingers. I sympathize with him and help him clean up his table. One of the gunners who hadn't eaten breakfast doubles up with the "dry heaves," a condition far worse than throwing up.

With the acrobatics over, our plane on a steadier course, we rendezvous with two other B-17s for formation flying. The gunners relax. Tight formations concentrate our firepower, discouraging attacks by fighter planes. It's a survival skill we practice often.

We fly north above the Mississippi River, narrower than I thought it would be. Far below, a barge and tug make their slow way up the river, leaving a small wake behind them. About one hour away from Alexandria we turn slowly back to a southern heading toward the base.

As we near Alexandria, a solid cloud deck forms beneath us at the altitude of the temperature inversion I'd charted soon after take-off. I feel smug and satisfied that I'd predicted it. I wish I'd told someone about it. Now alone, we fly over the soft white mass of clouds. As I look down on all that blinding whiteness, I spot the shadow of our plane riding the smooth cloud tops, and, around it, a curious rainbow-tinted halo, a phenomenon I'd never seen before.

We lower through the clouds, buffeted by the currents whirling around in the mist. We break through, and then fly just beneath the layer, the currents rising into it shaking the big plane. By the time our tires finally squeal on the runway, I feel as though I'd been active for a full day, but it's only noon.

Since the officers allow us little respite, I spend over an hour after lunch filling out mandatory papers. By 1500 I'm out on the skeet range where I must practice shooting clay pigeons until 1700 when my military intelligence class begins. After 1800 we're free to eat supper and return to the barracks. I'm exhausted. I'm always exhausted. I dash off a quick letter home, run through the shower and slip into bed. Beneath the cloud cover the evening remains warm and sticky. The sheets always feel damp. I push the blanket down, and pull one of them around me.

Tomorrow we must get up early again. The Bomber Command accelerates our training because more crews are urgently needed. Most of us feel that the invasion of Europe is close at hand.

BLACKNESS

Lights at the edge of the runway flicker by faster and faster. As we gradually lift, our wheels folding neatly up into their nacelles, our plane climbs into the night. I would rather not fly at night even though the blue-white dazzle of stars and the curious light patterns of villages and cities are spectacular. But when clouds obscure them, plunging us into darkness, only the pale glowing of our instruments indicates how our plane is flying. Hurtling through the void without any visual references makes me uneasy.

I much prefer to look down on the ever-changing scene below and around us at the shifting shapes of clouds. I like to know exactly where we are, to follow our path on a map, and match it with what I observe below---the sinuous turns of a river, a convergence of railroads, the shape of a forest, the outline of a lake, the grid of a city or the long ribbon of a major highway. Watching the countryside roll by beneath us is much like exploring the country, discovering new territories. I look down on the places we pass over then try to picture myself on the ground there, imagining what I might see. Night flying takes all that away.

When we fly at night, we don't begin until 2100. Each crew wings its way alone into the dark emptiness. We must remain aloft until 0200 before we are allowed to touch down. We eat breakfast at 0300, hope to slip into bed by 0400. We sleep fitfully until noon when we wake up to a dream-like day. The mainspring of our biological clocks has been sprung, our bodies telling us it's one time and our watches another. My stomach doesn't like it. The sun goes down too early, and we begin to prepare for another night of flying.

* * *

Gradually a solid mattress of clouds moving in below us swallows the city lights, leaving only nocturnal nothingness. I can no longer use pilotage, the most accurate way to navigate, relying instead on dead reckoning and the headings the navigator and I had plotted. Johnston has a radio compass in the pilot's compartment as a reliable backup. All I can do now is relax.

Sometimes, on nights like this, I'd climb up into the co-pilot's seat and practice flying the plane, or rather attempt to maintain altitude and heading by watching the compass, altimeter, gyro-horizon, needle and ball indicator and the rate of climb meter. As a rank amateur, I'd grasped the wheel and control column, pulling and pushing and turning gently in a futile effort to make the instruments do what I wanted them to do. On one night I learned how to transfer fuel from one tank to another, and on another how to take fixes with the radio compass, but tonight is not to be one of them.

A mild vibration, like a long shiver runs through the airplane, the shaking far different from ordinary turbulence. My stomach flutters as the vibration continues.

"Pilot to crew," Johnston finally says over the intercom, "We have a problem with one of our engines. We've shut it down, but we've lost oil pressure. We can't feather the prop. It's just windmilling around out there, tearing up the engine. Stevens, you and Warren get out of the nose and go back to the radio room with the rest of the crew while I see what I can do with this engine."

Warren and I slide under the pilot's compartment and around the top gun turret. Lucas, the engineer, stands next to Johnston discussing what to do about the engine. We squeeze through the bomb bay on the narrow catwalk. We enter into the feeble light of the radio room where the rest of the crew anxiously wait, their faces grim. Warren, our newly arrived navigator, remains quiet, undoubtedly wondering how he ever got into this situation. The shudder of the windmilling propeller still ripples through the plane.

"You'd better have your chutes on," says Johnston in a calm voice, "stay in the waist and stand by the door. We still can't feather the damn prop. We're heading back toward the field, but we'll have to watch the engine, and see what it does. If you hear the signal you'll have to jump."

My mouth sucked dry, I edge toward the rear door near the others. We stand in the dim light-- waiting.

Our chest chutes are firmly snapped to our harnesses. We listen for Johnston's signal, a ringing from a warning device that sounds like an old fashioned doorbell. Even though I'm firmly resolved to jump, I can't help but think of the worst. It's close to midnight, and even if I land without incident, I couldn't find my way in the dark. I'd have to wait for dawn. Much of Louisiana is covered with forests. What if I should snag myself on a tree, get hung up there? How would I get myself out of it at night? What if I should land in a bayou? I would have no sense of direction. How would I wade out of it? What about alligators? I run my moist fingers over the pull cord handle on my parachute. I want to be sure I know where it is in the dark. The other men are quiet except for an occasional clipped, dry-mouthed wisecrack.

"We're getting close to the field now, and the engine is at least not any worse, no sign of fire in it yet," says Johnston. "We'll try to make it to the field."

At least for now we've abandoned the idea of bailing out. The plane still shudders with its sickness, but our odds look better. I breathe easier. The prospect of jumping out into that blackness had been more like a nightmare than real life.

Still unable to feather the propeller blades to keep them from windmilling, Johnston lowers the trembling plane toward the runway. Just before our wheels touch the runway, the engine freezes. The propeller stops turning. As we roll in for a near-perfect landing, I silently thank Johnston for his skill and coolness, my confidence in him growing even more. With our remaining three engines, we taxi to the flight line.

Anxious to feel our feet on the ground again, we file out of the side door, the same door we might have jumped out of a short time before. The last one out, I grab the door handle to slam it shut. The handle feels slimy in my hand. In the dim light I can see that the palm of my hand is streaked with oil. A thick coating of it covers the entire right side and bottom of the fuselage. The plane wears a gleaming liquid skin of oil, the airport lights glistening in its slippery blackness. A broken oil line and other damage to the engine had spewed the oil out all over the plane, leaving none to lubricate the engine. Had Johnston been able to feather the propeller to keep it from turning, we wouldn't have had a problem, but windmilling in the slipstream, had moved all parts of the engine without any lubrication. The friction and heat damaged the engine. In its lower portion, bent push rods protrude through the finned cylinders, allowing even more oil to gush out. We'd been lucky that the frictional heat hadn't set the engine on fire.

A small truck meets us, delivering us immediately to another plane. We must complete our flying time, and, like a jockey who has had a spill rides in the very next race to conquer his fear and keep up his nerve, we mount our next "steed."

The lights zip by at the edge of the runway as we once again lift into the blackness. All four engines hum together, their clean power pulling us up to altitude again. Even though I'm not keen about flying at night, my confidence returns, settling into me again like a silent warm sigh.

FIRST ANNIVERSARY

Well, at this time last year I was just starting to crawl in my bunk for my first night's sleep in an army camp. I remember I was thrilled with it all, and I slept like a top. It rained that night, and no doubt it will rain here tonight. It was much cooler that night than it is here now though. So this is my first anniversary in the army. I was wondering then whether I would get into cadets, and here I am a bombardier on a B-17, exactly what I wanted. I guess I was pretty lucky.

I think back over the year about the subtle ways that I've either changed or remained the same. Being snatched from the hearth of a loving, protective family in California, then being thrown together with all sorts of men from all over the country with all kinds of outlooks and ideas certainly influenced my life. So too had being subjected to rigid discipline in strange and hostile parts of the country. I'd had experiences and seen sights I never dreamed imaginable. The lump of clay is still roughly the same, but the potter's fingers have done their work.

I still don't smoke, drink or "chase" women even though most men around me do. I don't gamble away my paycheck. I still believe in God, the holiness of the church and the power of prayer, though I'm far from being pious. I still believe in the ideal of marrying a good woman, forming a loving family, and reserving sex until marriage. Love for my parents and my home grows stronger rather than weaker. I write my parents nearly every day. None of my basic moral values have changed---my mother and father, the church and my track coach, whom I considered to be a great man, had shaped me in their images.

I met men from Texas, Rhode Island, New York, Oregon, Massachusetts, Virginia and nearly every other state, and listened with interest to their special accents, drawls and twangs---the slow talkers and fast talkers. From them I learned about life in other parts of the country---the raw life of Brooklyn streets, frog hunting in the Louisiana bayous, contending with winter snow in Michigan or the braving the rigors of farm life in Illinois. A few men didn't smoke while others lit their cigarettes at every opportunity. A few abstained from liquor, but others tromped noisily back into the barracks at night so drunk they could hardly stand up. A few who were faithful wrote loving letters to their wives; the single and the married men who considered themselves single returned to the barracks with lipstick smears on their faces.

I met Protestants, Catholics and Jews ranging from the occasional churchgoer to the devout. I met atheists who angrily claimed they had no religion. I hung on the edge of religious discussions and listened. "Everything in the Bible is absolutely true," proclaimed a devout Protestant. "Surely you don't believe that a whale actually swallowed a man, and spit him out alive," challenged a skeptic. "The Bible was written by Jews to make money," shouted an anti-Semitic atheist.

I saw men clutching fans of cards, stone-faced and serious, and others rolling dice, the sound of them muffled on army blankets.

As more and more men passed through my world, wearing the varying silks of their ways of life, I judged less and less. Without changing my own ways I began to accept men with values far different from mine. I began to comprehend the whole of humanity with its fascinating complexity of differences. I got along with the gamblers, greeted the men who drunkenly intruded on my sleep, talked to the men who have been with women in strange beds and flew with men who denied God. I realized that men of vastly different attitudes and ideals can work together, can merge their common humanity.

Feeling boyish at first, I learned that I could keep up with the other men both physically and mentally. I had no idea that I could learn so much, had the capacity to absorb the vast amount of information my training required. For the first time the idea of attending college seemed possible. I ran with the men, climbed any obstacle they could, leapt over pits of wet mud and held my own at boxing. I was as much a man as anyone else.

I'm proud of what I'd done, proud of being an officer and a bombardier.

I'd become more realistic. I think back about that day at Midland, the day of the Bombing Olympics. A flight of B-17s and one of B-24s roared over the field in a simulated bombing attack. Thrilled by the spectacle, my whole body caught up in the throb of those engines, I'd pictured the men flying in them as heroes, as something more than mere men. I'd imagined their features---their squinting, penetrating eyes, jutting jaws and handsome tanned faces. They looked like the heroic men in all the adventure movies I'd seen.

Now, as a crewmember on a B-17, I mix daily with the men from all the crews. None of them match the majestic models of my imagination. A few men are handsome, but most run the gamut of human types. There are short men with large noses, prematurely bald men or those with thinning hair, wisecracking men and jokers. There are tall thin men and others, already fleshing out, with hints of future potbellies. Some men are blond while others sport heads of dark curls or reddish hair over pale faces and freckles. Other men have large ears or ones that stick out. There are dark-jowled men who always appear to need a shave and boyish faces that appear never to need shaving.

With the romantic dust out of my eyes I see them now as men, men of all types. The rows of faces in the mess hall, the bodies clad in shorts shaving in front of latrine mirrors, the rumble of assembled voices before briefing begins---all different, all men, but just men---and I among them.

Although proud of becoming an officer, I feel no different. An18 year-old when asked on his birthday how it feels to be 19 ponders for a moment and says "I don't really feel anything. I feel the same." So it is with me. I'm used to it now. I felt honored at returning salutes from enlisted men at first, but now I find it routine and sometimes annoying.

I was right about flying. Despite occasionally having to fly at night or getting up too early in the morning, I love it. I never tire of looking at the land below me or of flying through the daily changes of weather. I like flying in brilliantly blue skies as well as bumping along in cumulus clouds or bursting through a rain shower out into the clear again. I like the challenge of navigating the airplane and bombing accurately. I enjoy the camaraderie of the crew, each member with his own function.

Despite my love for the Air Corps, the adventures of traveling to new places and the stimulation of meeting new people, I still can't break away from the persistent attraction of my home and family. It's as though I possess a two thousand-mile umbilical cord.

This will be my second Easter away from home. In the morning I will go to the sunrise service at the Methodist church in Pineville. That's just across the river from here. I hope I can persuade myself to get up at 5:00. I certainly hope I can spend my next Easter at home. Just between you and me, I think I will be able to. You just wait and see. I would just give anything if I could get home tomorrow. I am so homesick it is pitiful. That trip down to the railroad station that morning was the saddest trip I ever made. I wanted to turn around, and go back home.

Even in the midst of flying, thoughts of home bubble up.

Tell Myrtle that the plane I was in today had throat mike control boxes made at the Universal Microphone Company, Inglewood, California. I really showed the crew our town's name on them too. There it was as plain as day," Inglewood. Calif." I just happened to notice it as I pressed on the switch to talk.

Within the roaring glass and aluminum shell of the bomber's nose, my thoughts return to Inglewood---the peaceful street where the microphone company stands, the eucalyptus forest nearby leaning and swaying in the afternoon sea breeze, the cable swing attached to a high branch near Leslie's house, the steep grade of the Santa Fe Railroad where I watched locomotives struggle with their burdens of freight.

Twenty-two men from my block on Brett Street are in the service, serving in all branches in various parts of the United States or the world. So is nearly every male member of my graduating high school class. Most, I believe, yearn to return to their hometown, families and friends.

Warm raindrops begin to tap the roof of the barracks, and the soft rumble of thunder rolls across the sultry forests and bayous. It's too warm for a blanket. I push it down to the foot of my bed then pull the sheet over me. The blue flicker of lightning momentarily casts its soft light into the dark room. I stretch out, then relax, and begin the long journey to the next anniversary.

TWO WAYS OF SEEING BATON ROUGE

Our plane bounces in turbulence at only 1000 feet above the Louisiana countryside. Johnston attempts to stay in tight formation with two other planes but erratic bumps, lifts and drops make it difficult to stay close. A solid gray overcast at 2000 feet keeps us low, out of the ragged clouds.

Despite the choppiness, I fix my gaze on the scene below---the farms, fields, road patterns, railroads with their yards and switches, and the quaintness of small towns. Flying so low is almost like traveling in an automobile except the view is even better from the Plexiglas nose. I sit in my small bombardier's seat, fascinated with the tapestry of rural Louisiana passing beneath me. Horses and cows, spooked by the loud, sudden strangeness of us, scatter in every direction, loping across the fields for their very lives. Several days before, we'd flown low over a lake, flushing a flight of ducks, an obviously terrified mallard zipping right by the pilot's window.

We maintain the same altitude as we speed over the outskirts of Baton Rouge, then over the city itself. Its beauty impresses me, even on this cloudy, sultry day. Lovely residential streets with green lawns and canopies of lush trees flash by, then the bends of the Mississippi River, the grid of city streets and the tall Louisiana capitol building. I vow to return to Baton Rouge on the ground if we should ever have a free day or two.

Jostled in the tail by the violent currents, Stanowick, the tail gunner, crouches near his open escape hatch heaving his breakfast and lunch all over Baton Rouge. Witherspoon, the radioman, is sick too, but unlike the day before, he manages to keep everything down. The motion and strain of trying to keep our equilibrium has made us all a little woozy. Relaxing like an old rag doll, just letting myself flop with the motion seems the best way to handle it. Fighting each lurch and jolt is useless.

As we turn back toward the base, we fly into a blinding rainstorm. Because of poor visibility, we break formation and plow through it on our own, the rain beating so hard against the plane that I can see nothing at all out of the nose except uniform gray and streaks of rainwater streaming and quivering around the Plexiglas. Rain drips in from the leaky seals of the astrodome and around the gun positions. A puddle accumulates on the navigator's table. Johnston, flying on instruments in the intensifying turbulence, battles the controls.

Once out of the rain the pilots reassemble for more formation flying. I sit looking out of the window again, admiring the countryside and feeling relieved to be out of the storm.

Suddenly a dark object flashes in front of the nose. Short vapor streaks trail from wingtips. Then it's gone. I've gathered my wits enough to realize that we've been "attacked" by a fighter plane zooming upward close in front of our nose at such speed that the wingtips leave streaks in the sultry air. The silhouette image in my mind tells me that it's a P-47 Thunderbolt interceptor, probably from the training base in Baton Rouge.

Finding a good opportunity to practice their moves, two Thunderbolts continue to make passes at our formation. They streak beneath us, zoom from above, and approach in wide pursuit curves. We also practice on them, tracking them with our guns at every chance. I'm sure I've "shot one down."

Through with their fun, one of the planes flies along side, its pilot waving his hand at us before he peels off.

Back at the base, our engines stopped at the flight line, we emerge from the plane, slightly groggy. Some of the gunners are not interested in dinner. I feel sticky and uncomfortable. The temperature in the airplane had remained close to a humid 80 degrees at that low altitude. A good, steady, hot shower would cure me.

*   *   *

I peer out of the window at the Istrouma Hotel in Baton Rouge, watching people stroll down the sidewalk, only a few cars moving down the Sunday-empty street. Since the base commander moved our shipping date back another few days and intensified our training, we felt that this might be our last chance to get away before going overseas.

Podoske and I left Alexandria by bus in the afternoon, arriving in Baton Rouge in the early evening. The air-conditioned bus was very comfortable, the pleasant countryside green and rural. The Istrouma Hotel, adequate but second rate, satisfied our budget requirements and gave us a convenient base from which we could explore the town.

The Louisiana State Capitol is first on our list of the sights to see. Tall and slender, it looks more like an office tower than a capitol building. It's nothing like the domed California State Capitol or the one in Salt Lake City. I think about my visit to the capital in Utah in the cold and snow, contrasting that day to this balmy one. We stroll around the magnificent grounds and gardens. We look up at a statue of Huey Long, the idol of Louisiana. Most interesting to me are the steps leading up to the capitol building, each one bearing the carved name of one of the states and the date of its entrance into the Union. This is the third capital I've seen; someday I want to see them all.

In our ambling about town we meet several pilots who'd been with Podoske at either primary or basic flight training. All are finishing their training at Baton Rouge as P-47 Thunderbolt pilots. They might have been the ones who practiced on us three weeks before, and many of them may become our escorts when we fly our missions in Europe. Podoske envies their luck at being able to fly a hot plane like the Thunderbolt.

"You guys are really lucky," says Podoske. "I'm nothing but a co-pilot on a lumbering bomber."

The Mississippi River flows only one block from the capitol building and two blocks from the main business district. We gaze at the wide river and the forest of green trees that grow down close to its banks. We think about crossing to the other side on a ferry, but decide we don't have time. Baton Rouge is even greener than it appeared from the air. It comforts my eyes and relaxes my body, makes me feel good about the earth.

After a good night's sleep and a hearty breakfast, we board the bus shortly after six in the morning, light drizzle dampening the streets. The bus rolls out of Baton Rouge and over the Mississippi River on its way back to Alexandria. We soon pass over the Atchafalaya River, about half as wide as the Mississippi.

Out in the green farm country on a two-lane road the bus stops five times because of cattle or mules on the pavement. We pass one cow that had been hit by a car, the mutilated carcass shoved to the side. The lack of fences allows the farm animals to wander off at will unless they're tied. We hear that sometimes they even saunter into the small towns. The farms are full of spring colts, calves and piglets. At least two pigs at each farm have litters. Baby chicks are everywhere. It's a time of green and being born. I like seeing all the new life on our final pass in the United States. I'm hopeful.

TO ERR IS HUMAN

I didn't know they would put an article in a Los Angeles paper about the crash [at our field]. *I wasn't going to tell you because I thought you might worry unnecessarily about things. It smacked the road by the side of the field, but it was the pilot's fault. He just wasn't watching his air speed when he put down his flaps. He was only 300 feet above the ground and going slow when he put them down. Naturally the plane dropped like a rock. I didn't see the accident, but I saw the wreckage when they brought it in. Don't ever go worrying about things like that because it very seldom ever happens, and besides that my pilot is on the ball, and I don't think he would do a thing like that. Our planes are well cared for here, and it is very safe.*

Always afraid my mother and father will worry about me, I shield them from most of the bad news about flying. Even though they're proud of my being in the service, they're constantly apprehensive about my safety. Because our crew is about to go overseas, I know they secretly believe they might not ever see me again. They stoically withhold their true feelings in order to spare me the burden of their worrying. In a way, we protect each other. At home they keep themselves busy with the war effort, working night and day in our garage, silver-soldering fittings on short, flexible metal hoses for aircraft engines. In their way, they feel that they're helping me, and helping themselves to bring me back.

Errors are a part of our training. In time there are fewer as the trainee becomes an expert, then an experienced veteran. All crewmembers learn from their mistakes. Most are minor or, once made, easily corrected. If a plane is off course, I can give the pilot a new heading. If my bomb misses the target, I can make corrections in the bombsight. If a pilot's approach to the runway is too steep or too shallow, he can go around for another try. Pilot errors, of course, are the most crucial. Lapses at critical times pose the most danger. We're all young men in our upper teens or early twenties trying to master complex machines that can kill us if we make serious mistakes.

Mistakes unfortunately occur.

One pilot, believing that he was clever and invincible, buzzed a large lake, nearly skimming the water. He flew into a storm of frantic ducks, striking many and lodging several in his engines. The plane was so badly damaged it had be taken out of service. The pilot was not only grounded, but also court-martialed for his poor judgment.

Another bomber landing at our base rolled to the end of the runway and began to taxi back toward the flight line when its wheels suddenly folded. The plane squatted on the concrete. The co-pilot, in trying to reach for the flaps switch, hit the one for the landing gear instead. The propellers, still turning as the plane dropped, were mangled and twisted. The loop antenna was crushed, and the ball turret control column protruded out through the top of the plane. Although no one was hurt, the expensive airplane was severely damaged.

The pilots carry the burden of committing potentially dangerous errors, but most of them who have arrived at this point in their training have become cautious, levelheaded and wise. Their superior coordination and reflexes do the rest. Johnston, our pilot, has all these qualities, and my confidence grows in him day by day.

*   *   *

Podoske and I find a table in the mess hall where we can sit down with our full plates. The clanking of porcelain and the musical clinking of silverware blend with the babble of conversations.

"Why do you mix your food up that way?" I ask Podoske.

"I like it this way. I don't like to eat a bite of this and a bite of that from separate little piles. I like to mix it all together."

He stirs his mashed potatoes, gravy, peas and meatballs with his fork as I watch in disbelief. It seems to me that he changes his food into a kind of swill.

I look up at the other officers still waiting in line to be served. A certain bombardier with his pregnant wife waits with the others. I'd seen the couple before, and, for some reason, they'd caught my attention. Tall and slender, blond and handsome, he wears his uniform well. He's how I think the ideal officer and airman should look. But there is a gentleness about his eyes and around his half-smile. With a relaxed expression of kindness, he looks down at his wife and the swelling of his unborn child beneath her smock. She looks up adoringly at him, their eyes meeting, almost shyly. Blond curls frame her angelic face as she gazes up at him, leaning back slightly to counter the weight of her soon-to-be-born child. As they inch up in line, he sometimes rests his hand on her shoulder. At times, their hands touch, their fingers curling and meshing then withdrawing as though they're self-conscious in the crowd.

I eat my lunch and talk with Podoske, but I find myself glancing at them often. I keep my attraction to them private, not daring to mention it to Podoske who would not understand me and might laugh or make some kind of crack.

I know nothing about either of them, except that he's ahead of me in crew training and will soon go overseas. I think about their forced separation, the pulling apart of these two lovers, about the new baby he'll not be able to hold in his arms.

They represent what I want for myself---marriage, a wife whom I love and will love me in return, a family and a tenderness and adoration that holds it all together. I am sentimental, idealistic, even romantic, and their relationship holds me fast even in the turmoil of the grim preparations for combat. They are the embodiment of my ideals.

*   *   *

We pass over it as we come in for our landing. It's short of the runway, in the clearing at the edge of the forest. The blackened, twisted wreckage, still vaguely in the shape of the B-17 lies in a field of rank weeds. I feel my stomach churn as I gaze at the burned out hulk. I imagine their cries and the devastating sound of their impact. The crash had occurred the night before, lighting up the sky. No one knows what the error was or who made it, but because of it ten good men had perished, including the bombardier who had loved his wife so much.

Our plane settles into the runway for another safe landing, but the specter of the burned-out bomber disturbs me. It haunts me not because of the danger of flying, but because of that man's death and the sudden and cruel destruction of their love.

Her grief must be intolerable. The baby will never see its father. The whole tragedy saddens me. I want to write home about it, but I don't want to worry my parents. I don't tell anyone why I'm sad, why I'm a little quieter than usual.

Errors. No one ever knew when they would occur or what their consequences would be. A sudden mistake in judgment, a wave of fatigue, momentary laziness, a single distraction, a second of carelessness or an instant of inattention had the sinister power to destroy a bomber and a plane full of young healthy airmen.

THE NAVIGATOR

I am now up here in the nose of my plane, and we are cruising near Alexandria. We have just been on a navigation mission, and I was the navigator. It was the first time I had done dead reckoning at night in the air. It is a quarter after twelve now, and we have over an hour to stay up yet. We have to finish out the period. Our trip was from here to Shreveport, La. then to Texarkana, Tex., then to Monroe, La., then to Jackson, Miss. and back to Alexandria. I made out okay, and we hit the towns. I had to keep a navigator's log this time. There sure is a bunch of stuff to fill out.

Between Shreveport and Texarkana we ran into a hard rainstorm. The plane leaked, and I got water on my maps, logs, and down my neck. Gee, you couldn't see anything but inky blackness.

Tomorrow morning we don't have to get up until noon, so maybe this late hour won't seem so bad. There is some air coming in around the drift meter and around the guns. It makes it a little cold in here.

Papa, you asked me in your swell letter if I got hungry when we flew for five hours. I can answer that easily. I would give anything right now for something to eat. Sometimes we take sandwiches along, but we didn't this time.

At about one-thirty in the morning, weary from the long flight, we glide in for a landing, the wheels finding their way onto the outlined runway with the usual squeal of rubber. I gather my damp logbook and maps together, feeling quite satisfied with my navigation. As yet we and several other crews have no navigator, so the bombardiers perform the duty. I enjoy navigating, but not filling out the required complex logbooks.

Despite my griping, I'm fascinated with navigation. I like the responsibility of plotting a course to a destination then giving the pilot the compass heading we should fly. The idea that I can tell the pilot of a four-engine bomber and its crew where to go is a heady one. I calculate our ground speed and determine our estimated time of arrival to the destination. If unexpected winds carry us off course, I check the drift meter then compute a new heading. The thrill of "splitting a city" at the exact time I predicted is really satisfying.

Navigation is best when the weather is clear, and I can keep track of our position by pilotage: carefully comparing what I see on the ground with the features marked on my maps. I love my vantage point in the sky, my perch in the bomber's nose from which I can look down on the earth and behold hundreds of square miles at a time. I never tire of watching it. The sheer fun of checking my maps with what I see below never ceases. I have the pleasure of knowing exactly where we are, and, if the pilot asks, I'm ready with a pinpoint location.

After flying several times, I'd studied all the landmarks within a wide area around our field--- other air bases, army camps, and the geometric outlines of forests and the bends of the Red River. If the weather should ever close in on us during our return to the base, I would be ready to determine where we were even through a small break in the clouds. I learned these local features because of the absolute enjoyment of doing so. Navigation gave me more of a sense of usefulness than dropping bombs on deserted targets.

*   *   *

We were at Alexandria five weeks before our trained navigator arrived. Then he left immediately for a two-week furlough. Of our eleven weeks at Alexandria, he was away seven.

The day I met him, I wrote home about him.

We got our navigator, and so far I am very pleased with him. His name is Warren, and he is from South Carolina. He was a 2nd lieutenant before he took navigation. He was commissioned before as a weather officer. He had 8 months training at the Massachusetts Institute of Technology that was plenty thorough. He is sure a good man to have along on the crew. I think he is at least 25 years old; at least he looks that old.

I like him immediately. His soft Southern voice exudes a quiet dignity. He's friendly and accepting, gracious and charming. He understates his friendliness with a genuine half-smile and a playful light about his eyes. His face is slightly long and his features plain, his body just beginning to become rounded with, what looks like to me, middle age. I'm thrilled that my companion in the nose will be a fully trained weather officer. I'll have someone to talk to about weather, just the way I used to talk about it with my dad.

When Warren returns from his leave, I greet him like an old friend. He goes with me to the morning service at the Methodist Church in Alexandria. The same evening we go to the movies on the base together. He has quite a selection of books about meteorology with him and loans me several of them. Several days later I take him on the bomb trainer for two straight days to teach him how to use the Norden bombsight. He learns rapidly, and will, with time, be able to hit shacks regularly. I'm in awe of his background and intelligence. He had been an air conditioning engineer before he joined the army, followed by his subsequent training in meteorology and navigation in the service. We now have two learned men on our crew, Witherspoon, the radioman being the other. I have a special respect for both of them.

* * *

Close to midnight we wing our way westward toward Austin, Texas on a night navigation mission. When we reach Austin, we must set a course for Fort Worth then back to Alexandria. The nose is crowded tonight since Warren also has a navigation instructor with him. Both of us navigate. I use dead reckoning and pilotage, and Warren employs dead reckoning, celestial and radio navigation. The instructor constantly asks us, his voice raised over the vibrations and roar in the nose, for our present position, as though he's afraid we'll become lost. Warren stands near his table just under the small astrodome, taking fixes on the stars with his transit. The instructor stands with him, giving him pointers. I inwardly hope that Warren masters this procedure since it will be very important if we ferry a bomber over the Atlantic at night. From time to time the instructor also checks my navigation work, looking at my headings and asking for fixes on our positions. He compliments me on my technique.

Although I feel good about what the instructor said and have the utmost respect for Warren as a navigator and a person, I feel dispossessed. Before Warren arrived, I had the entire nose of the plane to myself. It was my room where I could do as I pleased. I used the navigation table for my maps and bombing calculations. I was able to sit anywhere, walk anywhere or stretch anywhere. I was able to sit undisturbed in my bombardier's seat, checking our course or simply gazing out of the Plexiglas window at the ground below or the clouds around us. The nose is my place, my territory, my home. Now I must share it.

With Warren here I'm no longer in charge of navigation. He'll give the pilot his headings from now on, a duty I'll sorely miss. Some of my importance on the plane is suddenly diminished; I've been replaced. Warren is such a likeable, agreeable fellow, however, that I soon get used to his being in the nose with me, and we learn to work well together.

But I can neither take my eyes off the ground nor give up my maps. Although Warren gives the headings and ETAs, I always check. Folding my map so it won't be so obvious to him, I meticulously compare it with the landmarks below, making sure that we're on course.

I want to know exactly where I am.

THE SQUALL

Jostling along on the shuttle bus from town to the base, Podoske and I talk about the movie we've just seen at a plush theater in Alexandria, "For Me and My Gal" with Judy Garland and Gene Kelly. The good feeling from the film flows over into our repartee. Light, airy and entertaining, it was just what we needed for a break in our rigorous schedule of non-stop flying.

As we sit in the darkened bus, the dimly lit heads of the other men jiggling and bouncing with the motion of it, I notice lightning flashes in the west. As we approach the base, that portion of the sky flickers constantly. The bluish light steals into the bus, illuminating the ghostly faces of the men. Will the rain catch us before we reach our barracks doors?

As soon as Podoske and I get off the bus, we rush toward our barracks, lightning stabbing closer, thunder growing louder. We sprint the last fifty yards, bursting through the door just as the first squall rakes the roof. The large clattering drops sound like pebbles. We perspire in the warm, humid air. Glad to be inside, we listen to the roar of the rain and the cannon-cracks of thunder as lightning strikes split the air nearby. The rain, obeying the wild currents in the storm and the erratic, gusty winds at the surface, falls in spurts, a torrent for a short time then a sudden ceasing followed by another downpour.

I stand at the back window watching the weather drama unfold. Waves of wind-blown rain wash past the outside lights so that they seem suspended in an unearthly mistiness while electric-blue lightning flashes dance through it. As the rain beats on the roof and against the tarpaper sides of the barracks, a lightning bolt strikes close by, the thunder like a bomb exploding. I automatically jump back from the window. It zaps down near the power lines, erupting in a shower of sparks, like a grand celebration! Our base is plunged into darkness.

Not finished with its repertoire, the storm lashes out with a sudden wind squall, striking with such ferocity that the fragile barracks begin to tremble as though they're about to blow away. As our quarters shudder, the wind drives sheets of rain against it, forcing itself through every opening and crack. Many officers, still in town, had left their windows open, as the weather had been sultry and uncomfortable during the day. Podoske and I scurry through the barracks with our flashlights, closing windows and pulling belongings out of the water. Much of the rain had blown in through the vents, leaving puddles on the floor and sorry pools on some of the beds.

An hour after it starts the tempest moves on, still roaring back at us with ever softer rolls of thunder, flashing its electric eyes ever more dimly. As the thunderheads shift off to the east, the temperature drops quickly. During the day the air had been so hot and stuffy that I could hardly breathe, but now it has a dry, cool crispness to it, the kind of cold that nips at my nose. The air smells fresh, and the lights on the base, now back on again, twinkle in its clarity. We may have to fire up our coal stove again to keep warm at night, a thought unthinkable earlier in the day.

Despite the storm's ferocity, I enjoyed it. I savored the twin juices of fear and rapt excitement. I reveled in the storm because I understood it. Reading about meteorology and keeping up with current weather charts gave me much of what I needed to know to appreciate it. The squall with its thunder and lightning, howling wind and drumming rain, its wetness and its smell, even its sheer violence, had been a living laboratory example of what meteorologists attempted to explain with their printed words, diagrams, charts and statistics.

For several days we'd been bathed in the humid shower-bath air oozing up from the Gulf of Mexico, it being like a huge bathtub of warm water steaming its sultriness into the air. The gulf air's moisture settled on our skins like sticky, invisible dew, blending there with the sweat seeping out of our pores. Our collars were damp and limp, and sweat printed stains on the backs of our shirts. It made us feel we couldn't breathe because its warmth and moistness equaled that already in our throats. It covered everything we touched with its clamminess. It brought out the bugs, especially the mosquitoes and June bugs, and fouled the air with a faint swamp-like smell.

While we stewed in the steam bath in Louisiana, a huge mass of cold, dry air, born out of clear, starry nights, edged out of Canada, slithering and sliding its way southward and eastward across the United States, carrying with it the frigid breath of the north. Heavy, dense and fast-moving, it began to invade the territory occupied by the warm, moist light air from the gulf. Somewhere a weatherman drew a long, curving blue line on his weather map indicating the edge of the invasion, a vigorous cold front moving toward the southeast.

The cold air crept relentlessly across the states, wedging beneath the lighter gulf air like a plow, forcing it to rise and cool, its moisture to condense into clouds and rain. The cold air was moving so fast and had been so massive that it lifted quickly and violently, spawning a squall line of towering thunderheads and Niagaras of rain.

The weatherman's "blue line", his cold front, passed over our field with its exciting hour of violence, replacing the tropical air of an hour before with the chilled, clear air from Canada. Even though I think about a short trip outside to the coal bin to stoke up our pot-bellied stove, I revel in the new air's dryness, its refreshing coolness on my face and its luscious feel in my throat. I can breathe again, and pull the blankets cozily around my neck. Tomorrow will be cold, but the skies will be clear and brilliant blue. Tomorrow night, flying at high altitude, keeping warm will be a problem, but it's all worth it.

The following day I write my parents about the squall, explaining it all to them, drawing them a diagram of a cold front in hopes they might understand it. I tell them that the B-17s on the flight line had held up quite well, but that a Piper Cub had lost a wing, and a small Cessna C-78 transport had suffered a gaping hole in its side.

* * *

I watched a number of cold fronts march through Alexandria, some so weak they had stirred up only a few scattered clouds and others so strong they had kicked up heavy thunderstorms with gale winds, heavy rain and hail. I saw hail fall for five minutes, whitening the ground, and I saw freak hailstones shaped like oversized candy Lifesavers that bounced on the dirt, porch and asphalt, rolling crazily until they fell on their flat sides. Sprinkles, drizzle, fog, low clouds or thunderheads all interested me. Coming from California with its benign climate, I had never seen such a variety of weather or so many abrupt changes as I had in springtime Alexandria.

I sometimes think about becoming a meteorologist after the war. I have renewed confidence in my abilities and the achievement of goals, but I also harbor doubts about my capacity to handle college mathematics and physics. After the war is a long, uncertain time away, and I have difficulty seeing any clear future. Whether I become a meteorologist or not, I can still enjoy the energy and dazzle of squalls and the thrill of the ever-changing weather patterns that sweep into my life each day.

ON THE EDGE OF THE
STRATOSPHERE

At 20,000 feet my temperature gauge reads minus eighteen degrees Centigrade, far too cold for me in a B-17 without a heating system. Even swaddled in my fleece-lined winter flying gear, I'm not warm enough. I sit in my bombardier's seat in the nose, checking my maps and peering out ahead for our first "target," the railroad yards and roundhouse at Shreveport, Louisiana. Having never flown this high before, I'm astounded by how much country I can see from one hazy horizon to the other and how much smaller objects appear below. People have literally disappeared, and automobiles, barely discernible, appear to creep like tiny insects along the highways.

Far ahead, the railroad yards begin to take shape. I adjust the bombsight and check the camera for the "bomb run." At the exact second that a bomb would have been released by my bombsight, I must take a photograph. Besides being stiff and uncomfortable from the cold, I struggle to move around in the cumbersome clothing. My oxygen mask with its short flexible hose, my throat microphone strapped around my neck and pressed against my Adam's apple, and the wires leading to my earphones, tether me to a short range of movement. My cinched-up parachute harness binds against my flying suit.

With the target in sight, I attempt to fine tune the bombsight with my thick-gloved fingers, keeping the crosshairs as steady as possible on the patterns of tracks and boxcars below. At the instant of release, I press the camera button for photographic proof that the target has been "destroyed".

Our combat formation of nine B-17s veers off to a new course, heading towards the railroad facilities at Texarkana, Texas. As our navigator is not with us today, I scrawl the time and the new compass heading into his logbook. Podoske, the co-pilot, thinking that he didn't have to wear his heavy clothing for this mission, suffers miserably from the cold. Blaming himself, he complains, and tries to rub the stiffness out of his joints. All he can do is take it.

Halfway toward Little Rock, Arkansas for another bombing run, Podoske and I are both hungry. Flying, especially on the long missions, always stokes our appetites. Both of us brought sandwiches, but we don't know how we're going to eat them with our oxygen masks on. At first we remove our masks just long enough to take a bite, slapping them back on quickly, then chewing and swallowing. Frustrated, we both take off our masks and begin to eat our sandwiches as though we're in the mess hall back at the base. After four bites we both become light-headed and bluish in the face. Quickly attaching the masks again makes us feel much better.

As we head back toward Alexandria after "bombing" our last target at Jackson, Mississippi, our bodies are almost numb from the cold. We had been at 20,000 feet on full oxygen for nearly four hours. Condensed water from my breathing had frozen around my oxygen mask, breaking off at the edge, and dropping little slivers of ice all around me. Combat missions would be even longer, and I think about how we're ever going to stay warm over there.

Our formation flies in low over the field, the planes peeling off in succession, and stringing themselves out into a well-spaced pattern for landing---the way it's done overseas. In some of the low buildings along the flight line, officers interrogate us about our targets and the details of the mission-

--again, the way it's done overseas. They had briefed us before the mission in the style used at the airfields in England.

* * *

The last phase of our training is a series of long high altitude missions, complete with detailed briefings beforehand and intensive interrogations afterward. The training officers become more demanding and serious, knowing full well that we need more seasoning to become combat ready.

At noon, we take off with nineteen other bombers then gradually assemble into the largest formation I've ever seen. We fly together at high altitude on a route that will take us over Louisiana, Texas, Arkansas and Mississippi for the camera bombing of military targets. An extensive deck of low clouds, unpredicted, spreads itself across our assigned targets, thwarting the possibility of the camera mission. Gigantic thunderheads rear up to the west and south, all of them so beautiful and typical that they might have been used for textbook illustrations. We continue the mission, hoping for a break in the clouds, as the navigators practice their dead reckoning and the pilots work on formation flying.

All goes well except for the "bombing" until we turn on our final leg back to Alexandria. We learn that the lead navigator, for some unexplainable reason, is lost. As he guides our entire formation, we are all lost, all twenty of us. For an hour we fly aimlessly, lowering our altitude and looking for breaks in the clouds in hopes of spotting landmarks. Finally we all descend to an altitude of only 2000 feet. Twenty airplanes, their eighty engines creating an unholy roar, skim over the green fields and farms of rural Louisiana. Terrified horses and cattle scatter in every direction. With the sky darkening and lowering and our fuel running low, we pass over the Red River, the same one that flows through Alexandria. Using it as our guide, we fly down it for the final sixty miles to our field.

Shortly after we land the rain begins, followed by the parade of thunderheads that we'd seen earlier.

Back in the barracks the rain pounds on the roof, and lightning knifes to the ground with explosive thunder. A clattering of hail bounces on the roof and on the ground outside. I think about our being lost and how uncomfortable it was. I vow to always know where I am, even if someone else is in charge. I wonder about whether we are really ready to fly overseas if we can lose ourselves that easily.

The commanding officers are wondering also. Inspectors from the Second Air Force, flying a fast twin-engine B-25, watch our high altitude formations from the air, slipping in and out of our bomber patterns with a critical eye. Tight formation flying is the best defense against fighter attacks, and the commanders insist that the pilots master it. The pilots generally fly well, but weather continues to be the nemesis of both the pilots and the navigators. The problem of not being able to obtain precise weather data for our missions haunts us always.

*   *   *

Our engines labor as we climb steadily with ten other planes for another camera bombing and formation flying mission to Baton Rouge, New Orleans, Mobile and home. We are to climb to 17,000 feet before turning on a course to Baton Rouge. At 12,000 feet we slide into a thick deck of alto cumulus clouds, so dense that we can't even see the plane next to us. By the time we emerge from the cloud tops at 13,500 feet, three of the planes in the formation are not with us anymore. We lose radio contact with them then have to assume they've flown off in another direction.

The eight of us that remain continue with the mission, still climbing. At 15,000 feet we reach the freezing level, flying under a higher deck of clouds that continues to thicken and lower. At 17,000 feet we all begin to leave vapor trails. Super cooled droplets from the clouds splatter against the Plexiglas of the nose, freezing instantly as they hit. Rime ice begins to collect on the leading edges of the wings. Waves and streaks of snow stream down just below us toward the earth, an amazing sight to me. At 18,000 feet we can nearly reach up and touch the cirrus. The sky suddenly becomes so milky that we have to fly on instruments to keep our bearings. As we climb, the visibility deteriorates and icing becomes more severe.

Finally forced to give up our high altitude mission, we circle down through a break in the clouds, and continue at only 5000 feet. According to the radio, flying in circles had disoriented another lead navigator who is now lost. This time Warren and I know where we are in case anyone should ask us, but the lead navigator's job is to find himself again. Finally the lead pilot claims he's picked up the Baton Rouge radio beam, and homes in on it. Around Baton Rouge the P-47 Thunderbolt pilots find us, zipping in and out of our formation with abandon as they practice their interceptor moves.

North of New Orleans our eight planes fly toward Mobile in good combat formation between two layers of clouds. Gradually the two layers merge, plunging us all into a blind translucence. We decide to climb to get out of it, but when we finally break through the soft fluff at the top of the cloud layer, only one other plane is with us. Eventually, through a break in the clouds, we spot the other plane from our element about 2000 feet below us. Seeing us, he gradually climbs to rejoin us. The other five planes had turned away for some reason and we lose track of them. Finally contacting the other planes by radio, we decide to reassemble over Baton Rouge. The gathering together takes nearly a full hour, during which time the P-47 pilots "attack" us again, seizing their opportunity to hone their intercepting skills.

A combination of weather, navigation errors and uncoordinated decisions by the pilots had literally scattered us all over the south. Had we been in a combat zone, we would have been naked and relatively defenseless. Had the P-47s been Messerschmitts, we would have all been annihilated.

*   *   *

I've never seen so many airplanes at one time. After rolling out of bed at 4 a.m., we take off early, climb to 20,000 feet, assemble into formation, and head north. Farther north, we join B-17 formations from two other training bases, forming a giant flotilla that from the ground must have sounded unworldly and ominous. All of us, in combat formation, fly toward Tulsa, Oklahoma where we are to camera bomb vital targets. Over fifty bombers stretch out in close groups toward Oklahoma like an orderly swarm of mechanical bees. I feel that we have been absorbed into the group, have become part of a greater organism where we have lost our individuality as a crew, but at the same time I appreciate the comfort of numbers and the protective security of it all. I try to imagine that combat is this way.

This is our last formation flight in the United States.

THE FINAL DAYS

Today we took our physical and got shot again, this time for cholera and typhus. Next week I have to take two more shots for the same thing. In April I have to take typhoid and tetanus boosters. My arm is starting to hurt already. I had one shot in each arm.

Well, things are really buzzing around here now. We had our final processing at this field today. We were issued some overseas equipment---blankets, mess kits, etc. Also had all our papers cleared up, and all shortages filled. It took all afternoon and evening to get it done. Shortly I will be sending a lot of stuff home, probably by Railway Express. Our baggage is necessarily restricted to a certain amount when we go over, so I will have to send some home. We are still supposed to leave the first week in May, but it could be even earlier than that. It seems as though they are rushing things somewhat.

We will still go to Nebraska for a while, but we will probably be restricted to the post. Things are sure in an uproar, and you just don't know what to think. When we get up to staging in Nebraska, we will have to start censoring our mail. I guess I won't be able to say much up there.

From the staging area we fly to the Port of Embarkation. That will be Presque Isle or Bangor in Maine or somewhere in Florida, depending on what route we will take, the northern or southern. If we take the northern route, we will go by Greenland, Iceland, Northern Ireland or Scotland. We will then be placed in a sort of pool either at Prestwick, Scotland or Bloomington, England, probably the latter. If we go the southern route, we will

389

go by way of Trinidad, Natal, Brazil, Ascension Island, Azores and North Africa. They will more than likely ship us to one of three places, England, Italy or India. It may be an entirely new theater for all I know. You never can tell.

The things I send home, you can just flop under my bed with the rest of the stuff.

I imagine that I will be able to tell you where I am when I get overseas. If not, it will be better that way anyway. In all probability you will know where I am.

*   *   *

The crewmen all sit in a large room, reading the fine print and wrestling with terminology. Few of us had ever seen a will before, let alone made one out. With the help of the officer in charge, we gradually fill in the blanks and name our beneficiaries, but the irony of healthy, vigorous young men writing their wills is unnerving. Even though we like to consider ourselves invincible, the documents carry with them the faint scent of death, an unpleasantness that lingers in the shadowy corners of the room.

We also fill out forms for appointing a power of attorney, so that if we are incapacitated, someone can act for us. I'm ready to send both forms home.

Most of us here have made out a will and a power of attorney that I will send home. That's just merely a precaution. I have made them out in both your names. You can read them, and get more out of them than I could tell you.

At least the final full day at Alexandria is so filled with activities that we don't have time to think about anything else.

We've had quite a busy day today, running around getting things signed, listening to lectures, getting forms and all that old stuff. You just about run your legs off doing all that.

We also had Air Force inspectors here today who questioned us about everything. We asked them about leaves, and they said we were supposed to get one before we go over, but it was seldom done. The same old story; nobody really knows. It is very doubtful right now because they are going to need crews probably for this invasion deal, if they pull it. I bet we get in on that during some part of it. Oh me.

* * *

Alone in the barracks, I sit on the edge of my bed, writing a letter, the pale afternoon sun slanting through the windows. The banging of the front screen door breaks the silence of the room, and I look up to see Flight Officer Seagrave framed in my doorway. He looks unhappy as he strolls into the room and sits down on the opposite bed.

"Do you have a few minutes, Stevens?" he asks.

"Sure," I answer, "What's on your mind?"

With a pained look on his face, his small mouth solemn and his forehead furrowed, he says, "I told them I couldn't do it, that I just couldn't go overseas. I just can't do it, Stevens. The thought of going into combat paralyzes me."

Seagrave surprises me. I had known him since bombardier school at Midland, Texas, and we had been good friends on the base. We rarely went on open post together because his whole life centered on women. He's a man dedicated to taking as many women to bed as possible, a goal that I didn't share. On an everyday human level we got along well.

"Who did you tell?" I ask.

"Almost every one in charge," he says.

"What did they say?" I ask, anxious to hear his answer.

"Of course they didn't like it, and they sure as hell didn't like me, but they told me they couldn't make me go.

They said I would be reassigned to some kind of ground duty."

I think about how long the fear of combat must have been tormenting him, yet none of us knew it. It had taken him until the last days of training to muster enough courage to say he couldn't do it. I certainly understand, and don't look down on him, but his sudden decision baffles me.

"They began attacking me personally in the office," he goes on. "They said that I went around with a sneer on my face, as though I was better than anyone else. It's not true. I don't sneer. That's just the way my face looks. Did you ever think I was sneering?"

I look intently at his pleading eyes. Two deep creases mark his cheeks below his nose, angling off to the corners of his mouth. I'd never interpreted his natural look as a sneer.

"No," I reply. "I never thought about whether you were sneering or not."

"I know," he continues. "They've trained me all these months, and given me a commission, and now I pull this at the last minute. I know what my crew must think of me. But I can't do it. There's no way I can go over there."

I sympathize with his agony, and try to reassure him that he'll find a good ground job. A trace of what he feels so strongly probably resides to a certain degree within each one of us. Even though some will call him cowardly, I have to admire the strength he must have summoned in order to admit that he was not able to face combat.

"Well, thanks, Stevens. I've got to go now."

"Good luck," I yell to him as he passes out of the barracks door. I think too about the guilt he must feel, guilt he might carry the rest of his life, especially if his crew is lost.

*   *   *

I sit in the base chapel at night, the only light, the flickering of candles on the altar. Other men are here too, the dim illumination of the candles touching their faces. The strains of "Finlandia" sweeten the darkness. I have never heard music as beautiful. No minister is about, nor is there a service---just shadows, candlelight, music and the men, each one quietly attending the private drama in his own imagination.

I'd never been devout. Like most boys, I'd suffered through Sunday school in my itchy wool trousers because my parents took me to church with them. As a teenager I'd gone to the Inglewood Methodist Church on my own, but mainly for social reasons. Despite my motives and habits, I truly accept a real God who cares about me and listens to my prayers. All during my service time I sporadically attended church on Sunday mornings, but now, with the reality of combat ever nearer, I feel more and more drawn to the church, the only place of solace that I know. I'm at peace in the dark room with the haunting melodies of "Finlandia". I feel spiritually connected with the divine, with God.

No, I haven't seen "The Memphis Belle", but I would like to see it. I guess that is pretty authentic. Naturally I will have some pretty close calls over there, but I am very, very confident that I will get through okay. You just wait and see. I like to feel that God is with me, and believe that to be true. Just that one part of the 23rd Psalm, 'Yea though I walk through the valley of the shadow of death, I will fear no evil, for thou art with me.' If someone has something like that to believe in, somehow his fear may be removed.

The words of the 23rd Psalm drift through my mind as "Finlandia" ends and the "Emperor Waltz" begins. I feel that if I can think of the passage enough, and say it enough, I'll somehow provide a holy shield for myself. When the music ends for the evening, I walk out of the chapel, somber but confident.

*   *   *

The olive-drab Pullman cars of the troop train backed into the air base spur near all the supply buildings during the early afternoon. Carrying our gear, Johnston, Podoske, Warren and I make our way along the string of dusty cars with the other men, looking for our assigned Pullman. The Air Force band blares its brassy notes into the soft afternoon haze in an attempt to lend cheer and importance to our send-off. I suddenly envy their position; they'll never have to worry about combat.

Warren and I sit down in a Pullman compartment facing Johnston and Podoske. Podoske holds a small sack of sandwiches in his hand, raising them up and warning us that if we don't want to go hungry on the train that we'd better get some too. We kid him about his worrying, but he warns us again,

"You guys are going to be sorry. Don't ask me to share these with you." We laugh and lean back in the comfortable seats, listening to the band music drifting in from the outside. Just before we depart the band breaks out with "I'll be Glad When you're Dead You Rascal You", a kind of sinister joke, much funnier to them than to us. We smile nervously, but tighten up a notch inside.

The train rolls quietly out of the rusty spur, the locomotive laboring and billowing out clouds of black smoke. A variety of feelings hover around me--- like insects around a light bulb on a summer night. One dashes into the light for a moment then flits out again into the darkness to be replaced by another. The insects of death and fear skitter around the others but only in the dim light away from the lamp, just close enough that we can feel their nagging presence, the acid thrill of them ruffling through our intestines, their strange deep, soft twist on our testicles, their unwanted intrusion into our thoughts.

Excitement about the adventures that lie ahead dominate our minds---new places and experiences, the vast unknown. A curious exhilaration bubbles out of everyone, each one of us infecting the other, all of us effervescing with the camaraderie of men who have grown close through the intensity of their time and training together. None of us really knows what combat is. We've seen the movies and the newsreels, and we've listened to the words of the men who've been there, but it's all an abstraction to us, a hazy macabre business so dreamlike that it hardly seems real.

On this day in May 1944 the train picks up speed down the main line while we all separately think of the long journey ahead, wondering how it will all come out.

ABOUT THE AUTHOR

Charles N. Stevens, or Norm as his friends call him, grew up in Inglewood, California. At 18 he joined the Army Air Corps. He entered in 1943 and was discharged after the war in October 1945. He served as a bombardier on a B-17 in the 8th Air Force, 351st Bomb Group, at Polebrook, England during the summer and early fall of 1944. He finished his tour of duty, completing 34 bombing missions over Germany and occupied France, Belgium and Holland.

He wrote extensively about his combat experiences in his previous book, *An Innocent at Polebrook: A Memoir of an 8th Air Force Bombardier,* published in 2004.

After returning from overseas he trained as a radar bombardier at Langley Field, Virginia and Williams Field, Arizona. He was to be assigned to a B-29 crew for duty in the Pacific when the war ended.

Following the war he enrolled at the University of California at Los Angeles, graduating with a BA in psychology. After a series of graduate courses he earned his teaching credential. Over a span of 32 years he taught science and mathematics in junior high schools and English and American Literature in high school. While teaching he earned a master's degree in English at California State College at Los Angeles.

He has two sons by a previous marriage, Jeffry L. Stevens and Greg E. Stevens.

He has five grandchildren, Brenda Stevens Sherry, Eric, Sharon, Michael and Beth Stevens.

He retired in 1984 and has lived a life of reading, writing, traveling and being a grandfather. He lives with his wife, Dolores Seidman, in Monterey Park, California where they have resided for 36 years.

Printed in the United States
205552BV00001B/1-72/P

9 781434 388285